For Juliana

For Juliana

Almost to the Almost, One Penny at a Time

Janet Spencer Barnes

Dedicated to Juliana Spencer Ramos
Who by virtue of coming into my life changed it forever.

Acknowledgements

With my deepest gratitude I have to thank such an incredibly widespread support system from my immediate family to our Facebook following. Within that array of personalities and sensitivities a 'story' emerged out of what was 'our lives'. I would never be able to list all of the individuals that have made my life and subsequently this story something I managed to live through but, as I have done throughout this saga, 'I will try...'

~ To Chris Medina for far more than I ever thought I could thank a person for. You saved my daughter's life in so many obvious ways and my sanity in much less obvious ways. To call you my 'future-son-in-law' is no longer enough of a term of endearment. What we shared was an entire array of emotions from tragedy to humor. The bittersweet love I will always have for you is nearly indefinable. Many praise you for 'choosing to stay' but we both know you never even considered it a 'choice' because you never wanted to leave. And for having that much love and respect for my daughter, you have made a permanent imprint on my heart. In addition to all else, you are my very dear friend and an incredible man. Although I have always been a very big fan of your music and talent, your character is what makes you famous to me. I am honored to have been the recipient of your humor, support, counseling, love and strength. You saved me.

~ To my children Adam, Dylan, Cheyenne, Delaney and Mackenzie, I am so sorry for what you had to sacrifice through all of this. You were so good to come home to, lean on and appreciate. You were forced to grow up fast and become understanding and self-sacrificing adults far too soon, and yet, you did. I will always carry the guilt of deserting you and yet you never faulted me for it but instead, thanked me for being there for Juliana. You gave that up for her, for me and for yourselves. You are all my angels and are every bit as important to me as my first born angel. I know you already know that but I wanted you to know it again. Our family is strong in love and commitment to each other and I am proud to call you my children EVERY DAY of my life. My love for you is unmatched.

~ To my sister Lori who from the moment she had to deliver the bad news, to the countless hours of fundraising and spirit raising, I love you more than I have ever been able to show. I suspect you know that now though I am sorry it took this to show it. My gratitude nearly matches it.

~ To my brothers Joe and Michael and their VERY significant others, my sister-in-law Toula and future sister-in-law Maida Ramirez, who tried to do all they could while giving me the space to grieve, grow and survive. I know how difficult it was for you to watch Juliana and me in this situation and yet I never doubted that you were ready at any moment to spring to action and appreciated it greatly when you did.

~ To my sister Diane and my niece Sheri who had to watch from afar and struggle with what they knew, what they didn't and what they couldn't do. No worries, your intentions were felt even from a distance.

~ To my niece Allison who tried so hard to be more than just family but also my friend. Being around you is as warm and effortless as it is enjoyable and entertaining. Your desire to make it all better came through in so many ways from 'hanging out' with me or Juli to helping edit this book. I am so proud of you and grateful for you in my life.

~ To Chris Ramos and family and Gloria Medina and family...out of the most unlikely places comes the support to make it another day. We were forced to learn how to be a uniquely configured family in unusual circumstances For Juliana and you know? It worked. Chris, we brought Juliana into this world together and I am so glad we were able to remain focused on Juliana as our priority. Our kids are amazing people, all four of them. Gloria, you helped me stay strong and positive in my darkest moments even though it was a hell of a way to become acquainted! So much mutual respect to all.

~ To Allison, Caitlin, Parker, Connor, Jimmy, Tess, Vickie…thanks for continuing to be my reminder that Juliana still belongs to, the 'next generation of our family' and always showing your love and support to us. I am so happy you are my nieces and nephews!

~ To my wonderful in-laws, the Barnes, Mori and Daviera families. I knew that we were more than you bargained for from the beginning and I am grateful you let us grow on you. Thank you for always making me and my children feel like part of the family.

~ To my wonderful friends Dawn Ferralez, Paula Leuder and especially Carrie and Ron Cummins and the entire Rosenberg clan (special shout-out to Herm) who stood by me when the nature of our friendships had to change, and you loved me anyway.

~ To new friends such as Mary Golembeck, Aimee and Yuriy Zymsly, Mike and Amy Cahill, Jim Dolan, Taylor Gestes and family, who came along just when I needed a new perspective.

~ To the many families that made sure we had delicious meals while I couldn't even think of eating such as the Dampf, Spencer, Pappas, Smith, Wilson, Rago, Ramirez, Pagan, Blazkowski, Mancusi, Kudra, Leuder, Slattery, Cahill, Zurisk, Medina, Knight, Westergren, Hall, and Mitchell families.

~ To the wonderful people who shared their special expertise out of the goodness of their hearts such as Jennifer Conway, Angela Mehalek, Christine Gialamas, Paula Mitchell, Jill Michalek and Gia Wilson. You all helped imprint your unique styles and assistance on Juliana's recovery.

~ To those who immortalized our year in special photos and videos such as Natalie Escabedo, Mike Schick, Bill Bronson, and my brother, Joe Spencer.

~ To our angels who came in and helped us take care of Juliana (once we finally admitted we needed help) such as Paula Leuder, Lauren Hall, Mary and Nikki Golembeck and of course, our Super Angel, Susan Knickerbocker (Ms, Knick).

~ To Juliana's friends who continued to visit Juli in the hospitals and at home (even when she couldn't visit back) with the everlasting belief that she will be back in our lives one day, especially Christine Ranos and Sarah Mitchell. Sarah, thank you for being a friend to my family as well.

~ To my coworkers who made sure I had a job to return to and a quiet place to 'lose it' when I needed to, especially Glenn Itano, Patty Gonzalez, Peggy Wind, Dana Chang and Shirley Sains.

~ To everyone who contributed to the successful fundraising including those mentioned in the story and those friends, family members, neighbors, co-workers and strangers who I didn't mention, I thank you immensely (especially since I spent much of those first months in a coma of my own!)

~ To those who contributed to the construction of this book: Ms. Knick and Allison Carroll for the edits, back cover photo by Joe Spencer of the Remodeling Station and Artwork created by Penelope Wrenn - Jetty Art Productions. As most things in my life now, it took a village.

~ To all of the 'Team Juli' members, 'Medina Maniacs', 'James Gang', 'Prayer Warriors', and other variously configured support groups both on Facebook/ForJuliana, ForJuliana.org and prayer teams assembled around the world, you will never know how grateful I am to you for stepping forward to send words of encouragement and gifts of support to bring my daughter back to life. I have been gifted by so many people working hard to keep our family going.

~ To God. Thank you for loving me enough to carry me through this ordeal and loving my daughter enough to save her for the rest of the world to love as well. We will make you proud that you did. I have always said that this is a job given to me by God and I was not willing to mess it up. I hope you don't think I have although I doubt myself daily. I know you saved Juliana for better things as well as I know that I am exactly where I am supposed to be, doing what I am supposed to do...For Juliana.

And last in this list to symbolize that he is first in my heart...

~ To the man that I will spend the rest my life with, my husband Don. You have tolerated so much without complaint or regret and somehow managed to sing my praises to everyone in the process. You took a woman with four kids and loved her and them as if they were your own. Then when the 'for worse' part came around, you made good on your vows while giving me all the space I needed to devote to just one person: Juliana. You stood by me like a rock and your love for me never wavered even when I wondered how you ever managed. You made sure that I never wanted, or needed, or worried about anything and stayed strong so I didn't have to. You patiently stepped aside while I was absent, distant, and broken and then when needed, you quietly just picked up the pieces and put them back together. I know you were hurt and grieving too and I left you to do that alone. For all of that, I am just as sorry as I am grateful. You embodied what a marriage commitment should be and our children should be proud of you for that. You are exactly the role model I believed you to be when I said, "I Do". For the record, I still do. I will spend my lifetime showing you how much I love you for it.

Foreword

A group of souls in heaven are reviewing their next earthly assignment. Two of them discuss the gravity of what will happen:

Angel 1: "So let me get this straight. We are all going down to earth and will be a family, right?"

Angel 2: "Yes, and I get to be the mom, you will be my daughter"

Angel 1: "Ok fine. And did I also understand that our family will have to endure a traumatic situation and deal with it publicly so that others may benefit?"

Angel 2: "That is what I understood as well. It sounds like quite a challenge. Are you ready to do this?"

Angel 1: "I am ready of course. That is our duty in His plan. So if you are the mother, then I want to be the one who gets injured. Together we can help make a difference; but I really don't want any of the others in this assignment to have to be 'the one' to live through that pain and recovery on earth."

Angel 2: "That is so typical of you to expect to 'take one for the team'. You are so giving of yourself. That is why I always want an earthly assignment with you. It is where we connect: through pure love."

Angel 1: "I feel the same way. Let's do this then, let's go make a difference…'mom'."

Angel 2: "I guess that means I go first, but don't leave me there too long since it seems my importance is all wrapped up in you, 'daughter'."

Angel 1: "Deal. I will be right behind you."

… It's just a theory…

"Janet, are you awake? I need you to wake up and listen to me." My sister Lori's voice was all business. It was just before 5 am on a Friday and she knew I was going to wake soon to get ready to work from home.

"I am awake, what's up?" I was too sleepy to be concerned but I sensed something creeping in…dread maybe?

"I just got a call from your father-in-law. He got a call from Christ Hospital and Juliana has been in a serious car accident. You need to get to the hospital right away."

Ok, so I was definitely awake then.

I got off the phone with her, calmly but swiftly woke my husband Donnie and got ready to leave. I am not a panicky mom by nature and assume the best so even though my heart was racing, I was certain that this was just another car accident of Juli's. Yes, there have been many. Her poor driving was legendary…in our family at least. As my husband got ready I called Juliana's fiancé, Chris.

"Hello…?" He was clearly disoriented and frankly, I was surprised he even answered. *"What time is it? Where is Juliana? She should be home now."*

"Chris that's why I am calling. Juli's been in a car accident, I don't know any details but we need to get to Christ Hospital right away. Meet us there."

The next phone call was to Juli's dad, another Chris. His wife another Cris, picked up the phone.

"Hi it's Janet. Can I talk to your husband?"

"Is everything ok?" She asked cautiously.

"No" She handed the phone to Chris and I heard her say, 'It's Janet'.

"What's wrong?" Since he does tend to panic, I downplayed my concern to keep him steady. Looking back I can say that I did that often as a way of keeping everyone calm in the hopes of that calm reflecting back on me.

"Juli has been in a car accident. I don't have any details yet, but we need to go to Christ Hospital. I am leaving now. Meet us there, ok?" I could hear the sobs that were starting. I don't recall what he said but I know that his fear was palpable.

The drive to the hospital for me was taking care of business. I left my 17 year old daughter Cheyenne home sleeping along with my 8 and 5 year old daughters. I called Cheyenne after we left so she wouldn't have the opportunity to come with us. I needed her to get the girls off to school as if nothing was wrong. I needed her most of all not to lose it, because she would. After all, we didn't know what was going on; maybe it was 'nothing'. A nagging thought told me it was definitely going to be 'something'. I warned Cheyenne, "keep it quiet until we knew more, don't panic and don't tell the girls. Get them off to school and if we need you to come up here, we will make sure someone gets you." From her panicked reaction I had no idea if she was going to be able to do any of that but I had to move on. My son Dylan was away at school in Hawaii. I definitely did not want him knowing just yet. I would not be able to manage a long distance update. And I was also not ready to commit to this being something anyone should worry about. Denial is a coping mechanism that would serve me well in the coming weeks.

My next call was to my father-in-law. The nagging thought was getting more like a shout in my brain and I had to piece together how the communication chain occurred. He told me that the Oak Forest police department called him and asked if he knew Juliana Ramos. He said that she was his granddaughter. They told him they were trying to reach us, went to the house and there was no answer, no activity inside when they looked in the windows with flashlights. Looked in the window with flashlights? This is not good. I have seen enough TV to know my original assumptions were flawed. Since we don't have a house phone in our room, we didn't hear anyone calling us. Not the police or my father-in-law. My father-in-law happened to have my sister's phone number and called her to try to reach me. She then tried my cell phone which I answered. He was clearly shaken by the whole experience so I let him know I was one less thing to worry about.

"Ok dad, that all makes sense. I am sure it will be fine. What did they tell you about the accident?"

*He answered, "They said that she has been in a **life threatening** accident and the family needed to get to the hospital right away."*

For the first time in this experience...the first of many times, and less than 15 minutes after the initial call, my heart fell out of my chest.

We all arrived at the hospital about the same time. Chris, Juli's fiancé, was followed by my son Adam who rented the same house with Chris and Juli. They shuttled us in a private room waiting for the doctor. For those few moments, a chaplain sat with us very serenely trying to give us peace through osmosis. It was more eerie than comforting.

"Can I get you anything?" she asked sweetly.

I didn't want small talk or beverages or comfort of any kind. Not yet. "Information. That's all I want." She explained that we would need to wait for the doctor which only made whatever was coming next feel grave. I looked at her trying to read if she was steeling herself to comfort a grieving family or preparing her 'there is hope' speech. She was a trained poker face and I needed more...NOW.

"Can you at least tell me if she is alive??"

"Oh, she is alive..." Her voice trailed off and I heard the word she didn't say...'barely'.

Knowing what she was trying not to convey should have scared me to death. Hearing her fleeting reassurance should have had me fainting or screaming. Seeing what she was trying to get across to us, prepare us for, should have broken me down.

Instead, the oddest feeling came over me. At that moment I was instantly absolutely sure my daughter would eventually be fine. Thank God I was so naïve for so long. It was a false positive that I would come to recognize as footprints in the sand.

The doctors came in and gave us the specifics. She came in nearly dead. Her brain function was the lowest it could be. The Glasgow coma scale is used to evaluate levels of consciousness from 3 to 15 and her score was the dreaded 3. "Patients with a score that low rarely live. Most likely scenario? She will not regain consciousness but if she does, you are looking at a return to minimal functionality" Aka, a vegetative state. That was the first time shock set it. I think it might have stayed with me for the better part of two weeks but it was a cushion from the reality.

They led us into the room where Juliana was being tended to. Blood streaked and smeared across her still unbelievably beautiful face. A large bandage covered her head and tubes were everywhere. Her face was swollen and her eyes were bruised. She was the most beautiful injured person I have ever seen, in person or on TV. That moment we dubbed her, _Sleeping Beauty_.

Within an hour the waiting room was filled. Cheyenne posted on Facebook, "Please pray for my sister Juliana" and that was pretty much all it took. The social network did its thing. I was as flattered as terrified of the attention. It was getting harder to ignore what was right in front of me. We waited through the morning for a battery of tests to assess the damages. She had no internal injuries. Finally, something to be grateful about. We didn't know what to expect but we kept talking to her and trying *to rouse her. After several hours passed with a parade of visitors, and Juli still had not been moved to a room. I learned later that they were doubtful if she would need to be admitted. Wow. While they waited for Juli to die, I waited for them to see it my way. The crowd of supporters grew and it was nearly unmanageable. At one point security needed to step in and control the mob. We were limited to only two visitors at a time until a doctor whispered something to the security guard who then turned to me and said, "I am sorry, I didn't realize your daughter's…condition. Let them come in and say their goodbyes."*

Now let me explain something. Much to my parents' chagrin, I rarely accept what people say at face value. By this point, their position was clear and I already had enough of it. So although the security guard was trying to be tender and sensitive, I couldn't help but think: "he's stupid".

Later that evening the mob of supporters moved up to the 4th floor waiting room and brought food, energy and support. Juliana was finally given a bed in the SINI unit. With the admittance to the hospital I guess they had no choice but to start to agree with me: she would at least make it through the night.

We spoke with the doctor on staff in the unit that night and he told us something that would hold us over when no other answer would suffice. He told us that recovery from a brain injury is a long and unclear process. Every brain is different as every person is different but what I can tell you is that Juliana has three big things in her favor: "She is young, she is healthy, and she is here." Yes the hospital was definitely top in its field for this sort of situation and we were very grateful for the medical care. But as I walked away I thought of the other 'here' he might have been referring to: Alive. Either way, in my mind, our good fortune was only just beginning.

I spent the next several days writing a journal for Juliana. I just knew that she would want all the details when she woke up. She was going to feel so bad for all that we went through. She would also want pictures, though she would have been mortified if I showed them to anyone before she saw them. I would sit by her bed and just tell her everything I thought and felt and wanted for her. I would normally have done that face to face anyway so it was the most natural thing in the world. Besides, a new feeling was creeping in when I had to recognize that the person I told all of my stories to wasn't really listening: I was starting to miss my daughter.

That night, Juli's adoring fiancé Chris and I slept on and off either in her room or on the couch in the waiting room. Since we expected her to suddenly wake up at any moment, leaving was never really an option because we needed to be there when she woke up. I remember my sister asking if I wanted to have someone set up a Care

Pages (illness and recovery support page) for Juli. I was almost offended and said, "NO, not yet. Let's just see how long this lasts." What I wasn't prepared for is the massive amount of calls, texts and visits from people trying to find out how she was doing. Managing that communication was more stress than my figment of a capacity could handle. Therefore, two days later we created a Facebook page that began as a way to keep everyone updated but evolved into my journal…a love letter…a reflection on everything that happened to Juli and to those that loved her along the way. What it became was something much bigger than all of us.

It was written as it happened but I have inserted commentary where the original blog left elements out. As the days go by you will see the posts become more inclusive of what happened as well as how it affected us. These entries became a true representation of the motivation in our lives beyond that moment.

Everything we did was always… 'For Juliana'.

Here is our story…

October 4, 2009 - 9:00 pm

Juliana is still in a coma and on a ventilator and feeding tube. Her motor function and responsiveness to pain continues to improve. Visitors are currently restricted to immediate family and Chris, but visitors will be allowed in the coming days in hopes that friends can help rouse her from slumber.

October 5, 2009 - 7:20 pm

Although Juliana is still in a coma she appears to be trying out for the Chicago Sting. Yes, her leg muscles are intact. In fact, she is also doing her best 'Incredible Hulk' impression by trying to escape from the arm restraints that are fastened for her own good. Sorry, trying to inject a little humor into a humorless situation; it's just one more way to cope. So, tomorrow Juliana is scheduled for surgery at 10:30 am to repair her facial fractures. They are going to wire her jaw and perhaps add a plate inside her mouth to stabilize her bones. (It supposedly sounds worse than it is but based on this description, who out there is signing up for this? That's what I thought) Anyway, the surgery will also involve moving the trach tube from her mouth to her neck and her feeding tube directly into her stomach. These things all have more precise descriptions but what do you want from me? I am a mom, not a doctor. The whole thing should only take 2 hours and she will be much more comfortable. Yeah I know what you are thinking but comfort comes in many forms these days.

The doctors are not recommending stimulation from visitors until after she recovers from surgery so for those of you asking if you can visit, we really need you to be a little more patient. This is going to be a long process so we appreciate your support and look forward to seeing you assist Juli back to full health.

October 6, 2009 - 3:30 pm

Juliana is out of surgery with the best possible outcome of all the scenarios presented to us. No wired jaw since her bite was perfect. They would have known that in the pre surgical examine except, well, her bite was perfect on their finger! Yes, she can kick AND bite...memories of preschool all over again.

...But I digress.

So, they did put in the trach tube and the PEG (feeding tube) which will make her more comfortable and allow her to heal. It will not allow for taco slurpees no matter how much of a good idea it appears to be. Also, No visitors for her tonight, except for her mommy. (No they did not surgically remove me...but then again, why would they.) I am absolutely giddy, can you tell? So tomorrow the rest of the work begins as we start to wake Sleeping Beauty. Hold off on visitors juuuuuuust a bit longer please though your support is really incredible. Have I mentioned that you guys rock?! Thanks for being there for all of us. We feel it, honest to God we do.

October 7, 2009 - 5:00 pm

So...imagine you need a million dollars...and you are pretty sure that you are going to get it...but you are going to get it one penny at a time.

Juliana's recovery is my million dollars.

She is moving her right extremities a little more today and she is exclusively on the trach collar. Those are good things. She is also off of the constant pain medication. That is also a good thing (well, depending on your perspective I suppose). Since she cannot tell us if she is in pain, we are becoming behavior interpreters though not sure we know the lingo. She has a fever that is coming and going and that is not really a good thing but just as everything else, we don't yet know if it's a bad thing. CAT Scans results show no change, which oddly enough is a good thing because it's not worse. Although she is moving, she is not yet aware enough to 'follow commands' the doctors give her like "open your eyes" or "show me two fingers" or "wiggle your toes". That is what the doctors are testing for each hour to check her neurological status. Knowing Juliana, she probably is still debating whether she agrees with the request and is considering IF she will follow.

I will get back to you on that.

Starting tomorrow, short visits for a very short time will be allowed. So for those of you who have been asking, only positive thoughts from those closest to her will be allowed through the glass doors. One thing we have learned is this whole thing is it is moment by moment and Juliana is taking her own time...wait, that's not new! In lieu of an in-person visit, a Facebook visit is equally appreciated.

Tune in tomorrow, I think I might be up to $100.59. Thanks for your prayers. She has already exceeded the doctor's expectations.

October 8, 2009 - 12 pm

Juliana had a rough and restless night followed by an equally rough morning so she will not be allowed to have visitors today after all.

As the day progressed from morning to afternoon I knew something had changed. I was getting scared in a whole new way and mother's intuition told me that something was wrong. Her right eye was swelling by the hour and it was beginning to come out of her eye socket. As the swelling increased so did my fear. I moved from knowing something had changed to being terrified about what it was. This was the first indication of things moving in the wrong direction. They nurses tried not to agree with me but by evening, it could not be denied.

October 8, 2009 - 6 pm

Relief. Juliana always said that was the best emotion. Think about it.

So if October 2nd was the worst day of my life, October 8th was the second worst. Juliana spent the night throwing up and the day swelling up. Her blood pressure began to rise, reaching an alarming 186/118. Her heart rate increased to 119. Her breathing dropped to 4 breaths per minute. I am pretty sure if the monitors were on me, my stats would have been the same. As they tried to tell me that "this sometimes happens with Neuro patients" (her new clique apparently), I tried to tell them, "that's NOT what has been happening with THIS Neuro patient so far so come in the room, examine her again and reassure me." So, they did...examine her anyway. Within 2 minutes we had the floor nurse, our nurse, three interns and the Neurosurgeon examining the day's statistical activities. Five minutes later I was signing a release form for them to insert an EVD tube into her brain to evaluate the pressure (think fetal monitor but for clique members only). The Neurosurgeon said he really hoped he would not have to take this step but it was probably the best option to know what was causing her new symptoms. Ok, so I will spare you the dramatic hour we waited and tell you that they did discover a dangerous amount of pressure on her brain and were administering medication to relieve it, putting her back on the breathing machine and a sedative for a while. He expects we will see improvement soon and within the next 6 hours we will know if we need to reassess, but is relatively confident that we are going to see improvement within a day or so.

Juliana is right. Relief. You feel it?

Maybe just a little...

'Reassess' we learned would be to remove a portion of her skull to allow the brain to continue swelling as it needed to. Without any release the swelling of the brain would press on the brain stem making recovery much more tenuous, if at all possible. The doctor gave us our choices: "You could wait and see how much more this pressure grows and then make a decision later, or you could let me put a tube into her brain to monitor the pressure and relieve some of it. Its up to you."

Really doc, ME again?

"What would you do?"

"I would do the procedure."

"Do it."

With a sweep of a cloth he removed his tweed jacket and revealed what would later be described as a large S on his chest and a flowing red cape. That doctor, that man who had previously been nicknamed "Dr Death" suddenly became a superhero to our delicate angel. We were forced to trust him with her life and for whatever reason, we did.

October 8, 2009 - 11 pm

I am officially 10 years older, 20 years wiser and 100 years more grateful. Juli is stable through the 6 hour window. Your prayers and positive thoughts are working. They pulled us through a rough one. Let's see what tomorrow brings. (I think I might be down to $50.00 though.)

After that horrific day of returning to square one, I spent the next day trembling. I was supposed to be happy that we made it through a crisis but I was instead developing a new sense of underlying terror. I avoided seeing my other kids because I was afraid I couldn't comfort them and they completely relied on my perspective to know it was going to be ok. That was my job and I was on shaky employment. Dylan, still thousands of miles away, was reassured to the point of being unaware of the gravity. We lived in denial together. I was holding on by the thread of hope that since Juliana and I had such a great relationship before the accident, by sheer will I could harvest the ability to pull her through….

October 9, 2009 - 9:30 pm

I just had a heart to heart with my daughter. I reminded her of all the times that she came home frustrated and overwhelmed by her problems and how we form a plan to solve them. She laughed at my need to plan things but she also relied on it.

So tonight I told her the new plan: Regardless of what she hears the doctors say, she is to fight. Regardless of what I hear the doctors say, I will believe. Regardless of the health scares, we will be brave and regardless of the duration, we will endure. We are going to continue to do that together with the help of all of your support. Juliana is still in critical condition, but she is stable. With the fractures on the right side of her face she may need additional surgery on her right eye. They say that vision in that eye is not likely, though without her being awake, they don't know. She is heavily sedated, back on the ventilator and will stay that way until she is stronger. Tonight they are going to put in a central line because her veins are not cooperating. The doctors continue to be more cautious than optimistic. But that's ok, I don't need them to be kind, I need them to be good.

7 days, 18 hours, Sleeping Beauty still sleeps...

October 10, 2009 - 8:30 pm

Here is how I measured my day: Heart rate 98, BP 107/63, Pulse-Ox 100, Breaths per minute 14, Central Line 4, ICP 16.

Translation...statistically it was a really good day.

Juliana had a procedure to allow for the reduction of swelling behind her eye. It required... (ready?)...cutting the side of her eye: flesh AND bone.... I KNOW! Authorizing that today made us cringe too, and we did hesitate because she has been through so much already. (Wait til I tell Juli this whole crazy story...she will never believe it.) They assured us it was the best chance to save her sight. What's a mother to do? I will tell you: Fight my daughter's fight while she regains her strength. Thanks to all of you who give ME the strength to keep doing that.

October 11, 2009 - 11:30 am

I love being right. For all of you who know me, you know this to be true. (My ex-husband is not on Facebook or he would surely confirm this). In fact, I suspect that all of you have at least a secret love of being right.

So this time, we are all right.

Juliana's latest CT scan showed, at long last, improvement. The swelling has gone down, they are able to see the brain stem and are (to quote the Neurologist who had previously given us very little hope), "very hopeful".

Welcome to OUR club, doc.

As I reported, all her scores were perfect. (Good behavior does pay off) and tomorrow morning they will take the EVD tube out. Then they can take her off of the sedation, get her back to breathing on her own, AND THEN we can return to the road back to consciousness.

I always told Juliana she was magical and my life had purpose when she was born. And don't get me wrong; I am appreciative for all that medical science is doing to help my daughter. The medical staff here is top notch (even if their propensity is to prepare you for the worst). But I really believe that WE are creating a miracle here.

Isn't it awesome to be part of something so incredible? Try being me. I am grateful.

October 11, 2009 - 10:30 pm

Chris described this best: a horrible roller coaster that alternates between bad and not so bad. Right now, I am hanging by a thread and it feels bad. Nothing new, no real reason to doubt, but this is heavy and I am weaker than I thought. Pretty big shift from this morning's update, right? That's the roller coaster. I don't know, this is all new to me. It's just that she is an amazing daughter and a friend and I miss her a lot. It's just taking its toll. As she continues to progress she will not need intensive medical assistance so she will be transferred to another facility for care and rehab. That could actually happen later this week. We are supposed to meet with the social worker tomorrow to learn our options. However before the doctors talked about that they felt it was necessary to cripple her support system by reminding us of her slim chances for recovery. If they are interested in patient recovery, why go there? We already heard it, we are doing our part to hope and believe and they want to be sure we don't believe too much. It's sad really, for them as much as us. The doctor and the nurse walked in to have a 'talk' with us. They didn't feel that we had realistic expectations of Juliana's situation and they wanted to discuss it with us. "Ok, lets step outside and talk." The doctor said, "Its ok, she can't hear us." Now I know very little about a person in a coma but I was NOT going to have 'the talk' in earshot when we wouldn't even let people cry at her bedside. "STEP OUTSIDE" I told him and then led the way out. Before he could speak I said, "From the beginning you have told us that 'You don't know'. You have said that the brain is still very unknown and it's unclear how much she will progress. You are done with her in a few days and I have to fight for her for the rest of her life. Why would you try to disable her support system before they even get started?" I was not letting him speak still and I knew the lashing out was for many reasons beyond this talk. I was still holding it together but the thread was nearly bare. "Doc, if YOU don't know...why can't I be right?" He just stared apologetically and I shook visibly. I have no idea if I believed what I said or even if someone else was speaking for me but I couldn't NOT say it. "You are right" he said. "Let's just wait and see" and then he walked away.

I don't know why I let it rock me but I totally did and tonight, I need you to carry the 'positive vibe' torch for me, I cannot.

Let's see what tomorrow brings.

Immediately following that conversation I sat resolutely at my daughter's bed speaking to no one. I shot daggers of fire at anyone who approached the bed and clenched my teeth so hard that my mouth bled. I was quietly imploding and doing so in silent torture like an armored tank at her bedside. People came in to talk to me and I would not respond nor release my intense fury. There must have been whispering amongst our support teams because my husband finally extracted me from her room and walked me to the 'quiet room' to talk. Without saying a word I broke. I spent the next four hours crying hysterically. I would neither be consoled, nor comforted and shamefully pitied myself as much as my poor wounded daughter. It was the first time I cried, really cried in the whole event and it was epic. I rolled into a ball and wailed with all of my heart and soul for everything that happened and everything that was yet to happen. I cried for all of my children who would forever have a broken mom, even if Juliana recovered fully. I knew then that in spite of my inflated confidence, the doctors and nurses succeeded in puncturing my resolve and I was starting to tumble off this mountain I didn't want to be on. I hated them for that at the time. I felt like they disabled the support system that would be required to help her heal long after they were done. It would be much later that I could see the compassion in what they tried to do. Being the fourth of five kids, I never truly had that feeling of being in charge, and never wanted it. With both of my parents gone I suddenly looked around and realized I was the parent here and I didn't have a damn clue what I was doing, yet six kids were counting on me to show them the way. It was too much. It was incredibly overwhelming and insurmountable...for that time. When my loud wails subsided, shock and catatonia set it. I was lost inside my own head. Dylan called and asked to talk to me but I could not and that panicked him and I. I could no longer pretend that it was all just OK. That was all he needed to hear to know what he had to do. Against my request, my husband put the phone to my catatonic ear:

"Mom, if I have to sell everything I have here, books, laptop, clothes, whatever, I will do it. I am coming home." I couldn't say anything. The sobs just started all over again.

October 12, 2009 -11 pm

The blink of an eye.

That is how quickly your life can change. Today started with the EVD tube being removed from Juliana's brain, then the sedation was slowly stopped. We watched her all day for signs of movement like she had prior to the swelling that set her back. We wanted to see her arms grabbing at tubes, leg kicking nurses, fighting her way back. We wanted to see that for her, for us, and to prove to the cautious doctors and nurses that the human spirit, HER spirit, was powerful. All day she was peaceful with only slight movements of her fingers, delicate wiggling of toes, and minor movements of her arms.

Then, during her every 2-hour assessment, ever so slightly...

She blinked her eye.

It's a very small step, but it is a step where they thought there might be none. It is the glimmer of hope that I needed to lift the cloud that was taking over.

And it all happened in a blink of an eye.

Thank you to all of you for being an awesome support system. Good people make all the difference in the world, well, in my world anyway.

For the first time in 10 days, I am going to sleep all night in my own bed...goodnight.

October 13, 2009 - 8 pm

From Wikipedia: A coma is a profound state of unconsciousness. A comatose person cannot be awakened, fails to respond normally to pain or light, does not have sleep-wake cycles, and does not take voluntary actions.

From Me: 'Waking from a Coma' is not an event, it is a process. And it could be a very long process.

Thought I would share my new knowledge with you, though with 1700 of you out there, I bet some of you knew all that. I know I sure didn't know that back when this all began and I was waiting for the soap opera 'waking' where the heroine snaps open her eyes and breathes a well-rested sigh...

October 13, 2009 - 9:45 pm

So you know it's gotta be good if I am back again so soon.

Juliana's left pupil reacted to light which is an awesome accomplishment... and then...THEN...she tried to open her eye! She tried!! This is so excellent. Keep doing what you are doing support team!

October 14, 2009 - 3:30 pm

As Juliana's mom, of course I will wait forever for her to wake up. I won't give up hope because there isn't an expiration date on parenthood. The medical field has their own ideas. So proverbial, good news/bad news time...

Good News: Juliana is on the trach collar (again), off of medication other than for pain. She is starting to make small advancements toward consciousness and she is considered medically stable. Yet, because of all this 'goodness', she does not qualify for a Long Term Acute Center (LTAC), which is the step before Rehabilitation where they prepare patients for the aggressive rehabilitation ahead.

Bad News: She is still considered 'unresponsive' since she can't participate in rehabilitation, regardless of the improvements she has made, and although she is not on the ventilator, she can cough, choke and elevate her blood pressure and heart rate to alarming numbers which require medical intervention (that was our morning and is starting to be our afternoon again as I type). Because of this 'badness' she doesn't qualify for a Rehabilitation Center either.

That leaves a nursing home.

I hate even typing that. They say that the elevated blood pressure and heart rate is to be expected when they are coming out of a coma and to be prepared. They say this could be a good sign but they just don't know and it's frightening to watch. Well let me tell you, there isn't a parent out there that would expect any of this and preparation is just not possible, no matter what they say. 2 steps forward and (hopefully only) 1 step back.

In the middle of it now so I will update later.

October 14, 2009 - 10:45 pm

Today ended being more peaceful than it started and that is a good thing. Just like a new baby, we are learning things about our Juliana...when her temperature goes up, so do her vitals. Next time we (Chris) will panic just a little less. Ok, I confess, I panicked too but Chris made me!

Her nurses have been really awesome. They actually treat her like a person, not a patient. Of course, when 20 of her closest friends camped out for 2 weeks in their place of business, we probably grew on them.

Tomorrow she will likely be moved to another facility where the hopes are that they will give her the rehabilitation steps needed to improve. We don't know where or when just yet but I will keep you updated. And...we will likely get her into an LTAC facility after all. Yeah, sometimes I whine for nothing, pay no attention.

I have to tell you, even though this is every mother's nightmare...no, every FAMILY'S nightmare, since so many of us are impacted, there has oddly enough been some good come out of this as well. Some relationships were mended, others were formed and the rest were appreciated anew. That is what magic is about. Did I mention Juliana is magical? Yeah, I might say it again too someday. But then again, you might already know it.

October 15, 2009 - 3:45 pm

We have all heard about assumptions...

If you have been reading along, you won't be surprised anymore at the ebb and flow of the chain of events. Last night when I posted the update, I 'assumed' Juliana would be moved today to Rush-May-Loyola Specialty Hospital (RML). Right after I posted it, I also 'assumed' I would be writing another post that she did something wonderful because she seemed soooooo close to opening her eyes.

But Juliana will not be rushed to go anywhere or do anything.

She had been having an intermittent fever for days and the blood cultures came back at midnight indicating she has an infection in her blood. What this means is she is back on antibiotics and will not be moving anywhere until she is once again stable. This might seem like a setback but it has a bright side. It gives her a few more days to begin to regain consciousness so she can hopefully go to RIC instead of RML. At least that is how the nurses try to spin this latest turn of events. I am not sure what to think really but it is the devil we know vs. the devil we don't. Our nurses love her like one of their own so that is a safety net for me at the moment. I just don't know what to expect at the next juncture.

As for my other assumption, everyone feels like she is on the verge of a breakthrough but until we actually can see her following commands consistently (play along and pretend like Juli might actually have done that in consciousness), we have to 'assume' that she will be going to RML when the infection clears.

Yes, I do know that I am doing that again.

So for those of you SINI waiting room campers, it looks like tonight and tomorrow night she will still be in bed 18.

Until we have a new plan...

That night, Chris and I stayed up all night talking. It would be the first of many times we did that in an effort to glue each other back together. It took many months before I admitted to him how I depended on his support. But this particular night I was wrought with guilt. All the mistakes of motherhood weighed heavily on my mind and I replayed all of the 'should haves' under sobs and sighs. Chris is a very insightful young man and having only seen him as 'one of the kids' up to this point, I surely overlooked the impact that insightfulness could have on a situation of this magnitude. He has been paying attention to people and specifically our family for the better part of 7 years and although I was unaware, he really already knew me.

"You always do that," he said.

"What?"

"You always take the blame and the burden on yourself, usually to save your kids from it. You have this way of making it all your fault. Don't do that now. This was an accident and regardless of how anyone might have prevented it, none of that matters now. It happened and we will go forward...together. "

That conversation lasted for hours and was one of mutual therapeutic benefits. We established our new strange relationship as partners in this unbelievable journey and made some choices that would forever influence the course of her recovery. The first of which is that all crossroads and decisions would be faced together so neither one of us would shoulder the burden of this responsibility alone. With me as her past and him as her future, we conceded to each other's value in every aspect of the unknown life of Juliana. The second decision was that no matter what, we would be only focus on recovery. Blame, cause, excuses would not be addressed, dissected or considered because to maintain full focus on where we needed to go, we could not let any of that useless negativity influence our purpose.

October 15, 2009 - 3:30 pm

Just listening to the Black Eyed Peas, 'Tonight's Gonna Be a Good Night'. Juliana made everyone in the family watch that opening segment of Oprah's new season a hundred times. We made that our anthem for a whole weekend. Juliana inspires those moments all the time. In fact, they seem to gravitate to her...hmmm. For those of you saying you don't know her, stick around and meet her when she is well. She is worth the wait.

She is still running a temperature and has an infection. It is under control, she is on antibiotics, and will once again be staying at Christ hospital at least through the weekend. All of her other vitals are good. Her right eye appears to be improving but that is another big unknown. To watch the Ophthalmologist insensitively 'examine' her eye this morning was almost enough to make me pass out in sympathy. I could see the pain on her face even in her state and I was extremely saddened by how hard this must be for her silently trapped inside.

She seems to be intermittently following commands, which the doctors and Rehabilitation Centers translate to 'not following commands'. We translate that to...pretty soon she WILL be consistent, of course. (Maybe the doctors need to find a little faith from our powerful Facebook support group... geez)

Chris and I went to visit RML Specialty Hospital in Hinsdale today. It was a sobering visit that really illustrates the long road ahead of us. That is where Juliana will likely be moving to once she gets released from Christ. It is intended to be a short term stay to get her off of the ventilator, provide preliminary PT and OT and continue the efforts to bring her back to consciousness. During that visit I still couldn't comprehend that this is our life now and struggle with that on the eve of her planned Bridal Shower. But more than that, I felt just really, really grateful that my daughter is alive.

One more thing: Many of you have commented on my strength and it really boggles my mind when strong is the last thing I feel. During the last 14 days and 13 hours I have often felt I was in a coma as well, just keeping my head above water. So for all of the strength I appear to have, what you are really seeing is the reflection of my incredible support system consisting of an amazingly awesome family, powerful prayer/support chain, and my steadfast belief that Juliana will recover.

Ok, tear filled eyes, screen blurry, update later.

October 16, 2009 - 12:30 am

Tonight started like so many others:

Chris playing his guitar and singing. Old songs, new songs, and songs he creates as he goes…The crowd gathers and enjoys and laughs and just loves the moment.

But this time the crowd was smaller and more inspired because we were gathered around Juliana's bed and listening to him sing to her, "Open your eyes, Open them wide, Open them so I can see the beauty in my life"

And

Wait for it

Nah

She didn't

BUT

She did officially and 'on record' follow commands!

This is a really great step toward regaining consciousness. (I know…this whole 'I can move, I can even follow commands but I am still in a coma' thing is very confusing. I swear I know people like that in my everyday life!)

So the Peas were right after all…tonight WAS a good night.

Tomorrow will be even better because there will be hundreds of people in one place thinking the same thought: Wake up Sleeping Beauty.

October 17, 2009 - 11:15 pm

First of all, I have to once again thank all of those who put together such a heartfelt support for Juliana. My gratitude can never truly be expressed. For all of you who were in attendance, I am now glad I came because it was extremely uplifting, yet again.

Juliana is still about the same, her progress was remarkable today but additional achievements may take a few more days. This is a long distance race, not a sprint. We don't plan to tire so, once again, we wait for Juli.

For those of you that asked (or were not there today), here is my message given at the benefit (Sorry, I promise I won't make them all this long):

"As you know, today was to be Juliana's bridal shower. That was just one of the many activities that go into planning a wedding. We have been planning it for a year and a half and were coming close to completion (ad lib coming…I planned it for a year and a half, Juliana started participating about 4 months ago, once again in her timetable). I was getting really stressed about the wedding, the cost, the details, the deadlines….but it only took one phone call to want THOSE problems back.

This has been a year of challenges for our family. This particular event has been called 'horrible', 'saddening' and 'tragic'. And yes, this is every family's nightmare. My beautiful, promising, vibrant daughter's life came to a screeching pause 15 days and12 hours ago. The original prognosis was grim. The first hours, they did not expect she would live. Beyond that, they didn't expect she would come out of the coma at all. Minute by minute, breath by breath, we held ours and prayed. To say that our feelings have been overwhelming would really be an understatement.

But thanks to all of this, all of the support, all of you, we have never fallen too far into despair. What started as just a mother's irrational hope for a recovery actually evolved to a glimmer, a possibility and, as of this morning, a reality. As small of a step as it may seem, Juliana was able to hold up 2 fingers upon command! For those of you who know her, anything 'upon command' is an accomplishment. But what this really means is that it's not just my desire for her to improve anymore. It is happening. That very simple '2 fingers' is according to her Neurosurgeon, a complex command. For the first time, those 2 fingers really meant 'peace'…peace of mind.

So for all of this incredible potential, I credit all of you. During the last 2 weeks I have been forced to recognize that 1. I am not as strong as I thought, 2. I am not as positive as I thought, and 3. The weight of the world is not only on me. You are all helping me carry it. I also realize all the wonderful things that are happening all around us. Relationships have been formed, strengthened and repaired. Its powerful, it's healing and it's real. I could go on and on but I need to save some details for Juli to share on Oprah. But I do need to take this opportunity to personally thank all of you for pulling together in support of my little girl, my family and me. Especially, I need to thank Lori, my sister-in-law Toula Spencer, my niece Allison Carroll, Juli's best friend Sarah Mitchell, Chris's mom Gloria Medina and my wonderful husband Donnie for working so hard to make this event successful. Even though money can't make her heal, the unknown factor in her recovery is provided by your support. I've said it before, I will say it again, Juliana is magical.

This room is electric, you all are wonderful, her recovery is tangible and I am grateful. Thank you."

October 18, 2009 - 7:30 pm

So you recall that yesterday morning we had a little 'confirmed excitement'. And perhaps many of you are watching for updates a little more frequently now, sure that any moment we will have another exciting development. But I have to remind myself (and you as well), that we may see many days pass where nothing new happens at all. That is the pace we have to expect. But in case you are curious, I can share some of the 'pennies' we have received in the last week: She is swallowing more often ($5), yawning occasionally ($5), making slight facial expressions (5$). The more 'movements' she makes, the better of course. We talk to her constantly, describing the day, her environment, events, herself. She moves her hands around the breathing equipment too. She used to tug on it but now she seems to just be curious so what she touches, we describe. Yesterday she was holding my hand and playing with my wedding ring. I explained what she was touching and thought she may somewhere in there wonder about her own ring. I told her that Chris is wearing it safely around his neck until he can put it back on her finger. She gently dropped her hand from mine and appeared to rest. It's our new language I guess, but I am learning with her. Is it odd to say it's beautiful to be a part of it?

Juliana being a night owl tends to be more active during the night. This is the time they usually give her the 'spa treatment'. They soaked her hair in conditioner for an hour and used de-tangler to finally get all the knots out of her hair. I awoke in the morning to find they had replaced my daughter with Dorothy from the Wizard of Oz!

As the day progressed, since she is very stable they decided it was time to sit her up so they put her in a cardiac chair which allows her to sit up but get secured in place. (Let's call that $20) It made me nervous to leave her side though because if she falls forward or sideways, she would not be able to correct herself. For a moment, she slid down to the right and I got to slip my arms around her back to fix her. It was a sweet and long awaited for…hug.

Priceless

October 18, 2009 - 9:45 pm

Expectations…

You know, I just set YOURS to not expect too much new information and then here I am, updating you just 2 hours later. It's not an eye opener (pun intended) but it is another example of an improvement that we were told not to expect.

You remember the comment from the 'pessimologist'…er…ophthalmologist that said Juliana would likely 'lose her right eye'? Well, she is NOW showing corneal reflex in that eye too. It's not a major advancement but it is an indication that there is a possibility of activity in that eye where our expectations were set to be none.

I have learned to expect the unexpected, again.

But don't expect another update tonight.

Or should you?

…hmmmm

Wouldn't THAT be cool…?

October 19, 2009 - 9:30 am

Sometime this afternoon, Juliana (and her entourage) is moving to RML Specialty Hospital in Hinsdale. Visitors are welcomed and appreciated. It's a very good place that specializes in weaning patients off of ventilators. That will be the main goal while she is there although we are hopeful that the increased activity and movement will also further her connection to consciousness. When she is more able to participate in rehabilitation, she can qualify for the Rehabilitation Institute of Chicago (RIC). That is where the real work will begin. It continues to feel like she is sooooooo close, (as all of you who have crouched down in front of her face when we were sure her eyes were about to open, can attest to). We have seen fluttering eyelids, her head swaying in response to direct requests to 'wake up'. She seems just under the surface but we can't seem to pull her out! The swelling in her right eye continues to improve so we are using that as our gauge of the swelling inside. It is really a test of patience for all of us sleep deprived onlookers. It has also been an opportunity to really watch Chris become an incredible partner to my daughter. To echo the sentiments of Juliana's dad, I will also be very proud to have him as a son-in-law. (Yeah so those of you that know us knew that was always true anyway but now more so than ever before). My daughter is going to be very happy to hear how dedicated and tender this fiancé is. Chris said to me one day, "Now I have to rewrite my vows. I planned to commit to all of the things that I will do but by the time we get married, I will have already proven that I have done it." Chris, you are my family, always and forever and I could not have made it through this without you.

Goodbye Christ Hospital, hello RML...

October 19, 2009 - 9:30 pm

Here we are at our next stop, RML Specialty Hospital. The transit here was fine, she appeared a little agitated when we got here and then she slept for a few hours. We have met a lot of staff and they seem very nice and to be caring for her ok so far. We know this is a positive step, and a good place, but it is scary. It's just that we did get a little attached to our core group of excellent nurses who got us through the roughest days of our lives. We have to get used to all new staff and new routines, but it's a small price to pay.

She no longer has as many monitors and tubes. That's another good thing we know, but they were our indication of when it was time to be concerned and time to rest confident she would be ok for a while. Tomorrow they will begin the weaning process to get her off the ventilator. Another very slow process but the first is to go on the trach collar. We know she was able to handle that before so hopefully that step will be easy. The physical therapy will also begin tomorrow but since this is not a rehabilitation center, we can't really expect vigorous exercise which suits Juli just fine since she is not really a 'vigorous exercise' kind of girl.

I don't expect much sleep tonight as I watch her every move and make sure she is safe all night. Much like the way we met...

October 20, 2009 - 11 pm

Today we learned a lot. We learned that even when you are technically not 'awake', you can still have an exhausting day. As planned, Juliana was switched to the trach collar for 12 hours. She tolerated it well, as we suspected she would and will do it again for 12 hours tomorrow. She also got her first session of physical therapy and we got our first session of learning how to help her with the exercises. She was visited by the speech therapist who talked to us about developing a language with Juli in her few minutes of responsiveness each day. We were also instructed to try to develop a routine with her and limit the time we spend trying to stimulate her to 20 minute increments. We are going to be capitalizing on all of her senses by using aromatherapy, music, movies, touch. After those sessions she will also now need 4 one hour rest periods where the room is dark and quiet and no one is to bother her. (I know that for just one moment you are thinking this coma gig isn't so bad after all, eh?) Anyway, this is so that she can use those hours to process the stimulation activities and heal. We have been told to describe everything and use details. Don't assume she knows who you are, who she is, or anything about her surroundings. Tell her. Sounds to me like what I have been doing for 23 years and had to learn NOT to do it. As I said, we learned a lot.

The new ophthalmologist came in to examine her and said she has an infection in her eye and gave her new drops. He said it is too soon to tell how her vision will be affected but his initial diagnosis is that there will be some deficit. He was gentle and kind and talked to her, not about her. In fact, I think we are going to be ok with all the staff here at RML too.

Her eyelids are fluttering more and more all the time. She seems to really want to open her eyes but is still struggling with how to do it. It's frustrating to watch what appears to be a very subtle struggle and not be able to help. I have no idea if we will get other 'signs' or if this is what to look for.

She had several visitors and started to get a little worked up so Chris decided to request a little quiet time for her himself. It's comforting to know that he has learned to pay attention to her needs. After 7 years together I would say that Juliana has taught him well.

Keep thinking good thoughts For Juliana.

October 21, 2009 - 9 pm

Many of you know us well, but there is a considerable group of you that don't know our family at all. The fact that you keep us in your thoughts and prayers anyway, is moving and definitely appreciated. For those of you who don't know us, let me just tell you, I had the perfect life for me. Maybe not the exact life I planned to have but it was actually even better than my plan! It was a great, happy and fulfilled life. I considered myself fortunate for that life and thanked God for all my blessings. I know that I have already had more good fortune than many people, so to ask for more would be greedy.

But I am. Asking for more that is.

So today, nothing new so far: Nothing bad, nothing different, and nothing worse, just quiet. I want to be happy about that but greedily I still want more. Every day and every night as I watch Juliana lying in that bed I look for any signs of improvement to convince myself she is getting better than this. Hoping that I am getting my great life back where planning a wedding was a stressful pleasure. (Definitely didn't appreciate that enough) I doze off and wake up thinking this new life might not be real, but it still is. I may never have that life back, and I can accept that. What I want now is whatever life I can get for my daughter that includes her own fulfillment, whatever that will look like. For that to begin I sit and wait, hope and pray, and of course, believe. It's faith in the unknown while being uncertain what I am looking for because hours (and sometimes days) go by with just pennies that are sometimes hard to recognize.

I found two on the floor this morning by the way, face up. I kept them.

October 22, 2009 - 4:45 pm

Did you know that I was the only one to get 100% on the Facebook quiz: "How well do you know Juliana"? I wasn't surprised and neither was she. She always says that we have a psychic connection. When I call her she claims to know it at the ring and calls it out in advance. I would need witnesses to testify to that. But true or not, she knows me, knows how I react, what I like, what I don't , what I believe and what I don't and always…how to get to me. I know all that about her as well.

And I know her better now.

I know that when her heart rate is between 75-85 you might as well not talk to her because she is not listening. I know that when it reaches 127, mine starts beating faster and neither of us is listening. I know that 1 finger means "yes", and 2 fingers means "no" and that it makes us ecstatic if once a day we can get her to answer us. I know that it takes 47 minutes to comb out her hair when it's wet and she is lying down. 40 if I give up on the knots and cut them out (which I would NEVER do Juliana, no matter what they tell you ☺). I know that she relaxes when you rub her feet or straighten her arms, even if she acts like she doesn't want you to do it. I know that every day when Chris plays the guitar and sings by her bedside she sometimes sheds a tear, and I do too. I know that when she is most alert, she is most afraid. And I KNOW that she is in there somewhere and wants to come out.

Two steps forward, on step back. That has been the path we have taken, and took yet again. Last night Juliana spiked a temperature of 101.9 and her heart rate went to 154. (The alarm sounds at 130 just to give you an idea). She first got Tylenol, then Ativan. When neither of them worked to slow her heart rate they started her back on IV antibiotics. That didn't lower her heart rate enough either so they gave her fluids. That did the trick. It was a scary, sleepless 6 hours. The 6 hours immediately following my complaints of a quiet day.

In spite of all I know, I guess I will never learn.

October 23, 2009 - 12 pm

Good night last night, good day today so far. It has been statistically sound, nothing new to report really and this time I am NOT complaining. (Just in case written gratitude counts). Juliana has had 3 days of success on the trach collar, 12 hours, 16 hours then 24 hours. This is very good news. They will leave the collar on for a couple more days and then if she continues to do well the next step is downsizing the tube. After that they will cap it off for a period of time and the final step is to remove the trach altogether. Those are the steps, now let's see if we take a straight road there or the typical winding path. For many patients rehabilitation starts before the capping or even the downsizing because trach weaning is not a prerequisite for rehab. The prerequisite is her participation. And that means she needs to 'wake up' or at least have more than a few moments of responsiveness each day. RML will assist us on stimulating responsiveness more after they complete the weaning process. For now we continue to follow the physical therapy exercises they showed us and of course follow our own stimulation methods. Since of the five senses she is mostly dependent upon touch and hearing, we are focusing on that. This means that everyone in the room is entertained by several concerts a day by Juliana's favorite artist, Chris Medina. Juliana will be excited to hear the new songs that are being generated on her behalf from this emotional time. Today, Gloria mentioned that it's been raining for days now. Chris said, "That's because heaven's crying because they don't get to have my angel". Have I mentioned before that I love that young man? You all do too now, right? Yeah, that's what I though. Yes Chris, congratulations, you are G.

October 24, 2009 - 8:45 am

Yesterday was a very productive day. Not as productive as the birthday girls wanted (Toula and Stacy, thanks for spending your wish on her) but we do get closer all the time. We found more and more successful opportunities for Juliana to respond. It's still hit and miss but we saw at least 10 times when she held up fingers in response to our questions. Her responses are still weak and delayed but progress will come slowly so we will take it. Just this morning when I felt I had a window, I asked Juli, "does it hurt to try to open your eyes?" and she held up 1 finger. That confirmed our suspicion that perhaps the eye opening we are looking for will not happen until her eye is healed. That is happening at its own pace too. We will see the ophthalmologist again on Monday and hope he indicates that the infection is clearing. If it is, the progress is very, very slow. Juli also got into the cardiac chair again though she slept through the whole experience. (When I say sleep that means her heart rate is under 90). We tried more extensive massage on her arms and legs and rubbed different textures on her skin. No reaction that we could see really but we are told it helps stimulate the senses so, even unrewarded, we continued.

We met a new family yesterday and shared experiences and when I told them of Juli's accident, they too had a family member who had been in a coma for a long time then returned to a productive life. There are more of them out there than the doctors lead you to believe. We will be one of those as well. Thanks for waiting with me.

October 25, 2009 - 8 am

So by now you have all realized that these updates are for me as much as they are for you. Each day as I think about what I want to tell you, I have to think about what I believe about this situation and the two become intertwined. I remember my dad telling me, "You never know what you believe until you begin to instruct your children." There is something about stating your opinion to a captive audience that forces you to check your facts before you do it. So these updates force me to consider what I know and what I am willing to commit to as my beliefs on paper, even if it isn't read by anyone at all.

I actually started a journal the day of the accident as a way of keeping track of this most unbelievable sequence of events thinking that Juliana would certainly want to know everything that happened and how I felt at the time. I wrote for 11 days, 59 pages. Then I stopped. Somewhere in the 54th page I noticed that I stopped writing TO Juliana and started writing ABOUT her. The shift in thinking scared me and I had to set it aside.

I was afraid I was starting to stop believing she was going to come back.

But here we are 23 days later (I can hardly believe THAT either) and every day she inches back, still just pennies at a time, but it's progress. Each day she may not do something 'more' but she in exchange may do something 'different'. I know that we also have to expect days when nothing will improve and even setbacks (oh yes, lest we get too comfortable in our progress...)

Our family meeting with the doctors to discuss our next steps is November 4th so we are hopeful she will have made sufficient strides in participation and consciousness to qualify for a rehabilitation facility. Currently, she only responds during certain windows of wakefulness, but her reliability for response is getting more consistent. Looking at where we are today might not seem much, until I look at where we have come from: the mangled car, the photos of her the first day, her prognosis upon arrival. Then I look at her now. That is why I can believe.

October 26, 2009 - 7:45 am

"Some things never last...if it goes for the good, it must go for the bad...I do believe it too." Keith Urban from "Live to Love Another Day". Those of you who know me know that I like to quote songs and apply them to situations. In fact, many of my parenting choices were suggestions from Garth Brooks! And those of you that know Juliana knows that she likes to quote...come on, you know it, you love it...'Friends'. She quotes that show all the time. Last season on the Bachelorette, Juliana and I were trying to figure out who one of the guys reminded us of. We kept saying, we know it's a friend of ours but we couldn't place it. Then it occurred to both of us at the same time, literally. It was one of those moments where I called her to tell her and she said, "I was just about to call you…" The 'friend' of ours was Chandler from 'Friends'. So many things shape your life that you aren't expecting. In fact I would say that 'Friends' overall have shaped her very interesting life. And now, her friends, her supporters, (all of you) are shaping the person who I will be for the rest of mine. See here's the thing. You can't go through something like this without being changed, obviously. "Life's about changing, nothing ever stays the same" Suzy Boguss (…see…). And though I have known many of her friends from the time they were children, I am so proud and inspired by the adults they are becoming. I am encouraged that they are our future; they are such a force here in the present! Even more than even that, I am encouraged about society if so many people can care about this one angel and her family. Honestly team, I am rarely sad about this anymore. I sometimes feel guilty about how much good I see in this whole situation. But I know that just as your body goes into shock to protect you from the pain of severe trauma, your mind does as well. Wait, that isn't fair. I will give credit where it is due. Those 'footprints in the sand'…yes, I am totally being carried. I even feel like I am floating. I feel like I have help breathing. I feel like I am in a bit of a coma myself sometimes but it is how the support works. Because Juliana was the beginning of everything important to me, if I had to focus on the devastation I could not make it. There really isn't strength enough in a person to survive that. Anyone who has been in a similar situation can attest to that. This is not something you survive alone. So the next time one of you thinks that I am being strong, share the wealth. It's you, it's love and support, and it's faith that is carrying this burden and helping us all heal. Life is good, people are good, and God is good. Don't doubt it.

Ok, enough pontificating on my part. Here's what you really want to know…Juliana continues to improve. She is following commands more frequently and more consistently and we know that means she is slooooooooooowly regaining consciousness. I actually don't care how slow it is, we are certain it will happen and that is good enough. (Chris might disagree with the pace, though he seems just thrilled every day when she gives him a sign of acknowledgement.) She also continues to be medically stable though the longer she remains in that bed, the greater her chances of developing an infection which could set her back. I am trying to make sure we don't lose sight of that. We did have an incident yesterday where she reached across with her left arm and scratched the inside of her infected right eye. Oh yeah, you all cringed too, right? It was not pretty. There was blood, there was pain and there was a lot of 'poor baby-ing' going on. Hopefully that won't have additional adverse effects on her healing. Did I mention in a previous update that I promised that the updates wouldn't be that long? Sorry, I guess I have to take that back. That's ok, friends understand, right?

October 26, 2009 - 10 pm

This month in (our) history…

Makeup, jewelry, business suits and 3 inch heels – OUT;

Jeans, sweatshirts, gym shoes and a pony tail – IN

Weight Watchers and LA Fitness – OUT;

Vending machine snacks and physical therapy – IN

8 hours of sleep in my own bed – OUT;

Sporadic sleep in a recliner – IN

Wallpapered walls, scented candles, tikibar parties – OUT;

Fluorescent lights, hand sanitizer and waiting room hangouts - IN

Cooking, Dishes, and Laundry – OUT;

Meals provided by caring family and friends, Disposable cutlery and laundry done by my husband – IN (um, yeah, so, Donnie and Juli always did the laundry so for me I guess that part was always out…hee hee)

Holding grudges – OUT;

Bonding – SO TOTALLY IN

And in other news…

Juliana's trach was downsized from a size 8 to a 6. This gives her vocal cords room to move if they set her up with a voice box which is really just a tube that will allow air passage in both directions and produce sound when the day comes that she tries to speak. The speech therapist was thinking she might do this today but she came by to evaluate Juliana's responsiveness but …parents out there see this coming… kids never perform when you want them to! So we will try again later, another day maybe. Today she is less active than yesterday all around. Her doctor assured us that after the last few days of increased activity, that a day or low activity is not abnormal and not to get discouraged. If we expect progress in a straight incline, we will be disappointed. Yeah, yeah, we know but it is still our inclination to expect forward progress and fear standing still because although one day this will ALL be history, we patiently wait while she re-writes hers.

October 27, 2009 - 4 pm

You remember when you were child and you had this impression of adulthood that included being in charge, in control and having all the answers? Some of us even thought we would finally be through with being told what to do. Well we all know how that fantasy turns out. I suspect that all parents feel as helpless as this when they have a sick or injured child. I believe she is in there and scared and might even be thinking I am the 'adult' here and is counting on me to have taken care of her and I feel very inept. I also see that this does not end when they stop being A child because they are always YOUR child.

Today we had a minor setback. Maybe calling it a setback is a bit dramatic when really it is just a day lost from recovery, which with the rehab clock ticking can equal a setback. As the nurses were getting Juliana in her cardiac chair to give her a different, more upright position, she grew increasingly uncomfortable. She has been in this chair 5 times before, 2 at Christ Hospital and 3 times here, all times with no issue or concern but this time for whatever reason they struggled to position her and her heart rate started rising higher and higher until she was clearly in distress. In the midst of this escalating discomfort, the neurologist decides to make her very first visit and evaluation. (Picture baby crying, dog barking, dinner burning and the doorbell rings, only 'Halloween' style) The neurologist is happy to see that Juli moves her arms and legs but none of us were happy to see that her tongue is turning blue because she is biting down on it so hard! It made it appear as if her mouth was swollen and gave the impression of a possible allergic reaction or seizure. (I didn't suspect either of those for the record). I suspected when they got her into the chair, they moved her too much or too roughly. I was not in the room when they put her in the chair so I just don't know. Yes, I am bruised from the self-inflicted kicks on that already. In any case, in order to calm her down before she could hurt herself she was given .5mg of Ativan which, you readers following along know, will knock her out for the better part of the day. (This happened at 10 am, she is still out of it as of this update). So the bad news is we were not able to stimulate Juli at all today regardless of our efforts, we just had to let her sleep. If time here was unlimited, it would be ok but it is not. The good news is the neurologist did see Juliana move around, questionably follow a command, and exhibit purposeful movement. Not sure which factor will ultimately matter most during evaluation. She ordered an EEG to get a baseline of what is going on in her brain but she said, 'really only time will tell because we just don't know'. It will be the first EEG she has had done so far (is anyone else surprised by that?). More good news I hope is that she is going to start on a drug that may stimulate her brain and awareness. She is already on high doses of Omega 3 twice daily but this will be just one more thing to try. We were also visited by the physical therapist who although was pleased with her current range of motion, was unable to really work with Juli because she was too sedated to participate. Then the dreaded ophthalmologist came in. (Does anyone else hear "ghost of Christmas past, present, and future here??) He wheeled in a cart of toys like no other doctor before him. He examined her eye with all of his toys and concluded that her eye was improving and it was just going to take time. He still maintains that he believes there will be significant vision loss but…he just doesn't know.

So, I guess adults don't know it all. Even the adults who are in the most respected jobs, and top of their fields sometimes only know how to go back to basics and shrug their shoulders.

October 28, 2009 - 4 pm

The room got bright then dark then bright again. People shared frantic whispers and waited for the assault. They clutched each other in fear as their palms sweated and their hearts raced. Frantically she grabbed for an arm to steady her. Then two arms, then there were bodies clamoring together trying to help, trying to make sense of the scene. The onlookers gaped in horror as the stabbing, once, twice, three times… and still it was not over! The blood. It trickled through her fingers, staining her garment and splashing to the floor. When the fourth gash was made it was at once both merciful and complete. Finally the panic was quieted.

The IV was in.

Ok, so forgive the Halloween dramatics but for those of us in the room, it was not very far from the truth! (back me up here Gloria)

Last night while I was at home falling asleep reading Goosebumps to my daughter Delaney, Juliana was playing charades quite effectively with Chris, Christine and Drew. Of course, all day I get the 'I am sleepy and I don't want to listen to my mother and follow commands' Juli, but they get the 'fun (finger) chatty' Juli. It was encouraging to hear about though and we really thought we were on a roll. She even appeared to respond to requests to open her eyes by moving her eyelashes as if she really wants to do it. Chris said that one time she even turned her head toward his voice when he asked her to. I was very excited to return this morning, hoping for more or increased activity but after the IV debacle which we endured for close to two hours, I left her to rest this afternoon. Tonight, again we play...or try to.

You know one of these nights I am going to put in a late night update that she did something remarkable, you wait and see.

Juli just likes to build up the suspense for the big finish. Not sure where she learned to be so dramatic...

October 29, 2009 - 9:30 am

Two days before the accident Juli and I were in the kitchen discussing motherhood. You see she is the nanny for my youngest two children and has played a central role in their upbringing: getting them ready for school, picking them up, doing homework, teaching them all the girly things that a working mom sometimes has to delegate. Although I was never a fan of 'letting someone else raise my kids' there was something less 'other' about Juli doing it because we shared the same philosophy and love for the girls. In addition to watching Delaney and my daughter Mackenzie she also started babysitting the baby of a friend of hers. She loved little Logan and took very good care of him, (though I thought she might have held him a little too much, it's a good problem to have). Anyway, she said to me in that discussion, "Does it seem like people judge you when you are a parent?" I had to tell her the truth that people are constantly observing and making judgments. It's just human nature to see, evaluate, compare and decide. She wasn't happy about that for sure but I told her that is goes beyond them being babies, "I get 'judged' all the time for the actions taken by my almost grown children." I told her. Naturally she scoffed at that. But let me tell you, when the parade of doctors comes through this room every morning to see my very still daughter lying in the bed, they are passing judgment that has profound effects. Just like when my kids choose education, work or career paths that may not be popular, I find myself defending their choices and fighting to create their reputation so the other parents will give them a chance. Now I am trying to create a reputation for Juli that is dependent upon her potential. Potential that those of us close to her can believe in but others have to be convinced of. I need them to believe in her recovery based on something they may not witness, only my testimony and faith, and that is not the way this process works. "Yes, doctor, she IS active, it's just usually later in the evening when all of you have gone home." Or "She does follow commands sometimes, and she will respond to us but she has to be 'in the zone'. Yes, I know that the staff isn't seeing it but you only come in for one minute a day, trust me, WE see her all day." That is the daily plea for them to continue to try new things and not discount her too soon. Even while we were at Christ hospital, the staff had to learn to 'have that feeling that she would recover'. Child advocacy is exhausting as many of you already realized. It makes me see how easy my life was before this. My children were always healthy and strong so I never had to fight this fight that some of you are already familiar with. It's humbling and strengthening at the same time.

Today the physical therapist will be sitting Juli up on the edge of the bed. Ummmm….really? Yes, really. Just one more crazy coma myth busted. They will hold her up there and check her vitals and posture. The idea is to see how she reacts to a familiar position and movement and hopefully use that movement as stimulation. They want to see if she can control her head, neck and trunk and if she can attempt to right herself when she begins to sway to the side. Will the activity stimulate her to bigger and better things? Will they think she has failed if she cannot? Stay tuned…I will update you later on the early verdict.

October 30, 2009 - 6 am

Next Friday is my daughter's 18th birthday. No, not Juliana…Cheyenne. You didn't know about my other children? That is understandable since Juliana is the main attraction here but even I have to admit, my other equally loved children have generously relinquished their right to the family limelight for the foreseeable future. Cheyenne will reach this long anticipated milestone, no longer interested in celebrating. Just like the rest of us, she just wants Juliana to wake up. And then there is my son Adam who is 15 months younger than Juli. He lives with Juli and Chris so for the last month, he is missing his sister too while living alone in the house that Chris says (except for the music equipment) is really "all Juli". Then there is my son Dylan who went away to Hawaii Pacific University a few months ago only to abandon it to come home to support his family. And then there are Delaney and Mackenzie… Juli is their nanny and has been for 5 years so they are at a loss without 'their Juli' and, as a result, without their mommy too since I am with Juli most of the time. So you see, the fabric of all our lives is complex, our place in the family is unique and the impact we make on the world is profound. So the next time you think that a particular decision is yours and affects only you, think again. You can see that not only has my life changed forever but also that of many people around her. 'Who can say if I've been changed for the better? (I do believe I have been changed for the better) But because I knew you, I have been changed, for good' …Wicked

Yesterday the speech therapist came in to put the speaking valve on Juli's trach. The idea is if Juli chooses to vocalize, she can. They were only able to leave it on for a few minutes the first day but she did cough a few times and it had a sound. The therapist tried to elicit an 'ow' from Juli by doing what they always do, pinch her toe but she didn't vocalize yet. They plan to try a few minutes each day and if there are times when she seems more interested in talking than others, we can request to have it put on. The thing is, it changes the familiarity of the airflow so it could get uncomfortable for her breathing so we have to take it slow. Just one more thing. Immediately after that the Physical Therapist came in to sit her on the edge of the bed. One stood in front and positioned her feet on the floor, hands at her side and the other knelt on the bed behind her, holding up her head and supporting her body. They gently shifted her weight from one arm to the other, then moved her hands in her lap, and just tried to give her the sensation of supporting herself. It was pretty nice to see. They will do that again next week a couple of times but they said 'it has to go slow'. Yeah, I got it. I mean, it's been 4 weeks today, I am familiar with the pace now. Today she is supposed to finally get the EEG. I am a little nervous about the results. I have been of course glued to the internet researching everything and I know that this test will help them determine the amount of brain activity and they may make a prognosis again. After having heard the doom and gloom several times and dismissing it (which makes it sound like it didn't affect me when, uh yeah, it did) I guess I have to ready myself for the possibility of another dose of their reality. Then I will add the unknown factor of her sheer will to get through this and ours to force her. Then we will be back to where we ought to be, changed for good to our new normal.

October 30, 2009 - 10 pm

"Hi Honey, how was your day?"

Well, if a picture is worth a thousand words, this video is worth at least a million pennies (is anyone keeping track?).

I dare you not to cry.

The post that day was a video taken by Chris on what Juliana was able to do in her semi-conscious state. The doctors continued to believe she was unresponsive to commands but we knew that was not true so Chris was determined to prove to the doctors that Juliana was following commands. He stayed up each night through her 'awake' period and talked her into cooperating with him. He had previously tried to explain to the staff that he gets her to respond by 'asking' her if she could hold up two fingers, instead of 'telling' her to do it. They clearly didn't give that much credibility, so he recorded Juliana following commands: move your leg side to side, lift your leg, wave. In addition to sharing it with our growing readership, he walked the floors of RML showing it to every one of our nurses, doctors and caretakers. The video was three minutes long and if they initially grew impatient with watching the desperate attempts by a determined fiancé, their reaction always ended the same: Awe. When they saw Juliana wave, natural as can be their own hands flew to their mouths in shock and pleasure. Most would shed a tear as well. Chris would just laugh that deep sincere laugh of pride and victory. The doctors changed their documentation to reflect Juliana's viability in the semi-conscious program at RIC. It was neither the first nor the last time that Chris would be her hero. All those that watched this video ended the same way: in tears.

October 31, 2009 - 11:45 pm

Told ya you'd cry. Well I cannot top the update from last night but I can tell you that we are still moving in the right direction. As many of you described it, Juliana seems closer to the surface all the time, (though that wave seemed eerily above the surface to me, I don't know). The videotapes were especially helpful to convince the skeptical doctors and nurses that she is responsive since their 'notes' indicated that in their 1 to 5 minute visit each day she was unresponsive. I really have to credit Chris for thinking of new and different things to ask her as well as making sure he recorded it. They now see what we see and will hopefully make decisions accordingly. She responds better to him than to anyone, which I guess bodes well for their marriage. Tonight we were able to get her to move her leg on command, raise her arm with minimal assistance all the way over her head, and then back down at her side.

She is starting to more frequently touch her face. I suspect she has heard the concern about her eye, though we try desperately to avoid the discussion in her presence. We just try not to have the 'oh, her eye looks so much better' chatter around her because we don't know how she will interpret 'better'. So today she nervously (that's just my interpretation of her movements + her expression) moved her fingers across her face as if she was trying to figure out where everything was. She even rubbed the top of her sore eye...ouch! She didn't flinch so maybe it was just painful to us. Although it did not happen immediately, she was able to point to her ear when asked. We came very close to having her touch her nose as well but there were too many interruptions and we ultimately had to let her rest. We have learned that her quiet time is important for processing the stimulation she receives. It has been a very controversial rule to enforce when you have such a variety of schedules amongst the visitors. So sleeeeeepy now, good night.

November 1, 2009 - 10:30 am

Juliana just finished 55 minutes with the speaking valve on her trach. Yesterday she tolerated 45 minutes and that was pretty good so this additional 10 minutes is better. She didn't handle it easily though, her heart rate was accelerated and she was quite agitated but she kept it under the danger zone so they recommended we continue to stretch it out. With her heart rate in the 120's off and on for the past hour she is now exhausted. The doctor from RIC came by for a quick evaluation just prior to that and he said he hopes to see her downtown but she is not ready just yet. That was momentarily disappointing and another indication of the elongated path we are on, but it is still a day by day process and we are not out of the running yet. The doctor explained that the stimulation should occur at 15 minute intervals with 15 minutes of rest in between each segment. He said that the rest periods are key to her recovery. As I indicated in the last update, the downtime is hard for us when we have a rotation of visitors and stimulants. We have to incorporate all of the following with rest time: bathing and other nursing care, visitors chatting, music playing, reading, television, physical therapy, aromatherapy, massage. Since either Chris or I are here at all times, we do our best to manage the stimulation schedule and try to not to exceed her limits but it's really a pattern that everyone has to be part of otherwise it is just a struggle. And to be quite honest, I am not sure I can tolerate another struggle. I had a visitor earlier in the week say to me, "You must be getting a little frustrated." I confidently responded, "No actually I am not." That really was true at the time but it seems that since then, some of my resistance has faded. You see, yesterday was Halloween and I left here to take Delaney and Mackenzie trick or treating. It was supposed to be fun and all about them but I still find it so hard to be part of my former life. I know that is unfair to the rest of my family who have a right to keep living but I have not found my new normal. I am so grateful that my husband and kids have been patient with me because it's hard on all of us. The life I created and chose is what has to be delayed. (Imagine spending more of your time with your ex-spouse than your current spouse for a month and counting, with no end in sight....yes we are mostly rising above it but not without effort). It's just not possible to go back to anything that was before. It's all got to change now. I am sorry that this may seems a little dark in comparison with the great news we shared the other day and if she were the only person in my life, it would be just completely positive. But the long journey to her health will require many sacrifices and adjustments and each day that this continues on illuminates the future and dims the past. Don't get me wrong; I am still confident in her recovery, I am just less confident in mine.

I will update tonight to report on how productive her day was in an effort to erase this negativity. Excuse me while I go give myself an attitude adjustment...

November 2, 2009 - 11 am

One month ago today. That is a long time if you think of the moments of healing from then to now. Not such a long time if think about the moments of healing ahead. A dangerous side effect of the super information highway is, well, information. We have heard stories of miraculous recovery and those of saddening defeat. Everyone has a story, everyone has tragedy and sorrow and many have accompanying success. It is abundantly clear that the distinction in people is not what happens to them, since life happens to all of us, but what you choose to do about it. That is true for all the events of your life, not just those that are catastrophic. I experience it every day in the faces of my little children as they struggle to accept what is happening in their life.

So what is happening you say? Well, my eldest daughter continues to fight her way back to us. She is alert more moments in the day, more active during those moments and the ability to bring her to arousal is easier every day. She frequently waves goodbye to people though you never know in advance if you will be the lucky recipient. She always has been unpredictable. During her hour with her speaking valve we thought she was trying to talk and opened her mouth to produce sound today for the first time but it was very questionable about her intent. It was new and more purposeful so we call that progress. She continues to have opinions and shares them with us in her own way. She was frustrated with Chris last night when he was trying to prevent her from pulling out her trach (how dare you Chris). She actually swatted him away when he tried to kiss her hand. He said, "Juliana, are you mad at me?" She promptly gave him the finger...er, the index finger that is. Then he apologized and she lowered her finger slowly, he continued apologizing and she squeezed his hand. Husbands everywhere take note: Even in a state of limited consciousness women can be ticked off and you still need to fix it!

So what's up next? Well, hopefully we will get results today or tomorrow on her EEG. As interesting as that will be, that will tell us where she is, not where she will go. So to that, we will use the information judiciously. We should get another opportunity for Juliana to sit on the edge of her bed, additional time with her speaking valve on her trach tube and, hopefully we will move on to capping off the trach. We have a family meeting middle of this week to discuss our next steps.

Another positive...we had a wonderful doctor today say what we have been thinking: "It doesn't matter about the valleys from day to day. It matters about the peaks from week to week, focus on them." Hallelujah doc, you have successfully avoided liability while supporting the path to recovery! Was that so hard? Others should take a lesson.

And for all of you who had to bear my whining yesterday and sent me a message of encouragement, thank you. I had a great visit from a new friend and it was equally uplifting. Additional medicine came from a normal night at home where my husband made a great dinner, I caught up on my guilty pleasure, General Hospital (there is a funny story there I will share with you someday) and my girls and I shared cuddling before bed. I actually felt joyful for a few minutes. Then the giggling stopped, Mackenzie said she wanted to pray for Juliana and started crying.

Sigh...it's not just Juli...it will take us all time to heal.

November 3, 2009 - 7 am

"Times they are a changin..." Bob Dylan. Juliana continues to have an adjusted body clock so she sleeps more peacefully at night and is more active during the day. That is good for showing her responsiveness to the doctors and nurses. It is also good for us who sleep in the room to start to get a complete night's sleep. In addition to her active moments changing to daytime, they are also becoming more frequent. It is easy to rouse her now to a point of 'awareness', if you can call it that. We still do not have the long awaited for eye opening moment but everything else indicates to us that she is getting closer to being more awake. It seems like her slow ascent out of this coma is happening out of order, even maybe backwards. But expecting the unexpected is what we have come to expect. I had a dream the other night that she woke up and was physically functioning, perfecting and talking intelligently and seemed very healthy. The problem was she was a 70-year-old man who was 2 feet tall. I asked the doctors what was going on, since we came in the hospital with a 23-year-old girl. They responded as they always have, "you just don't know what is possible with a brain injury." I did dream that, I kid you not.

So the bad news/good news for today is she is still in a coma but she is still a 23 year old girl. Hey, it ain't much but it is something.

Now that the news of her waving has spread through the unit, the nurses and therapists are vying for the next pageant wave. It's encouraging to see the professionals finally expect something from her. Yesterday she made a nurse jump when she started adjusting her trach collar and Juli slapped her hand away twice. "Sorry," I said, "She has an opinion." Yes, she always has though she was never a slapper...hmmm...if I add this to the biting and kicking we saw early on she might just get evicted from this place.

She is also holding up her head, or lifting her head more often. She tried yesterday to lift her head and shoulders off the chair. In doing so, her head was tilted down and her nose started dripping what appeared to be clear water. We started by just wiping it and didn't think much of it. Then the nurse left and came back with a collection jar and said the neurologist wanted to see if it was spinal fluid or just accumulated water from the swelling in her head. No one gave us more information on that but neither option sounded good. We weren't able to collect any because there did not appear to be any more. If we ever talk to a doctor again...sigh...I will ask. I feel like we have a lot of accumulating questions and we are in a perpetual wait until you talk to the doctor state. We have yet to receive the EEG results and we still haven't heard really information on the specific damage to her brain. In fact, the amount of time we actually spend talking to the right doctor, could be measured in less than 10 minutes. Let's hope their bill reflects that. I asked about what is needed to move on to capping the trach and, after a long route to get to the answer, I learned that she has to tolerate the speaking valve all day. We aren't there yet. She did better yesterday and had a good portion of the time breathing calmly but then she 'forgets' how to breathe and tries to breathe out through her throat still and struggles until her heart rate is too high and we need to remove the valve.

Delaney and Mackenzie came to visit Juli last night and Mackenzie climbed in bed with her and chatted and played with her hand and asked her, many times, to "please wake up". She held back tears and sang her a Christmas song. I hope exposing them to this is the right thing to do. I know it might help Juliana but I don't want to damage the little ones for her gain. If I was sure this was short lived, I could spare them. But as long as this goes on, it will be part of my life and as a result, part of my other kids' lives. (Geez, a whole page already...wow, I really broke that 'short update promise made earlier!). Well, what can I say, things change.

November 3, 2009 - 10:45 am

SHE OPENED HER EYES

She was sitting on the edge of the bed working with her Physical Therapist and she opened her left eye!!! We even got it on Video! Oh yeah, we did, we got it on video!! It was only for about 15 seconds but it was awesome.

Maybe we will post it later.

Gotta go, busy busy busy being super excited...and I gotta call a BUNCH of people!!!! AHHHHH

I remember waiting for her eyes to open and hoping that it was going to be an awakening. I guess it would sound silly to say that Hollywood gives you an unrealistic impression of what coming out of a coma looks like, wouldn't it? I remember being so incredibly excited when this happened and then instantly sad that Chris was at work missing it. As it was happening I called him hoping he would be able to answer.

"Guess what your girlfriend just did?" I asked him euphorically.

"Who?" not sure why that confused him but…

"Who? How many girlfriends do you have? Anyway, SHE OPENED HER EYE!"

"Oh My God, she did?" He was as shocked as I

"Yes and it was beautiful" I said.

"That is so great, SO great. Oh my God that is so great…" his voice trails off and is replaced my quieter more distant sobs.

Now that I know how this all unfolds, this is just one more time I was grateful for my naiveté because the moment she opened her eyes…was magical. Reality would have certainly stolen that.

November 3, 2009 - 8 pm

So I have finally settled down. Not the euphoria of course but at least the frenzy. Let me tell you something that I am going to ask that none of you forget: HOPE is a guaranteed return on investment. Guaranteed. It costs you nothing and yields you anywhere from simple peace to grand miracles and everything in between. Everyone has troubles. Everyone. No person's burden is any less important than another's even if it is less dramatic. All of you have the right, no, the obligation to apply hope to your life. Seriously team, if you are a parent, or a child, or a sibling, or a friend, or a single solitary person who depends only upon yourself, you have an obligation to walk around this earth on this day with the hope that better exists and expect that it will be part of your life.

That is where my treasure started, with nothing but hope. You see what I have received in return, haven't you?

Now I have to make sure that you have a clear picture of what happened today. First of all, Juliana has tolerated the speaking valve all day. She is going on 12 hours without any issues. That is excellent. She also sat on the edge of the bed for about 20 minutes and held her head and neck and trunk steady for a portion of that. She did much better than the first time and the Physical Therapist was very pleased and impressed. In fact, she was also a witness to our miracle and was even happier to be part of that. When I told Delaney and Mackenzie, "Guess what happened today? Juliana opened her eyes." They both quickly responded with, "Then she is awake now?" So, coma lesson number 3 (or is it 4...?) Opening your eyes, even in combination with everything else that she can do, is not considered 'awake' or 'out of the coma'. It is one more step toward that, and in our estimation "a guarantee" that we will get there but we still have a road ahead of us. Also, today's 'eye open-ing experience' was momentous of course but it was also very subtle. It was a half-way, half-window into the still blank stare. It sounds bleak in those terms but it is really just a way to indicate that it is just a start. We are also not going to post the video of her opening her eyes because in watching it back, there are things that we think Juliana might not want published on the internet. I am sure you will understand.

Last night, Mackenzie lay in bed with Juliana for a while just playing with her hand. Its precious of both my youngest and my eldest daughter, who have been very much like mother and daughter themselves in many ways. In fact, one day about a year ago Juliana said she had a very serious request that she would like me to consider. "You have to promise me," she said, "that you won't answer until you thought about it for 2 days." I said, "ok" but thought 'uh oh'. She said, "Promise me mommy (yes she is 23 and still calls me mommy), I don't want an answer because I am serious and I need to know you have considered this from all angles." Ok, now whatever she was leading up to was going to be big and I was really scared of the two days of agonizing debate that I was going to have to go through.

"I want to keep Mackenzie."

Blank stare (me)

"I am serious Mommy"

Blank stare (still me)

"I mean, you can still pay for everything she needs and of course see her whenever you want but you have so many other kids and I already love her like she is my own…"

I skillfully hid the smile, though, you can feel free…she can't see you.

"Well, what do you think?" she asked, genuinely expecting my consideration.

I started with "I thought you wanted me to wait two days to tell you" and ended with "Are you out of your mind?!?"

As odd as this was, it was also a very good 'mommy moment', I want more of those.

Thankfully, I have millions already.

It was a moment that we privately videotaped we like to call the 'wanna be mamma' and MY baby girl. Well, they are all four my baby girls regardless of their place in the family.

And now, back to our regularly scheduled program…

We finally got the results of the EEG today. Good news: According to the neurologist, 'it's not that terrible'…hmmm…well, ok, we accept that answer. In fact, the left side has no damage at all. We accept that as well. (In fact, I will take two please). Bad news: She is having subclinical seizures. The doctor wants to put her on anti-seizure medication, which she was already on at Christ hospital as preventative but stopped when she reached RML. We were hesitant. We couldn't see the seizures and we were afraid to do anything to impede the progress that she was making. I spoke to the neurologist for quite a while tonight, who by the way had the good grace to step out of Juliana's room to talk to me on the phone. (Again, is that so hard?) She assured me that any side effects that might occur are far less destructive than what a seizure would do to her in this fragile state. We ended the call with the tough and potentially unpopular choice to trust the doctor and use the anti-seizure medicine.

Then she went back in the room with Juli and Chris and Chris did what he has been doing so well all along: Win over the staff. Oh yes, he sold that doctor on his love and faith in my beautiful daughter and she hugged him with tears in her eyes. (Ok so it was not just his winning personality it was the video proof of her abilities...he shows EVERYONE). And she was so impressed, so happy, so RELIEVED (Juli would be proud of how hard he works for her) that she said she was changing all of her notes. The video sold her on the revised prognosis. Another convert... She also asked that we download the videos to a disc so it can be officially included in her file for proof. (Uh, Mike, I know we told you to delete the files but, you didn't yet, right?) Anyway, it was a good day all around. It was a damn good day.

I HOPE yours was too.

November 4, 2009 - 5 pm

We had our much anticipated 'family' meeting with the staff at RML. During this meeting the Physical Therapist, Speech Therapist, Rehabilitation doctor and Care Coordinator each describe their experience with Juliana. Then we reviewed the notes provided from Respiratory, Infectious Disease, and Neurology. The objective of the meeting is to determine what the best next steps for Juliana's recovery are. We didn't hear anything surprising in terms of what Juliana is capable of. We did learn that had we not videotaped what she could do, showed it to each of these professionals, they wouldn't have believed us and the outcome would have been different. Not the outcome of her recovery mind you, but the outcome of the care provided to her. Makes you think, doesn't it? What they told us was that they are actually pleased with how quickly she is progressing. (Yeah, well, try being on this end doc) They also said, based on what she is already able to do, we have every reason to be hopeful for a very good recovery. They indicated that in a week or so we would be looking to move her to a rehabilitation center. Our first choice is of course the Rehabilitation Institute of Chicago (RIC) but we have to evaluate a 2nd and 3rd choice just in case. They are submitting the application for RIC this week and we should know soon if she gets accepted into their regular program or their 2 week evaluation program. The care coordinator and doctor feel that she has a good chance at qualifying for the regular program, again, based on the footage we were able to collect. Camera phones rock! If she gets accepted into the inpatient regular program it could be for a month or longer. That is of course largely dependent upon her progress and her insurance. They always have to go there, it's really unfortunate. Now if she doesn't qualify for the regular program she would most likely qualify for the 2 week evaluation. At the end of the 2 weeks, if she has not progressed significantly then she would be released to a sub-acute hospital for rehabilitation. We also have the option at that point to bring her home for rehabilitation. So our next steps are to select alternatives to RIC (which we really already have) and also to select a sub-acute hospital in the event we need to go that route. We are really more interested in bringing her home if she gets released after 2 weeks at RIC but we will reserve that decision for after we try out the sub-acute. Ideally, we would stay at RML for 2 more weeks to give her a little more time to heal, then get a solid acceptance to RIC in the regular program and kick some serious rehabilitation butt there. I hear the accommodations for family members are quite comfy and they have a real cafeteria…yeah!

So far today, Juliana has followed commands pretty consistently and has exhibited one more noticeable sign of awareness. You see, sometimes she drools. Ok, she will probably be ticked that I mentioned it but, freedom of speech, creative license, power of the pen all that stuff. So anyway, today I noticed that anytime she has saliva accumulating in her mouth she reaches up to touch her mouth. If she does actually drool, she tries to wipe it, every time. So, very little is going by unnoticed. We did try the talking valve again today and, even though yesterday she went from 8 am-11 pm with no issue, she never got comfortable with it today. In fact, after a couple of hours of on and off labored breathing, Gloria asked her if her breathing was making her uncomfortable. She held up…1 finger. Then when they removed the valve and her breathing was more regular, she was asked if she was still uncomfortable and she held up 2 fingers. We had witnesses too.

So, its early and there might be more to report later but for right now, we feel pretty good that our 24 / 7 attention to this girl has actually helped, again. Imagine if we could do that all the time with all our kids, regardless of their age…apart from having no life of your own, it would have many benefits. For example, I might not be in this situation at all, if we could.

Sometimes it was harder than others to be in the situation. When I was at the hospital with Chris I could be honest and let go, or we could rationally be grateful for all the Juli has achieved so far. Other times when there were visitors I could be 'on' and keep a happy forward facing outlook. I was doing it for them but it was working on me too. But when I am alone with just 'me' I get inside my head and can't let go of what used to be. It is so strange to be going through the biggest heartache in my life and NOT have Juliana there to talk through it all with me. There was no way to relate to anyone anymore. The isolation was disabling.

November 5, 2009 - 12 am

It's quiet and dark; she sleeps through the night,
    I watch her in silence but sleep I do not.
    I see her in photos, some old some new
    And miss her all over though she's just cross the room.
    She's taking this journey, in some ways alone
    And I feel I'm searching for a course of my own.
    She plays with her hair, she touches her face,
    I stare at the normalcy to make it make sense.
    How can she be there, and seem to be close,
    And hear me cry out yet stay so remote?
    I thought I could *will* her, back into this realm
    But I have to admit, I am not at the helm.
    So trust through my fear is my burden to bear
    Because so much of myself is because she is here.
    I am Juli's mom, that's where I began,
    And still she defines me as only magic can.

The impending epidemic of Bird Flu had everyone in a state of panic and hospitals everywhere began to restrict visitors.

November 5, 2009 - 9:20 am

Just an FYI, effective today, RML has modified their visiting rules: no children under 18 (sorry Cheye for one more day) and only 2 people at a time.

What they haven't been able to tell us for sure if it means that only 2 people can be signed in or only 2 people in the room. Since Chris or I are always here, that is one...

Navigating through this as divorced parents was challenging at times. Juli's dad Chris always meant well but our methods were different. Prior to this next update we had a pretty heated discussion about the things they were doing to push Juli forward. Chris always wanted to lean more towards the safe and slow option and I pushed the envelope. Combine that with the fact that, well, we are divorced, and the unfamiliar and frightening territory we were both in, I am surprised we didn't fight more often. He just didn't like seeing her struggle at all. I didn't either but I kept thinking that it was for a greater good. I never really did figure out if that is the truth or not but I just went with what I could live with...and what I could sustain.

November 5, 2009 - 11 pm

Sometimes, progress is uncomfortable. It is uncomfortable to experience, to watch, and to negotiate. When a baby is learning to walk, you learn to hunch over them. When a child is learning to recite, you learn to mouth the words. When a teenager is learning to drive, you learn to use your imaginary brakes. When you are encouraging your child to heal, you learn to consider the benefit vs. the cost. Children typically don't like medicine, washing out cuts, setting broken bones, or getting stitches. But our obligation to them as parents and caregivers is to do what is necessary, even when they don't like it.

In our particular situation we are in a balancing act of doing too much vs. too little. I have mentioned before that we navigate the schedule of stimulation and rest. Well we also have to evaluate the effects of the stimulation on a 'minimally conscious' individual (that's her new clique). Sometimes, watching Juliana experience certain stimulation like a change in breathing apparatus or a new position is uncomfortable when she struggles. We don't enjoy it any more than watching our children get stitches but you hold their hand, try to distract them from the discomfort and let them know that yes, they are strong enough to handle this. It is the age old dilemma of protect vs. promote. Do you give your children wings or chains? Do you give them opportunities or restrictions? We all know the answer is, well, honestly: **Both**. This is tense under normal circumstances but then you throw into the mix opposing opinions that must unite for a common goal. Now *THAT* is uncomfortable! But we still must do what is right for them even if it hurts...us. Ah but what is "right" is remains the debate...

Again today Juliana periodically had a hard time breathing while she had her speaking valve connected. Her stats were steady but we decided to remove it and instead, accept the suggestion that she be examined by an ENT doctor to ensure there is no blockage. We know that she must learn to adjust to this way of breathing since it is closer to normal. If she is removed from the stimulation without having to try to succeed, she may not. However, to be certain that there wasn't a new problem causing her difficulty, we will delay that step until we can be sure. If we can rule that out, we will need to watch her uncomfortably adjust again, (unless she doesn't...if you recall, Tuesday, she tolerated it for 15 hours without any issue so she can do it...will she though...)

Ups and downs they tell us...expect it.

Speaking of ups and downs...Juliana also sat on the edge of the bed for a while again today. Remember, that was the activity that brought about her momentary eye opening? Well, not today. In fact, not since then. No matter, we know it will happen again, just not today. Although we will wait, the anticipation is just a bit...uncomfortable.

November 6, 2009 - 5 pm

Over 2700 members? Really? How? Incredible, that's what that is. So that is an awful lot of people ready to wish my beautiful daughter CHEYENNE, a very happy (and SAFE dear GOD make it safe) 18th birthday!! You know, Juliana planned to throw Cheyenne a party for her birthday. She always wanted to look after her sister and often read her the riot act trying to keep her, (return her), to the straight and narrow. Not that Juli was a saint mind you but she made it her business to set Cheyenne straight anyway. When Juli wakes up, she will feel bad for all of the impact to others and for all of the hurting we have experienced. But she will also feel very bad that she missed her sister's very important birthday. Cheyenne has been talking about it for 16 years! But when she gets a chance to hear about all of this, and the fact that 2700 people were thinking about Cheyenne on her birthday because of her situation, well, she lets hope she feels just a little bit better about that at least. You see, my beautiful 18 year old daughter has had a rough year. The details are immaterial now but what Juliana will be so very proud to learn is that when I needed Cheyenne, she was a perfect, mature, and supportive daughter. If I didn't appreciate her before, I do very much so now. Juliana did a wonderful job mentoring her little sister, even when it was hard to do so. In so many ways, Juli dabbled in playing mom to all of my kids. I suppose that means I occasionally allowed Juli to take the lead, but as the oldest of 6, that is bound to happen and I was TIRED! (Don't knock peer pressure when applied to the family unit) I have known for years that if the kids were invested in each other, we would all reap the benefits for years to come. My parents never allowed my siblings to fight, physically or verbally, with each other. Most of the time, we even obeyed that. They maintained that "'one day, your brothers and sisters will be your best friends". HA I said. HA HA HA, I said. But darn it if Phillip and Felicia weren't dead on. I can't even count the number of times I have considered one or all of them my best friend. In fact, I can't remember the last non camping vacation that one of them wasn't on. You see, when one plans a trip, we all tend to jump on the plane!

And darn it again if I wasn't bound and determined to instill in my 6 children that same expectation for that same purpose.

So far, so good.

They are all devoted to each other, very close and dependent. And because of that devotion and dependency, on this day more than any other, Cheyenne is missing her mentor, her sister, and her friend.

So Juliana arranged for a little gift for her…

Today, during physical therapy, she was able to hold up her head, neck and trunk by herself. When moving from side to side she was able to use her arms to stabilize herself. According to the therapist this was very, very good and she was extremely impressed by her strength. And when Juli was getting tired and holding up her head was too much, Chris said, "Juliana today is Cheyenne's birthday and as a present to her, I want you to try very hard to pick your head up and keep holding it up." And wouldn't you know, she picked her head up and held it steady for the rest of the therapy.

And just as Cheyenne wished (on her Durbin's cheesecake last night), Juli briefly opened her eyes again. Yep, she did.

I suspect that was Juliana's way of saying Happy Birthday.

November 7, 2009 - 8:30 pm

Juliana continues to confound and amaze us. We can pretty regularly get her to wave to anyone who asks. She is the friendliest coma girl I have ever known. (Ok, I know what you are thinking but I bet she is the friendliest coma girl YOU have ever known too). In addition, when she coughs, she covers her mouth and when she drools, she wipes her face. She has always been polite but who knew those traits were so ingrained that at this juncture, that would be what surfaces first? In addition to her personality and manners, we are seeing other 'skills' return. Check this out: Chris told Juliana that he was going to lift her eyelid and he wanted her to touch the camera. (As you have witnessed, we use the camera like a third arm, just in case.) So, he pressed play, lifted her left eyelid and…yes, yes she did. She stretched her arm out and to the left and touched the camera! Let's tally up what we have here: Well, uh, she can SEEEEEEEEEEE, that is a good one for sure and based on her orbital fractures and compromised right eye, they weren't sure if she would have any sight at all. (But then again, their expectations were so low, breathing made her an 'A' student.) She also knows what a camera is, equally good because her memory is likely to be impacted even if only for a while. She also displayed hand eye coordination which is an excellent sign as well. And let's not forget that she is still following commands which although is 'oh so last month' is still important to the long rehab road.

She also continues to answer our yes/no questions with 1 finger for yes and 2 for no. Although we can't be sure she is answering correctly, we assume she is. And that is where the story gets a bit darker. You see her beloved fiancée talks to her daily in soothing tones with loving and tender language. He sings to her every day and even makes the nurses swoon. He professes his love and devotion in all that he says and does. (Yeah, yeah, he's a rock star, we know, blah blah…Just kidding Chris, you know I adore you as well) So, he said to her "Angel, would it be alright if I gave you a kiss?" Now mind you, he has kissed her many times in the past 5 weeks but never asked her permission. Since she was asked, she answered.

I know you see where this is going.

Yep, she gave him… 2 fingers: No. Oooh, ouch, strike one Mr. Medina. So then, he said, "Juliana, do you know who I am?" She hesitated for a bit, then she gently, almost shyly, held up…

2 fingers.

Strike two.

Um…

Awkward…

Stop there Chris, this is hurting all of us.

So let's just recap: My daughter is beautiful, friendly, and polite and doesn't want to kiss boys she doesn't know. That doesn't sound so bad, does it?

Well…Today she told me she doesn't know ME either.

It doesn't feel good to 'hear' but Chris and I agree: We made her love us once, we can do it again.

Stay tuned for that to all happen before your eyes.

November 8, 2009 - 11 pm

Think of your best memories. Think about them in detail. Remember the people, the places, the events, the mishaps. Describe the colors, the smells, the details you thought were not important. Remember the date, the time, the weather. Recall how you felt, what you thought, what you wished, what you got.

That is your life so far.

Now before you forget again, or put them back in the recesses of your mind, share them. Either with your kids, your parents, your friends, pen and paper or videotape.

This is the exercise we find ourselves going through now as we try to reconstruct Juliana's memory. Now, we may be very premature in doing this. After all, she is still technically comatose and cannot confirm what she knows or doesn't know. (Chris and I are going to give her some time to study then we will give her a "do over" on that last memory test). But we realize that it may be necessary to remind Juliana of who she was and the details from her past that made her so special. By reminding her of her past, she can gain context for place and time and hopefully feel safe coming back to the present. Now of course, we have no way of knowing if this is effective or necessary or all a bunch of hooey. But it can't hurt. And it feels very good to remember. You just kind of let your mind wander and it fills in the rest of the story like the pictures behind the narration. It was a wonderful exercise to help confirm what I knew anyway: Juliana has had a pretty awesome life so far.

I started today by playing home movies from the 90s. It consisted of Juliana's 4th – 6th birthday parties and lots of cute kid faces in between. Since she doesn't have her eyes open, I needed the videos to have enough commentary to help remind her. I have to think about that next time I record something.

Then in between visitors I reminded her of our trips to Disney, Vegas, Chestnut Mountain, camping, Road America, her cruises, her birthdays, her crazy misbehaviors that she thought I didn't know about. (No, I am not going to tell you!) Man I miss my daughter. As I was helping her remember, (well, helping me believe I was helping her), I tried to see if any spark of recognition came over her. I waited for my interpretation of what memory recall would look like. I wanted a sign that the message was received and the memories were doing the trick but what I got was a more calm, quiet and relaxed Juli. It wasn't until I got home tonight that I realized that I might have actually seen the exact reaction I should have seen if it were effective. Quiet, calm still, reflective. Maybe the memories are taking root and reforming connections in her brain that were broken after all? So much of this is guesswork that we can never be sure if what we are doing is right, we just know we have to keep doing *something* because regardless of how much ground we have gained, we are still just...so far.

November 9, 2009 - 10:30 pm

Juliana had a pretty productive day. Her trach was capped today for several hours and she tolerated it perfectly. A few times it seemed like she was making noises. Was that her attempt to speak? We won't know for sure until it becomes more obvious. She also had OT and Speech come in today and she 'performed' for them very nicely by obeying commands and moving when Chris asked her to. Even the therapist realized that he gets all the luck. Juli spent about 20 minutes 'standing' on the tilt table that allowed her to be completely upright. She had very good control of her muscles while standing. She was able to hold up her head the whole time. That is supposed to be good stimulation and it sure seemed to tire her out for a few hours. Then, before you knew it she was moving all over like she just wanted out of that bed. I can only imagine. Her eyes were fluttering so much we just kept staring at her, sure her eyes were opening at each pulse. She wore us out. Her hands were moving all over as well and at one point, she was rubbing her head and her hair and then she put her left hand over her left eye and lifted her own eyelid! Now, I can't say for sure if it was intentional or not but it sure looked like she meant to do exactly that. A few minutes after that, I opened her eye and waved and said, "Hi Juli, can you wave to me?" and she did. Heeheee. It's the little things...Chris bought some different textured gloves for us to try to massage Juli with the different textures. One in particular was very soft and I maneuvered it onto Juli. Well then she wouldn't let me take it off... (Probably because it's so cold in here she was holding out for the other one AND the matching hat and scarf). I wanted to see what she would do so I took it part way off and she tried very hard to wiggle it back on. I helped put it back on and that seemed to satisfy her. She continues to pull herself upright in the bed and the stronger she gets, the more I am nervous she will go forward OFF the bed. Geez...this has made me a nervous wreck. I remember when I never worried about anything.

We got some good news today. Juliana has been accepted into the AMiCouS program at RIC and will be moved there Wednesday, if a bed is available. That is the two week trial for the Assessment of the Minimally Conscious State. The goal is to get her aroused enough to put her in the regular brain injury program, which could last an additional 2 weeks. During that time she will get intensive Physical, Occupational and Speech therapy. In addition, they will teach the family how to continue therapy and help her care for her needs. They will also assess her medication and see if there are any adjustments to be made. RIC is thought to be the leader in brain stimulation so we are very fortunate to have been accepted. One of the conditions of this program is that prior to beginning, we have to define our plans for Juliana beyond RIC. I am confident that she will do well enough to remain at RIC for the extended brain injury program since she seems to really be steadily improving now.

Either way, after RIC, we decided that we will bring Juliana home.

If my assumptions and calculations are correct, that would put her back in our house the weekend that was supposed to be her wedding. But what I know for sure is that I don't know anything at all.

November 10, 2009 - 10 pm

And then 40 days later...........

Tomorrow around 11 we will have a new temporary home because we are heading to the Rehabilitation Institute of Chicago, RIC. We are excited and nervous. We have heard they do remarkable things and have been extremely successful in waking people in a minimally conscious state. For the next two weeks, we are banking on it.

So, you know Juliana's right eye is injured and still swollen, bloodshot and sore, right? Well, she sneezed.

You feel that? So did she. She cried. In fact, very gently, she sobbed. Chris could see the tears coming out of her eyes and even hear the noises coming through her capped trach and hugged her gently to comfort her. She put her arm around his neck and hugged back. He really loved that. Then he told her he felt bad that it hurt her and told her he would try to take care of her and protect her. Then the boy could not leave well enough alone and asked her AGAIN if she knew who he was. Still 2 fingers but he still doesn't care. He figures with almost 8 years of experience, he will totally know how to win her over, much faster this time. He better hurry though. The wedding was only postponed a year.

She is getting much more active and cooperative. Today she was able to show 1 finger, 2 fingers...all the way to 5 for the doctor when asked. She even waved at the doctor. It's really the fact that she isn't speaking or opening her eyes that mostly what is keeping her in this shade of darkness. As part of her therapy we were told to bring photos of everyone, labeled with names to use them in her therapy as reminders of her family and friends. She will be wearing her own comfy clothes and shoes which will be so much less 'patient' and so much more Juli. Maybe that step is for us? They also hope to work to eliminate some of the outside tubes. That means if possible they will slowly eliminate the trach, the feeding tube, and the catheter. Tomorrow will be a settling in day where they begin evaluating her. Then starting on Thursday she will receive 3 hours of therapy a day. Chris and I have worked out a schedule so that one of us is always there to participate. Their goal is to rehabilitate the patient and prepare the family to continue rehabilitation. That includes all that it would take to help her move around the house. They will also order any equipment we need for caring for Juli once we bring her home. This is all still so surreal, you know? We were just ordering her wedding cake, now we are ordering her hospital bed. It's not a turn of events you can even prepare for. I am just still a little stunned that this is the direction our life took. And it has been more than a few times that I thought I was not a good enough mom to handle all of this. And I still sure don't have a clue what I am doing. I am just so grateful I have an incredibly strong network of family and friends that are 100% here to help. Never take anything for granted.

November 11, 2009 - 11:11 pm

Change is hard. Even if it is a good and necessary change, it can still be stressful and scary. Leaving the known, the safe, and the comfortable. Some people love change and welcome it. Some people get bored easily and are only happy with change. I am not one of those people. Neither is Juli. We are very much creatures of habit and are on edge until we reach our comfort zone. We started this journey at Christ hospital and eventually grew to trust the staff and learn the machines and know the routines. Then we nervously moved to RML and did it all over again. Today we moved to RIC. The place that we ultimately wanted to be, remember? The place where 'the magic will happen'. The last stop before bringing her home to complete her rehabilitation. But with this move comes everything new: doctors, nurses, staff, equipment, terminology and cafeteria. (We were comforted to see the same coffee machine we grew accustomed to at RML, though it has city prices!) They even call things by different names here: the equipment, the medicine, the procedures, even her medical state. (Now I feel like my 40 day medical degree is totally useless.) So we start all over again with the comfort of knowing that although we are at the beginning from RIC's perspective, we have come a long way baby. Now our biggest challenge is that all of the progress that Juliana had made while at RML, which made the nurses so proud of her, and invested in her, is our new baseline. Now she will have to work hard to impress again and win her way into their hearts.

Not that I doubt her ability to do that … ☺

So our first very busy day here was spent with all the doctors and nurses coming by to evaluate her. They all wanted to see what she could do. They asked her to squeeze their hands, hold up a finger, open her eyes, talk. They might as well have asked her to get up and dance because she was having none of it.

Tomorrow she starts on her therapy schedule which will begin at 9 am and last until 2 pm, with breaks in between. Any visiting should be done in the evening, though if she does what she should in therapy, she may be tired in the evening. Let's actually hope for that. I have been told that the therapy program is just as much about 'waking' her as it is teaching us to handle her if she doesn't. Good thing THAT'S not going to happen. During one of the initial evaluation sessions the attending physician said, "Sorry, but I have to ask you this: In the event she does not progress, are you prepared to take her home just the way she is?" Talk about giving it to me right between the eyes, doc. "Well, let's just say, I am more prepared than I ever planned to be, and yes, I am her mom and so...next question." Growing up, did you ever watch those 30 minute sitcoms, like Brady Bunch or Full House where the problem started at one end of the show and ended at the other and you came away thinking, 'Ok I got it now. Sure, I can do that, I can be a parent'. I must have missed an episode. That's ok, we are writing our own. It will be a cross between, Eight is Enough, Greys Anatomy and the X-files because you just can't make this stuff up.

They just came in to tell me that they discovered she has an infection starting, which explains the slight fever, so they are starting her on Bactrim. They have also begun to regulate her sleep/wake pattern with medication to ensure she sleeps all night and works hard all day. Next week the trach weaning will continue in earnest to hopefully remove it all together since she is doing just fine on the capped trach. Oh, they call it 'corking' here... yeah that's one of the new replacement terms we learned. Anyway, it's on its way out so they can call it whatever they want as long as they call it 'old news' pretty soon. The rest of the lab work will start tomorrow so they can confirm her current medication is still appropriate. Once they get a handle on that, they will augment her brain stimulation medicine, hopefully by Friday. So, as I am writing this my fears are starting to subside (or maybe I am just emotionally exhausted since the day has had plenty of drama... don't ask). It's all so much to take in. But our view here in all of its wonder and magnitude puts it in perspective: To my right there is the bustle of Lake Shore Drive, the lights of Navy Pier and the shimmer of Lake Michigan. That is my brain stimulation. To my left there is my daughter sleeping peacefully, trusting me to take care of her, even when I am afraid. That is my medicine.

November 12, 2009 - 11:59 pm

(Ok so it's really 1:30 am on November 13th but I felt guilty about falling asleep without the update so woke up and am writing this pretending it was today but it was really yesterday. This is the X-files part...or the rambling sleepy person part. Regardless, here it is)

Juliana's slight temp elevated to 101.3 and held there through the night. They gave her Tylenol at 10 pm then again at 3 am and 8 am but her fever remained the same. Her fever persisted through her 9 am and 11 am therapy, coupled with the fact that they gave her a sedative for sleep the night before, made for a low participating morning. We put cold rags on her head and her feet and when the doctors rounded I asked for Motrin instead. They explained to me that Tylenol and Motrin are the same except they prefer to use Tylenol because it "works better". I said, "but this time it doesn't seem to be working at all, so can we at least try the Motrin?" They reluctantly agreed to try the Motrin at noon. I am sure her temp going back down to 99.1 by 1 pm had nothing at all to do with it.

During OT we dressed Juli and did some basic care exercises to see how she would react. She was given a hairbrush and asked to brush her hair, a toothbrush and asked what she would do with that. She wasn't participating much but because the OT hadn't seen her before, she was pleased with the little she did. I knew she could do more but was not bothered that this starting line appeared low. It will make it easier for her to impress them when she shows them what she can already do. The OT decided that it would be better if Juliana was watching what we were doing so she tried to tape her left eye open. It worked a bit but she used silly hospital tape. (Duct tape is what she needed but I guess this is not the Boy Scout version). It did make us think though that just because she isn't voluntarily opening her eyes doesn't mean we should lose out on the opportunity to utilize visual stimuli. "Maybe her eye muscles are weak, the therapist said. Let's just get her back in the habit and get her interested in seeing. After all, we know she can, right? " We tried to see if she could track with the photos that we brought but not quite yet. That would be our homework, we agreed.

I was also shown how to transfer Juli to a chair. It resembles folding them over and hoisting them sideways. Not so bad, I think I can learn that one too. After OT we had the opportunity to stroll through the unit for a bit until

PT started in the 'gym'. More transferring, more assessing, more of the same stimuli exercising she had been doing at RML but somehow it was starting to seem routine, and less of an event. Juli was still not quite helping but again, the baseline was not terribly concerning to us since we had two things we could blame it on. Next was Speech therapy. Just like a coma is not what we thought it was, Speech therapy is not really what we thought it was. It's more like Cognitive therapy. Ok, good, this works. During that hour, Juliana did fairly well. She started to behave like the Juli we have been seeing. She gave the doctor thumbs up and 'high fives' several times. She also had many localized responses to the stimuli which we learned, is good. We decided to start using thumbs up and thumbs sideways for yes and no respectively. That would also be our homework and we would start using that in conjunction with her visual stimulation.

Just as Juli needs to associate these activities with something familiar, we do too. So now that this all resembles school, it's a little more familiar and the fear is moving to the back inch by inch. She can do this, we kept thinking, and we can do this too. Our challenge will continue to be to keep the medical issues at bay while the brain heals and relearns what it needs to learn. We have heard so many stories where infections are the main detour from progress. With her fever and infection that detour is amongst us so we have good reason to be concerned. She has also tested positive for MRSA which many of you know, can be a very dangerous situation to be in. She had a lung x-ray and they showed that although her lungs are clear, the lower lobes are starting to collapse a bit from not taking full deep breaths for so long now. They feel that with therapy that will get better but they will keep an eye on it. All in all, a busy and informative first full day at RIC. I went home for the night and another wonderful family makes us a delicious dinner (thank you Slatterys). Have I mentioned that our family and friends are extraordinary? And being a 'food fan', all of the meals have been both delicious and helpful!

Having another biscuit, going back to bed.

November 13, 2009 - 7 pm

Terminology clarification alert: The transition from unconsciousness to consciousness is a continuum without distinct boundaries. It has certain defining criteria in order to apply usable labels to the stages. Based on those criteria,

Juliana is in a Minimally Conscious State, (MCS). This is not considered 'In a Coma' and also not in a Vegetative State. Nothing suddenly changed other than what you have been reading; it just means I got a little better informed. (What can I say; I have never done this before, so consider the source on all this information.) So from my most recent internet education on MCS the prognosis is good. Still lengthy, but, good. For individuals with a Traumatic Brain Injury (TBI) research shows that if they progress to a MCS, their recovery is very good. There is something inherently warped about the fact that nothing factual has changed, just my awareness of the facts and yet, it still feels like something just improved...hmmm....must be my confidence level. That has a physical effect too I realize. It's that relief thing again. Juliana was definitely onto something there. Ok, so this means, hard work is guaranteed to be necessary, but will also yield a payoff.

This weekend we are planning to gather some of her friends to videotape memories they have with Juliana. We figured, while she doesn't have her eyes open, she can hear. When she does, she will see and when she is well, she will appreciate. (Thank you Donnie for coordinating that). It is incredible how one person's altered state can alter so many others. As sure as I am that Juliana will be whole again one day, it doesn't remove the gap I feel from her absence each day. We don't dwell on that because we still have families and lives that must go on but it sneaks up on you and stings when it does. Enough of that. Today's Progress report: During OT they had Juliana in the bathroom attempting to wash her own face and brush her own teeth. She held the washcloth and rubbed it on her face. Then with toothbrush in hand she followed the instructions to move it back and forth over her teeth. As I stood outside the bathroom watching Chris encourage her and praise her for completing these tasks that come so easy to all of us, I was overcome with love for both of them. You always hope your children will grow up and find someone to love them enough to take care of them in sickness and health never really planning the necessity. Not a fun way to find out but it doesn't leave any room for doubt. During Speech she practiced swallowing....yes, everything has to be learned again. It took a little time but she seemed to start to get the hang of it. She still has quite a few reflexes getting in the way "but with practice..." they say. They are going to leave her trach capped all night and see how she does. The only obstacle to removing the trach all together is proof that she can protect her airways by swallowing properly.

They removed her catheter, (we did try that once at RML and 5 hours later they put it back in) so we will see what happens next. I will spare you the details of what else she has to relearn but you can conclude what the reality is here. To go along with our internet medical education, we are also learning how to administer medicine, change bedding, and provide feeding through her G-Tube.

The case manager came in to discuss discharge planning. If Juliana does not get extended to the longer brain injury program, she will be sent home on Wednesday November 25th, the day before Thanksgiving. So I have 12 days to pray as hard as possible that she is allowed to stay here a few weeks longer. As much as I would love to give up this city living, she just needs a little more time here. Help me on that, ok?

November 14, 2009 - 11 pm

Something is changing. I can't quite put my finger on it but something seems to be getting more...level. With Juliana, that is. Some of the behaviors we had grown accustomed to where she clenched her fists and drew up her arms seem to have subsided. Her constant constricted arm muscles and fists are less tight and bound. It's very subtle and I almost didn't notice it, until, I did. Although she wasn't quite agitated, she seems a bit calmer. It's very hard to describe and even harder to notice because it's really seeing what isn't happening, but it's there. Does it mean something you wonder? I don't know yet, I wonder that too. I can only assume that the change is attributed to the change in medicine where they added a stimulant and increased her seizure medicine and of course the passage of time and the continuation of healing. What I won't assume is what the result of this change in behavior will mean long term.

We continued our rehabilitation education today and I alternated between nervous and excited. Strange, isn't it? I mean, the many elements of life and logistics that must be taken into consideration for attending to my daughter while she heals is still staggering to me. If she truly comes home on Wednesday November 25th I will probably be terrified. I am sure 'Team Juli' (as so many of you have dubbed us) will figure it out but I am a planner and I need to visualize my plan. And so far, that vision is hazy.

Juliana still has not opened her eyes since November 6th though it sure seems like she wants to. Her dad has taken to calling her "Blinky" because she spends all of her awake time blinking as if she is really opening and closing her eyes. I keep looking under her long lashes to see if maybe she is peeking out at us but if she is, she hides it well. We really feel that her right eye is holding her back, maybe making it too uncomfortable to open the left but will need to understand more from a Neuro-ophthalmologist. So, we open her left eye on occasion and let her look at pictures or people's faces. In fact, sometimes she 'tells' us to open her eye by putting a thumb up for yes (formerly 1 finger in case you missed an update)

We worked on getting her to hold a spoon and bring it to her mouth. We got minimal results with the therapist but we continued to practice with her in the evening and she seemed to get the hang of it in a very basic way. She seems very capable of fine motor manipulations with her left hand and was almost twirling her spoon in an attempt to maneuver it to her mouth. Many generations of food fans in her blood make that as natural as breathing.

But here is the real excitement. Juliana and I had a seriously dynamic 30 minutes. I am still feeling a little high from it. Although it couldn't possibly translate in words what I experienced, let me see if I can do it justice.

So after her bath I was massaging her feet like normal. I noticed that she was breathing very hard and getting more and more...awake...She folded up her left leg so it was completely bent. I walked up to the head of her bed and noticed that she was slowly getting more jittery. She grabbed my arm and started shaking it. My heart was pounding because I didn't know what was happening so I tried to ask her. "Juli, are you ok?" She squeezed my hand. "Can you hear me?" Thumbs up. "Can I open your eyes?" Thumbs up again. "Can you see me?" Thumbs up and three slaps on my wrist. I am telling you, my heart just about jumped out of my chest. She indicated to us that she could see before but the way she was letting me know was...urgent. It felt like she was stuck behind a glass enclosure and was desperate to get out. I could tell she was getting more and more aroused so I went and grabbed the pictures and started quizzing: "Do you know who this is? (Picture of Mackenzie)" No response. "It's Mackenzie, your little sister. (Pause, eyelid rest, reopen) "Is this Mackenzie?" Thumbs up (that's not cheating, even though it seems like it because the therapist told me to do it). "Juli, can you point to Mackenzie?" Poke, right in the nose. "That's GREAT Juli, you make me so proud! Do you know how much I love you?" Although that was rhetorical, guess what I got? A thumbs up. "Juli, you ARE there, I KNEW IT! (Tears flowing) Can you just please come back to us, we miss you. Are you trying to talk? Can you try to talk?" Her mouth opened slightly but no sound. She was getting more and more fidgety with her hands working her neck, shaking around her face, through her hair. I knew that she needed a break so I said, "Can I ask you one more question and then I will stop opening your eyes and let you rest?" She hesitated. "Just one more question, I promise." Thumbs up. I held up a picture of her and Chris, opened her eye and said, "Can you point to Chris?" And she reached across with her left hand and tapped on Chris, who was on the right side of the picture.

Don't stop reading, it gets better.

I was of course very excited and texted Chris telling him to call me when he could. Less than a minute later my phone rings. I wonder who it could be. Oh, you guessed it, right? So I told Chris, "I think we are on the verge of something here." I replayed the story and he considered driving right over. I told him she was quite shaky and maybe he could just talk to her and try to calm her down. So I held the phone to her ear. She grabbed it from me and held it up there with her index finger extended and the other fingers wrapped around it as natural as can be. It was very surreal. She listened for a few minutes and then pulled the phone away from her ear, and intentionally, pressed the disconnect button with her thumb. I SWEAR. It was totally intentional and direct. I was shaking. I called Chris back and said, "You would not believe what I just witnessed! She was working the cell phone like nothing was wrong! Then she hung it up, what did you say to her?"

He said, "I talked to her for a minute, told her I loved her and then told her to press any button so I knew that she hears me."

I laughed and I cried. I do that a lot these days.

November 15, 2009 - 4:15 pm

What a day already. After last night, I was really excited about what might happen next. Turns out, I was right to be. She did spike a fever again of 102.3 at one point through the night. They were able to bring it down to 100.8 but it wasn't until morning with the combination of Tylenol and Motrin. I am realizing why we heard incredible things about RIC. I was a little discouraged at first because I was used to traditional medical care and although the nursing care is good enough, they are more interested in preparing us to nurse them at home. This is just one of the many similarities I have seen to the labor and delivery process. I will let you stew on that a bit. But this place is definitely less focused on medical issues and much more focused on rehab (obviously) not only for the patient, but also for the family. They make sure their staff are all thinking and acting in the interest of the individual's improvement. I am seeing that unfold in various ways but they are doing what they do in addition to making us feel empowered to help her too.

Her dad and I spent a few hours in the morning just taking care of her: getting her dressed, transferring her to the chair, talking with her. During that time, I happened to notice that her right eye was open a bit more. I got closer to her face to see if it really was open and saw someone looking at me… it was Juli! She had BOTH eyes open. I probably scared her with my reaction but geez, I just didn't see that one coming. Again it was just briefly, but she did it. We were very excited as you can imagine. On the heels of last night I suspected that we were making advancements but it still is so great to see. She also responded to the spoon by opening her mouth and some yes/no questions for us. Not necessarily new but it is happening more often, more… aware.

Then around noon the Speech therapist came in. She asked what kind of a day she had and I told her about the events the night before and also the morning. She worked on the same things that we have been focusing on. Thumbs up, thumbs down, high fives, spoon acceptance. Then, since we told her that Juli opened her eyes shortly before she arrived, the therapist decided to try the photo recognition. She reliably answered questions on identity. The therapist was impressed. Then we showed her the picture of her and Chris and asked her again to point out Chris. He was further away from her this time and still, she reached across to point him out. One thing we did notice is that her depth perception was a bit off. That could be a result of her right eye not working correctly yet. Again, it's too soon to tell. Then we showed her the picture of Mackenzie, who she acknowledged and I moved it, just a bit to the side and…she followed it! Tracking! That is tracking! We were so thrilled. Shortly after that, she opened her eyes again and again and AGAIN! 'Something tells me I'm into something good'. Pennies are raining down on us now. The therapist took that moment to tell us that, "I realize you guys are only here for the 2 week evaluation but all the therapists agree that we are seeing good things. I am not promising anything, but, it's looking good for the extended program."

Writing this now feels just as good as when I heard it.

November 16, 2009 - 10 pm

I am once again reminded that life can be an unkind roller coaster. There is give and take, yin and yang, to and fro. Never does life stop surprising us, with both good and bad. Today we lost a very dear friend, Bill "Herm" Rosenberg. My prayers and love go out to his whole family who relied on him for guidance and love. Everyone will miss him so much. You don't come across people like this man very often and I am proud to have called him my friend. What is our loss is surely heaven's gain, of that there is no doubt. So with this world's loss on my mind, and how his family is grieving this wonderful man gone too soon, I am sad and will just say good night.

All my love to you Rosenberg family.

It was my day to work in the office and so that is where I was when I got the call from Juli's rehab doctor. "I don't want you to be alarmed but we are seeing increased fluid build up in her brain and we believe it is best to put a shunt in. The shunt will be inserted in her head and will travel under her skin to deposit the fluid into her abdomen to be absorbed. Feel free to get a second or third opinion but I don't see this as getting any better, and you really need to act fast."

"How fast"

"No later than tomorrow."

"How long will the shunt have to stay in?"

"Forever"

I was standing perfectly still, phone in hand and I could hear the dripping of my tears on my shoe. I kept thinking of the saying that 'God only gives you what you can handle' and wondered how close He was going to cut it.

November 17, 2009 - 11:30 am

Results of the latest CT Scan, not so good. We are in the process of transporting Juliana back to Christ Hospital to have a shunt inserted in her brain to drain the accumulating spinal fluid. I will give you my version of a medical explanation of that later. Need to pack up her lakefront room right now. Surgery will be tomorrow. Oh, just real quick though, this is ultimately a good thing. Not so good that it is needed but the fluid may have been impeding her progress. Considering all the progress she has made, can you even imagine the rock star she will be after this procedure?

Gotta go….back to our favorite nurses at Christ!!

November 18, 2009 - 11:00 am

Juliana is out of surgery and all went well, per Dr Shiable. We are on our way back up to see her now. Thanks for all of your prayers and positive wishes. A little extra help in heaven probably didn't hurt so if there is Facebook in Heaven, thanks Herm.

Update more later…

November 18, 2009 - 11 pm

We have not hit one straight road yet. I should expect it more but yet each time it takes me by surprise. (Just like the freezing cold temperature inside this room). The surgery went fine. She looks great, the swelling decreased in her eye and her face seems less swollen too. She slept most of the day and then was just as quiet and sleepy through the evening. When the nurses did their hourly assessment, her reactions were good but very sedated as you might expect after general anesthesia. Then around 9 pm, she started vomiting. It wasn't pretty as you can imagine since her ability to help is limited. The nurses were calm and seemed only mildly concerned but paged the doctor to be sure. He was also calm and unconcerned but would know more after the CT Scan that would be taken after midnight. After the vomiting and the subsequent clean up, she was worn out and was VERY calm…too calm… .'scare your parents' calm. They checked to make sure her pupils were still reactive (they were) and that she still reacted to stimuli (she did). She would not however follow any commands. The longer she was still and silent, the more uncomfortable we grew.

The closest conclusion we can come to is that she reacted to the combination of the anesthesia on an empty stomach followed by the continuous tube feedings. But as she lay there looking more and more like a sleeping wounded baby, her head wrapped as it had been on the first day, we are again reminded of this fragile state and that we are still deep in the woods.

Assuming that this is nothing more than what they are suggesting to us, and the scan they take tonight looks good, we should be going back to RIC this week. We will just stay focused on that right now even though the eerie silence is deafening.

November 19, 2009 - 3 pm

Somewhere around noon she started coming out of the fog. I don't know why I forgot how hard sedation hits her. Remember the Propofol? Remember the Ativan? Remember the Trazadone? Juliana's experience with each of those sedatives took twice as long as they expected for her to kick the effects of the sedation. Maybe I have short term memory loss myself! I have to tell you, in the dark moments, it's not so easy to jest. Luckily they pass and I can chide myself. I am happily my own target. In fact, I have discovered that sometimes, I don't play well with others. You see, this is hard on many people, not just me and some of those people are really relying on me to provide open and frequent communication. I have to admit, I am not always happy to do so. And I am sure I will get messages from some of you saying not to be so hard on myself that I am doing great but honestly, sometimes I am not and I am ok to admit it. What are you going to do? This is new, difficult, all consuming, tiring and sometimes (not always) sad and I am just making it up as I go…with a LOT of help, advice and support. So, from one imperfect human being to another, thanks for taking this journey with me. For those of you who will read this and recognize I am referring to you, I am sorry. My dark side is currently under control. There, doc, can I count that as therapy so you can check that off your list of things we need to do?

In any case, this latest hurdle seems to have been a figment of my poor memory and Juli is working through the kinks herself. She is getting ready to move to a regular room for the remainder of her stay here with the plan to go back to RIC tomorrow. Then we will see how this latest medical intervention has affected her. The doctor said, "The CT scan showed that things are 'moving in the right direction' ". Hmmm….I think we have paid our dues and earned a little more medical terminology than that, doc. "The fluid is draining, the swelling is going down and the result is her eye should have more opportunity to heal. We will get another CT scan in a few weeks but there is no reason to expect this to need additional intervention at all." That's a bit better.

So, today we get off the multi-wired monitors, tomorrow we get off the IV, then shortly afterward the catheter can come out (again) which will put us back to where we left off: trying to get rid of the trach.

Changing of the guards: Chris is taking over. Now he can charm another wing of nurses.

November 21, 2009 - 12:30 am

Since we decided from the beginning that Juliana would always have someone with her, we had to make plenty of tough choices. Not the least of which was to compromise our sleeping arrangements. Somewhere during the middle of our stay at RML, Chris and I chose to start switching off who would spend the night. It has mostly worked well giving me some time to remember how to put my little girls to sleep.

So last night, Chris stayed and tried to figure out how to sleep in the new room. It is small, cozy and has plenty of one person chairs…hmmmm….. he did a little rearranging and before you know it, he was able to fall asleep half on the bed with her. He said it was a great couple of hours. I suspect it probably was.

We expected that she would be moved back to RIC today at 3 pm. Sometime just after 3 they told us that since she had a fever within the last 24 hours, she would need to stay at least another day. Now ideally we would prefer she stay until Sunday afternoon since the rehab schedule at RIC is lighter on the weekends. That way the remainder of our 2 week trial period wouldn't be squandered on a less intensive day. However, we know by now that this entire journey is happening at its own speed so we stress less about what and when, or at least make the attempt to. The compromise would be that Christ would provide PT for the day or weekend so that she could at least maintain some of the progress she had made. Just prior to the surgery she was so alert that Chris asked her at one point if she would marry him, to which she gave him a big thumbs up. He was happy of course and reached down and hugged her. She reached up and grabbed the chain on his neck that holds her engagement ring. He said, "Angel, do you want your ring? Do you want me to put your ring back on your finger?" She again gave him the thumbs up, so he put it on her hand. I KNOW, sweet, isn't it? Movies just don't do stuff this good and we are living it and you are reading it as fact. How cool is THAT??

But here we are, post-surgery and have not returned yet to that level or involvement. Since we knew that she was still not back to full steam, we were content with staying at Christ a couple more days....Ok so you see how this goes, we start to expect and plan and....um, yeah, they told us she will probably return to RIC tomorrow morning at 9. Whatever. We are just passengers on this bus anyway.

Most of the day she was sleepy with bouts of awareness and that was calmly satisfying. But later in the evening, as had previously been her pattern, (the pattern RIC was breaking) she started to perk up and regain activity. She even hugged her dad when he left and waved goodbye. That was encouraging to all in the room and Chris felt comfortable enough to leave for a bit to get something to eat and leave Sarah in charge. During that time, Sarah chatted with her and Juliana fussed with her face, running her hands up to her left eye. Sarah asked, "Are you trying to open your eye?" Juliana gave a prompt thumbs up. This was new to Sarah who, despite the many hours logged in Juliana's presence had yet to see her in that 'ultra-aware state' so her heart raced in excitement. Then Sarah asked if she wanted her to open it for her. Another prompt thumbs up. Now mind you, not all thumbs up are created equal so sometimes, they excite us more than others. We know the difference between, 'I hear you and am obeying' (weak thumb wiggle) and 'Listen to me people, I have something to say'...THAT is the prompt thumbs up I described. So anyway, Sarah opened her eye and waved and Juliana waved back. Sarah was thrilled and emotional at the same time. Chris came back in the room to see Sarah's reaction and hear her recounting the events and said (well I was not there but I will do my best Chris impersonation...) "Angel, can I open your eye?" Thumbs up, promptly. He opened her eye and

waved and said, "Hey angel, hi, you're so beautiful, hey…oh baby, I love you."
And he smiled at Juliana.

And then…

She smiled back.

Come on, gimme at least a buck for that one

November 22, 2009 - 2:30 am

Things are not always what they seem. In fact, sometimes, we are forced to remember that faith IS believing when you don't have a tangible reason to do so. Juliana is back at RIC, sans the lakefront view, ready for the next step in her rehabilitation. If we take inventory of where we are, she appears to have taken steps in reverse: She has a catheter, a non-capped trach, less mobility, stitches in her stomach and her head, a little less hair. All of these things add to her appearance of new vulnerability and it takes a moment to remember that God is the project planner here, I am not and what appears to be a backward direction is really just a refining of THE direction. This whole event could have shaken my faith in God. (Ok, so to be honest, I had my moments …) but for the most part, this has strengthened my belief and much of that strength I have drawn on from all of you. So many people have prayed for Juliana in a variety of ways; from a moment of silence in their own head, to asking their congregation to speak their requests out loud. Although I have mentioned how grateful I am for the support, I feel a responsibility to give credit where credit is due. (Now I don't mean to preach, but I am a mother and sometimes it's just part of the lingo)

In the beginning…(whoa, yeah that wasn't intentional) I often felt that I was not able to breathe there was such heaviness in my chest, and yet I had breath. I was not able to move, certain my limbs would stop cooperating and yet I walked. I was not able to speak, yet I had words. For all of those things, I did not think I was capable of doing and yet, I was able to do them all. When I took stock of that, I was actually surprised and a little excited by it. I thought, 'wow, I have never physically felt the power of God as much as I do now because I KNOW I cannot get through this alone.' That was my indication that someone else was in control, and it was tangible. Then as the days went by I saw amazing things happen in Juliana's recovery but more shocking, I saw it in all of the people and relationships that surround her.

Only divine intervention could have caused it all. I am sure some people are thinking, 'ok, so if there is a God, why would he let this happen at all'? To them I quote my dad: "You have to break a few eggs to make an omelet". We are still in the early stages of this whole ordeal so I believe the positive outcomes have only just started. The ripple effect has been tremendous already but to see it, you have to look through the eyes of faith. And that is what I choose to do and it makes Juliana look less vulnerable and weak and more of an instrument in an awesome plan.

It's all in your perspective.

November 22, 2009 - 10:30 pm

Since it was Sunday they informed us that nothing happens at RIC on Sunday so not to expect therapy. Every day of the last 8 weeks have been therapy for me so I wasn't concerned. We got Juliana dressed and plopped her in a wheelchair. Not the fancy adjusted one she had when we were there a week ago, but a standard, less comfy, less fitting chair. "Nothing happens on the weekend" includes getting a customized wheelchair. Then we spent the morning fighting the secretions in her trach…ewww….yup, it was icky. The bummer about that was we were this close to having the trach out altogether and now we went back to a cuffed trach with an HME. THAT was sooooo three weeks ago. Anyway, we whined just enough that our nurse paged respiratory and they came in to swap out her trach for a capped/corked one. We aren't allowed to have her keep it on overnight without doctors' orders so we weren't quite back to where we left off, but closer than we were. My goal is to have that trach out by the end of the week. It's Juliana's too (I have her proxy). We still had to deal with the catheter being back in but strap that sucker to her ankle, roll her pant leg down and you forget all about it. Tomorrow I will see if we can get that out.

But the real news is on the cognitive front. Today felt like a day of real progress. Juliana spent most of the day with her eyes open. Not wide open all the way like you and I when we are awake, but somewhere between peeking and squinting…without the squint, you know? This is quite a leap from 'opening several TIMES'. Today she just kept them open for considerable stretches and then added to those stretches with more stretches. Today was a mark it on my calendar day for progress.

Once we realized she was going to keep her eyes open, the ideas started churning. Not the least of which was, 'her favorite downtime-pastime is watching TV and the only thing on was football'. Shoot…gotta wait til the weeknights. We settled for taking her strolling through the unit to enjoy the view of the lakefront and everything else she has been part of in her slumber. It was so nice to sit in front of her, talk to her and feel like I was having a conversation, knowing that I could count on her seeing who is talking to her and the expression as they talked. I pulled out all my 'mommy faces': concerned, proud, amused, comforting, stern and determined. Yeah, I am pretty sure she would recognize them all. We also discovered that Juliana wants to talk. (Ok, so we knew that since the check on her first grade report card) but similar to her indications to us weeks ago that she was 'trying to open her eyes but it was hard', she confirmed for us that she is trying to talk, she just isn't able to yet. I explained to her again that just because she can't do it now doesn't mean she won't ever be able to do it so she needed to be patient and keep trying. We have heard her 'voice' in her accidental sounds like a cough and a grunt a few times so we know that her vocal chords are ready to go. The signal between head and mouth needs to be corrected and she will be back to interrupting me in no time. In fact, I asked her if she could say, "bye Mommy" and she gave a little "eh". I was very happy of course but not satisfied (I know it's the greed again) so I asked her again to say "bye Mommy" and she again gave me a little "eh". We repeated that routine a few times until I was satisfied I knew exactly what she was trying to say to me…"eh". I will take it and we can work on the rest later. Christine and Sarah came in to work on holding and maneuvering a drinking cup. They followed the same patterns we have in the past of repetition, brief commands followed by moments of rest then assisted movements then…watch, wait and wonder. Eventually, she did get the cup to her chin but it was a hard fought battle. We can expect everything will be.

…And they said nothing happens at RIC on Sundays. Guess they didn't count on Team Juliana.

November 23, 2009 - 9:30 pm

I am not sure if you know this or not, but the updates write themselves. Sometimes, one moment (and literally it may be only a moment), defines the day. Sometimes it is many moments. Sometimes, describing those very few moments might leave the impression that the accomplishments are cumulative. But that is not the case. For example, I have told you that Juliana can do the following: answer yes/no questions, open her eyes, try to speak, move her arms and legs, hug, smile, recognize family in photos, play with her hair, hold the phone, accept marriage proposals, even give the nurses the middle finger....wait...what? I didn't tell you that story? Yeah that's a funny one... for later. But anyway, if you add up all of those things that Juliana can do, you might think, "I thought I was following the story of a girl in a coma... no?" But then, you walk into her room and you find a once vivacious girl without the ability to do anything for herself and it has a very clinical reality to it. Each of her accomplishments cannot yet be added up because they don't together amount to a fraction of what she once was. Don't get me wrong, I am thrilled by all she can do of course but the reality is, no matter how positive all of these steps are, she is still just learning how to live again, one moment at a time. She still lacks the consistency and awareness of consciousness and with almost two months under our belt, it really illustrates how lengthy this road really is. So I want all of you to stay positive, because in spite of the way I have described it, I still am. But the reality is, you have several more months of reading ahead of you so you might want to pace yourselves.

In today's news, Juliana had a very successful PT session with her dad and Gloria leading the event. She followed commands, sat up straight and gave lots of fingers when asked. She even opened both of her eyes wide enough to make Gloria call Chris and me like she was voting for the next American Idol, (that one's for you Jules). The middle of the day was a bit more sedate where she had back to back PT and OT. Chris and I both practiced transferring her to bed and then back to the chair. A couple of more times and we will be experts. I even did it unassisted, (with Chris to spot me) at the end of her day in the chair. As I was getting ready to transfer her I said, "Now Juli, you will have to help me." Once I got her on the bed, with my arms still around her, she lifted her left arm, put it around me and hugged me. Still not aware, still not conscious and darn it if I still didn't love that hug.

During her evening meal of the gourmet and delicious Jevity 1.2, I could see Chris out of the corner of my eye start to take apart her wheelchair. He removed the foot rest and placed her gym shoe feet on the floor. Then he asked her to move her chair. (So in typical update fashion I should tell you that she did just that, right?) Have I become that predictable?

Well she didn't, so there.

Chris showed her how to do it by moving her feet backward one foot behind the other and showing her how to push off from the floor. (I attempted this on Sunday but I didn't have any luck.) It didn't look like Chris was going to either and she wasn't going to do it.

Until she did.

And once she got the hang of it she did it better and further. We cheered and laughed and of course...videotaped.

So the story about giving the nurse the middle finger...eh, I will save that for a dry news day.

November 24, 2009 - 10 pm

They told us that once the shunt was inserted there was a 50/50 chance that Juliana's progress would improve dramatically. That meant that either she would continue progressing as she was, or faster. Pretty good odds, right? So then I wondered, when will we know if she is progressing faster? From other families I have asked it ranges anywhere from immediately out of sedation post-surgery to a few weeks. Ah, yes, the familiar "we don't know". So knowing the best case scenario was 'immediately' but that she certainly wouldn't get worse, naturally we were concerned when the days following the surgery she was exceptionally calm and still.

Today gave us hope that we might be on the right side of 50.

During speech therapy Juliana was so responsive and expressive that the speech therapist was going to find out if we can get an augmentative communication device to give Juli visual cues to tell us what she is trying to say. I haven't seen the method they might offer us but I have seen devices before and it could be a book with pictures, or sounds or letters that she can use to spell. I will get back to you on that. The cool thing is that she is doing THAT well. After she got back in her bed she was holding her head as if she was in pain so Chris started a series of questions to determine where the problem might be. After about 10 questions that she answered easily and consistently he concluded that she had pain behind her right eye but not so bad that she wanted pain medicine. Good for her. We were successful in getting rid of the catheter today and the trach is targeted for Friday. Let's hope...

Then during PT she did even better than speech. She was able to do, or try to do, every single thing the therapist asked her to do from holding up her head to lifting her leg unassisted 10 times to their count. She was given specific directions like, "move your left heel under the mat" and she was able to comply. She was even able to use her right side, though weaker as expected. While sitting upright on the mat with her feet on the floor she was asked to put her hands down on the mat. She did as asked with her left hand fingers extended. Her right arm, still tight with muscle tone was not as accommodating, though she did try. So...she leaned to the right to bring the mat to it! The therapist was very impressed and continued to say that through the session. Good. We like impressed. Impressed will get her to stay longer, we hope. At the end of the therapy they put her feet in bike pedals and although she couldn't push it forward, she was able to pedal it backward for three rotations.

In the later afternoon Chris noticed that a spot on the right side of her face was starting to swell in infection. We had assumed it was a slow healing scab but, as assumptions go, we were wrong. It was a piece of glass wedged in her skin. They removed that and it did not require a stitch. Good thing because I am sure she will find a way to tattoo the caterpillar like scar they gave her on her stomach but her face, maybe not so much.

So we had a really really successful day. Could it be the shunt? If so, we might be on the verge of the waterfall of improvements they told us could occur. I will try not to get too hopeful just yet. But I think a huge contributing factor was that she had her eyes open for most of the therapy and locked on Chris. She's in love with the boy. She's going to marry that boy someday. Take a look back 2 years at a very special video our favorite videographer Mike Schick managed to post for us. This can be found on www.YouTube.com called 'Chris Medina proposes to Juliana."

November 25, 2009 - 11 am

This just in: Juliana has progressed from Minimally Conscious and is now officially considered CONSCIOUS!!

Because of that, she has been accepted into the regular brain stimulation program and her current discharge date has been moved forward to December 14th. That could move forward again, depending on her progress and of course, overcoming the real obstacle: insurance limitations. We aren't losing hope though because we have lots of irons in the fire on that one. The truly important thing is that from a medical and rehabilitative standpoint, she is progressing VERY well.

She just finished a session of PT and she was able to catch and throw a ball as well as support a portion of her weight with her legs. To quote the therapist…"Very Cool".

And finally for this mid-day report, to all of you who compliment Juliana, Chris and me, your support is like a warm blanket. But I have to say that Team Juli is bigger than just us and I would hate to have any of those individuals overlooked. So…spread the love to her dad, future mother-in-law, step-dad and step-mom, siblings, aunts, uncles and close friends. It takes a village and thank God, we have one.

Thanksgiving Day 2009

I have always said that is my most favorite holiday because, well first of all it's all about food and I love food but mostly because it actually centered around remembering what is good in our lives and why we should be grateful. Feel free to disregard this post as it is not about Juliana's progress but more a declaration of love and gratitude to be included for our memoirs. Here is what I am thankful for:

-My children. Juliana said to me just this year: "I always thought it was dumb when people said this but now it is so true I can't NOT say it…you are my best friend." She will never know how intensely that moved me because spending time with her was one of my greatest pleasures. Anyone who saw us together knew that. I loved my 'Juli time'. And it made me excited for the other kids to grow to adulthood so I could have the same bond with them though I suspect that Cheye-time, Delaney-time, and Mackenzie-time will look very different than Dylan or Adam time. (It's a mother daughter thing you know). I have said this for 23 years but I will say it again. If God wouldn't have gifted me with Juliana to take care of, I never would have known that being a mom was what I was meant to do, and then I wouldn't have had the pleasure of also loving Adam, Dylan, Cheyenne, Delaney and Mackenzie. Those kids are my life and I hope the rest of you all get the joy of knowing them. Not a day goes by where at least one of them doesn't make me so happy that I physically feel joy. I am grateful for that opportunity. Just as my tattoo says, "I have been blessed". Each of them have shown who they are through this situation and your efforts are not overlooked. I am very thankful for all that you have sacrificed for me and for your sister to bond together the way a family should. We make a great team.

-My parents. Although I did my best to rebel, I also did my best to absorb and humbly learned that my parents did the best they could and I didn't turn out so bad as a result. So God, tell mom and dad thanks from me.

-My sisters and brothers. Could I have made it through anything without you?? No absolutely not. Diane, Lori, Joe and Michael, I love you fiercely and am so grateful for my lifetime with you, not just the support over this last year but for all the times we shared from many many vacations to the horrible Leukemia battle Joe faced earlier this year. I am grateful he has beaten the odds and will continue to support that effort in the celebration in January.

-My nieces and nephews. You have been almost as close to me as my children and I am so grateful for the people you have become. I am intensely proud of you and thankful for how much you have shown your love to me. Happy Birthday Connor!

-My large extended family of aunts, uncles and cousins. Some of you I see often and some I only see on occasion but I know for certain that if called upon, we are a formidable army of one.

-My in laws. You accepted me when it was probably shocking to do so. I mean, Don brought home a cocktail waitress with four kids! You could have (probably should have) tried to knock some sense into him but instead, you bought all my kids Christmas presents and called us family. God, tell Irene and Linda thank you for me. (Um, still wondering if there is Facebook in Heaven).

-My great friends. I have oh so many from those I have known since childhood to those I gained when I married Donnie and you have all been there for me throughout, offering any help that you can provide. And to Carrie, girl, you know I love you dearly.

-Juliana's friends. You have stuck by her, stepped up and changed your young vibrant lives to push my daughter back to this life. I will forever be proud of you and grateful she chose such devoted people to share her life with. Learn from this and be better for it.

-My neighbors. You showed your support and brought us dinners when I didn't have the time or energy to make them myself. You saved my family from far too many 'cereal nights'.

-My coworkers. You not only show your constant care and support but made sure that I had a job to come back to. The effects of your efforts are lifelong.

-This entire Facebook support group. From this tragedy I have renewed old friendships and gained acquaintances and throughout have leaned on your combined strengths and experiences. Many of you don't know me or my kids and reached out to support me ANYWAY. That is a true blessing. I welcome the emails and the posts because they are a constant reminder that people are good. I love hearing from you and your stories of recovery or just stories of your life. Make no mistake, this is not a story about a girl in a car accident. This is a story of the impact of this tragedy on a society brought together. Who couldn't look at this group and feel the power that is generated? (Can't thank Oprah yet because she hasn't called yet…her loss, right?)

-For all the prayers, donations, masses said in her honor, visits from pastors and religious symbols to assist in this miracle. I am thankful for all that has been done to show your support to my beautiful daughter. I am far more honored than you know to be included in such a miracle.

-The medical staff who went above and beyond for my daughter. You did, and continue to do, so much more than your job and as a result, we have come so far. You know who you are because you have been invited in to read along…

-My ex-husband. This one is tough because, well, he is an ex and is supposed to be my enemy, right? Well, thankfully, you were here for your daughter and tried your best to make the last 9 weeks less stressful for me. We may never be buddies again but I hope we will never be enemies either.

-Gloria. Well well well….it took 8 years to get to know the woman who raised my very loved future son-in-law but I have to say, it was worth the wait. You are a hell of a woman and it has been a riot getting to know you. I can't wait until you can really get to know your future daughter-in-law because the two of you will love each other. You are too much like me for her to not love you.

-Christopher Medina. I loved you from the start but we have shared a most profound experience and out of that grew enormous respect and love. You (and this whole Facebook community) know how I feel about you and I look so forward to the day that Juliana sees the man you have become, because of her.

-And finally, my husband, Donnie. So much of this has fallen on you to silently just accept. You lost Juliana, and me at the same time and you don't even complain though I know you are sad and hurting and lonely. I am so grateful that you understand my need to be here with my daughter even at the expense of our time together and our time with the family and you have compensated in every way possible. I promise you, it will get better and we will have our life back before you know it. So thank you for understanding and tolerating my absence and all its repercussions. This is the 'for worse' part to go with all the 'for betters' we shared. I am "Donnie's Girl" and I love you with all my heart, just like my tattoo says. Yes, I wear my life.

Thank you for reading along and sharing it with me. Happy Thanksgiving.

November 27, 2009 - 11:55 pm

It was a very good couple of days for Juliana. We continue to get more indications that she is aware of her surroundings and trying to reach out to us. Her daily accomplishments are simple yet profound as she reclaims the details of her life. If she only knew that what she was accomplishing was far greater than just her life coming back into focus, she would be as awed as I am. I will be very interested to get her perspective on some dramatically changed relationships in the months that she was sleeping. Those are the things we would have sat cross legged on my bed for hours dissecting. As I think of that wistfully, I wonder how our relationship will have to change as a result. We had evolved to a peer/friend relationship but now we have been transported back to caregiver/care-receiver relationship. Don't get me wrong, I would rather have this role than give it to anyone else. In fact, I won't step aside for anyone else to do it. But I am also growing more accepting of the idea that we will need to evolve all over again and it could be different next time. And in that evolution, I will struggle with sharing her along the way. (Remember I don't play well with others?) Heck, I struggle with sharing her now! The mother cub/territorialism syndrome is fully ingrained in me and making that adjustment to widen the circle is uncomfortable for me. Even the inclusion of her nurses isn't very cozy. It probably doesn't help that these nurses aren't like the ones we had at Christ or at RML. They are less invested in the patient and are focused on teaching us but they all have their own timetable and method of execution and each of them are 'right'....sigh.... That is where I like to invoke the mommy rule: "if we can't reach an agreement, we do it my way."

The therapists (whom we DO love) continue to be pleased with her progress as she answers questions of date and time orientation and appears to recognize her family as well. We as her support team try to devise new and creative ways to challenge her. Chris had her holding one end of a rope and asked her to do the opposite of what he does. He pulled up and down, side to side and diagonally. No problem there, she was on it. Then he asked her to do the SAME thing he did and he tugged on his end of the rope 7 times, counting TO HIMSELF. Wouldn't you know, she was counting to herself too because she pulled back, 7 times. He was play fighting with Dylan when Dylan said, "Juli, are you going to let Chris do that to me? Hit him!" And her little balled up fist, (no bigger than a peach mind you), gave Chris three rabbit punches to the side of his face! Ok, bunny punches.....newborn baby bunny punches...

That's Juli though. Even in this state, she will fight for her people.

I brought in a white board hoping to focus on fine motor and language to see what she knows and what she has to relearn. I wrote 'Juliana' and asked her if she knew what the word was. She gave me a thumbs up but then answered yes to "does this say Ramos?" So I wasn't convinced on that one. Then I gave her the marker and asked her to draw a circle. She had done this earlier with Chris so I wasn't surprised when she easily made the circle. She followed it with a square and an attempt at a heart. This was left handed even though she is a righty. I told her to draw anything she wanted. I should have probably given more guidance because there is no way to tell if she is drawing intentionally or just scribbling. Or so I thought. Clear as can be, she drew a rainbow. I think she may have started adding clouds and rain and other things as well but I stopped her when the marker was heading off onto the pillow on her lap. I colored one side green and the other black and gave her the eraser and told her to 'erase the whole black side then hand me back the eraser'. She did that as well. I tried to assess her ability to see out of her right eye but I didn't want to disturb it too much so it was a weak attempt at best. Even so, I was not able to get any indication that she could see. Not losing hope there though. Then finally, I asked her to write 'mom'. It was chicken scratch but it was most definitely 'MOM'. I was so thrilled. Tomorrow I will have her do it on paper so I can keep it in her baby book. Hey, should I start a new one for her rebirth? Hmmmm, we'll just let this be her baby book. Maybe by Christmas, she will be typing these updates herself. Nothing would surprise me anymore.

November 28, 2009 - 12:30 pm

Quiet day today so far. Juli spent all last night sleeping completely sound. In fact, she never even moved her head. Hmmmm. You see, they reintroduced Trazadone at bedtime to force a full night's sleep. They want that kind of sound sleep so she will be well rested through the day and fully participate in therapy. We will see how that works out since she has speech therapy at 2 pm. Maybe by then she will be more awake. That is the method here, medicate her up in the day, down at night. It's not my preferred method and I still am not comfortable with it all but none of this was a chosen path so now we trust the experts...mostly. The problem is, (and if you have been reading along even YOU know this) Juliana doesn't snap out of sedation as quickly as most so, she got her rest last night and then is spending the day with nothing but rest. I don't understand how the nurses can pass by our room for several daytime hours without stopping in but at night, they have the need to come in every hour to do something which would wake anyone up. I mean, think about it: I am sleeping across the room and they aren't even bothering me and I wake up. So certainly Juli will wake up when they are taking her vitals, taking blood, moving her around on the bed, checking 'other things'. Geez, maybe just eliminate the sleep drug AND the nightly visits and we can all have a good night's rest?! (Yeah another side effect... crabby mommy) But that is the way it works in the real world, and this is definitely an altered reality. Sorry, just needed to vent to 3000 of my closest friends.

I tried complaining to Juli but she just snored. (Don't tell her she snores)

November 28, 2009 - 11:15 pm

Well! This afternoon started out with Juliana giving back her lunch, for the second day in a row. Oh yeah, and you know what happens when you try to help someone throwing up? You end up in the line of fire. Once we both got cleaned up and redressed it was time for speech therapy. I was thinking we wouldn't have much luck with that therapy because of the residual sleepiness and the vomiting but, once again, I was wrong. For all of the things I have learned about myself I must try to remember, 1. Have higher expectations and 2. Being wrong doesn't always feel bad.

During speech they did the typical 'open your mouth for the cold spoon' to elicit the swallow response. This time, they did it with a little bit of thickened cranberry juice. By the third pass she was opening her mouth a little more readily and swallowing a little faster (emphasis on little…a little with coaxing). She continued to indicate with a thumbs up that she wanted more so we kept going until we switched to Orange juice which she let us know she preferred. We were pretty happy with all that but you can't taste drops of juice for an hour, not at the prices I am sure this place charges, so we moved on. The therapist had her throwing the ball to her, then handing it sideways to her brother Adam. She did really well with that. Then we moved on to the whiteboard. That's where she really rocked. We discovered that Juliana can write her name which is evidenced by the photo I posted earlier today. Can you really appreciate what this means? She knows her name, how to spell it, how to write it in cursive (she even dotted her 'i') and she did it with her left hand when she is right handed. We were thrilled with that but it gets better. The therapist said that with Juliana only opening one eye her depth perception would be off, which we figured, but also that she might be seeing double. In order to help her visually answer more accurately the therapist concluded that any comparisons we ask from her should probably be stacked and not side by side. So, she wrote two names on the board, Adam and Steve and told her to circle her brother's name. She did. She wrote 23 and 30 and asked her to circle her age. Right again. Then we asked her which month she was born in, November or March. Trifecta. (Shout out to my dad on that). So let us recap: She recognizes numbers, letters, can read and write, knows her birth month and prefers orange juice over cranberry. Isn't this the craziest thing?? The therapist said that she is progressing quickly and she is ready to move onto more difficult tasks. Wouldn't you know, I finally get a child in advanced placement classes and she had to go into a coma to do it? (Don't try this at home kids).

The other new development today is that Juliana is starting to vocalize. We noticed her coughs taking on a bit more of a tune as she practiced the sound that she heard come out. Then today, after weeks of trying to elicit a response, she started very quiet, very brief, very subtle humming. If I hadn't become so 'penny wise' I might have actually missed the progression. If I were a betting woman (hey, I AM a betting woman), I would say, by Christmas, my daughter will be talking. It could be sooner though. After all, I am getting really good at being wrong.

November 29, 2009 - 11:45 pm

Great, great not so great. That is the ride of this wave. Third day in a row, roughly the same time, Juliana threw up…hmmmm…yesterday they took a look at her meds and said there shouldn't be any conflict with foods, nothing that needs to be on an empty or a full stomach. But today she had medicine at 12, still no food by 1:30 when she threw up. The doctor and nurses are unconcerned but think that medicine on an empty stomach could bother anyone. Seems logical, ok, lets modify that and try again tomorrow. Juli also started the day with a fever of 101.5. Another fact that the doctors and nurses don't seem too concerned about although that did prevent her from getting an extra unexpected hour of Physical Therapy they were ready to give her. They took some blood and urine to test for infection. She was also still more subdued today, probably a result of the Trazadone (sleep agent) that she hasn't grown accustomed to. A side problem is, when Juli is not well, Team Juli is worse. Yep, we crack under pressure. It is not always pretty and I am really tired of apologizing for it. It's just not always the ideal situation for camaraderie, you know? Sometimes it's a little like "Survivor". We are all truly acting with the same purpose which is to get that million dollars prize: Juliana's recovery. We just all have different methods of trying to get it and working together through the ebbs and flows. Alliances are made, alliances are broken, plot twists and unexpected obstacles test the endurance and skill of each of us. Sometimes it gets petty. Sometimes it's intense. Sometimes we want to vote someone off the island. Mostly we just want to fast forward through the episodes to the finale where Sleeping Beauty has fully returned to herself. If the only thing to navigate was Juli's care, this would all be much simpler but life is complex and relationships are dynamic so no matter how much we try to keep focused on the goal, it gets muddied by the fact that none of us signed up for this, or wanted this togetherness, at all.

Hopefully by tomorrow Juli will have adjusted to the Trazadone and will be fully awake for her therapy like they wanted. Hopefully the tests will come back with nothing new to concern ourselves with and her fever will stay away. Hopefully the time adjustments with her food and medicine will prevent further bouts of vomiting. And hopefully, Team Juli can keep it all together until the end of the season.

Now let's move on to the BIRTHDAY EPISODE….Happy Birthday Chris. We will put this on the list of 'holidays to do over when Juliana recovers' although I am sure the card, balloon and hostess cupcakes she got you will go down in history as your most memorable birthday gifts from her. At least she didn't forget.

November 30, 2009 - 7:30 pm

Juliana didn't feel well enough to throw Chris a party today. She did however throw UP for the fourth consecutive time today. This time is was lunch with no meds. So the only common denominator is the time of day, which as it turns out, may be entirely coincidental. It appears that she has another infection that might actually be the cause of her nausea and her lethargy. Just in case it is the quantity of food (which wouldn't make sense for yesterday's upset stomach because she hadn't eaten since 6 am) they are reducing her quantity and increasing her caloric intake to compensate and feeding her every 8 hours. The antibiotic she needs is an IV med 3 times a day which means she had to get another IV. And in case you thought this was really a hospital…let's just say, putting in IVs is not their greatest talent. I will spare you the Halloween reenactment this time but it did take them an hour and a half and four sticks to get it to work. But pretty much today she was lethargic and didn't fare very well in her therapies. The birthday boy grew a little older with concern, or with birthdays, or both…yeah, both.

Juliana did ok with OT later in the day but still not as good as she had been doing. We also discussed with the doctor removing the Trazadone and we are all in agreement: It's out. Now I want one of you out there to remind us how much sedation affects her, in case we forget, in the unfortunate event we have to go down that path again. We also scored an appointment with a neuro ophthalmologist on Thursday December 10th. I am very happy about that…I think. I am glad we got the appointment but am a little worried about what we might find out.

You lucked out, short one tonight. I am exhausted and still have much to do with Juliana before we can call it a night.

Oh, yeah, and one last time…Happy Birthday Medina.

December 1, 2009 - 9:15 pm

A couple of years ago Juliana had an ulcer in her esophagus from undigested antibiotics. It started a bit like heartburn and she couldn't even tolerate swallowing her own saliva. She ended up going to the doctor after about a week of extreme pain. They discovered what the problem was and gave her medicine to start to heal her. They told her with that particular antibiotic she needed to drink a full glass of water for that very reason. The healing was slow so the pain continued. During that whole time she couldn't eat either so she was also incredibly hungry. The whole episode lasted almost 3 weeks. During that time, she never missed a day of work. The same thing happened again about 6 months later. (Ok, a FULL glass of water Juli!). This time she went to the doctor sooner but knew what she was in for and the length of healing. Again, she never missed work. Now that is not to say she never missed work but she was never a lay in bed and be sick kind of girl. After her perforated septum surgery she was in misery and still came to my house every day to babysit and clean for me. (Now don't think that, I am not a slave driver…she wanted to come!) She just toughed it out. The girl can handle pain.

She started today with a fever of 101.9. I left for work at 6 am and Chris came in to take over. I was nervous through the day because we still didn't know for sure what was causing her fever and her 3 days of minimal activity was punctuated by last night's refusal to follow commands. I prepared to hear about another bad day but was what I heard was quite different. What Chris described to me was the girl we know, sick as a dog, fighting her way through everything they asked her to do. During one of her therapy sessions she indicated that she needed to stop, cued Chris that she was going to throw up, got that out of the way and got back to work. That's our girl. God I am proud of her. The rest of the day was just as much of a fight, but in an incredibly good way. She was taking control and pushing her way through with encouragement and respect of the therapists who all knew that she was sick and were impressed by her determination. She answered questions with yes and no, drew a star when asked, indicated that she was born in England, and preferred to listen to Fall Out Boy. It excites me that she is understanding and responding but equally exciting that she is showing SHE still exists. Throughout the day she participated in all of her therapy sessions although she did tire a bit more easily, the effort was applauded. She also indicated to Chris once that she wanted to stop and was in pain, but that she didn't want pain medicine. After a few minute break he asked her if she was ready to continue and she obligingly agreed. In addition to her scheduled sessions, two additional therapists stopped in who had "heard about Juli's progress" and wanted to have a chance to work with her. One thing we heard prior to coming to RIC and has been felt every day is that the therapists there are in it for the win, every day. They are working with the patients because they truly want to see progress. One PCT told me the other night, "you know everyone is talking about Juliana and expecting her to be our next 'superstar'".

Might as well, she already has a fan club.

December 2, 2009 - 10 pm

2 months ago they said she probably wouldn't live. If she did, she would most likely not wake from her coma. If she did, the prognosis was very poor. Plan for it, expect it and prepare for the worst.

2 months later…She drinks 11 sips of nectar, knew the date and place, pedaled for 15 rotations forward and 15 rotations backward AND…she stood. She did it three times and the third time, she even tried to take a step. Now I am not trying to imply she picked herself up and stood on her own, but, when pulled to a standing position, held in place by her PT around her waist as if they were dancing (and Juliana does NOT dance), she stood. She was strong and steady and was able to remain there for almost 5 minutes. She got tired, her PT sat her down, held her posture while sitting and then a few minutes later, stood her up again. Then on the third time, without being told she picked up her left foot ever so slightly and tried to move it forward. Her

PT was thoroughly impressed. He wasn't planning to try that today except he noticed when he got her from the chair to the mat, she helped him stand. "Juliana, have you been holding out on us?" Maybe. Tomorrow he wants to try standing her at the parallel bars to see if he can get her to take a step. We also got our next family conference and her discharge date is still set for December 14th. We will have another one next week and that will be our last chance to be extended again. I am not sure what to wish for because as much as I want her to stay, I want her to come home.

I gotta wrap up, I am almost out of battery and I left my power cord at home. And Juliana is reaching for the keyboard... here she is.rewwwwwww-wwwwwwwwwwwwwwwwwwwwwwwwwwwwwwwwwwwwwwwwwwwwwwww ww3333333333333333333333333333333333333333333333333333333333333333 33333wjuliana (I typed her name, don't get too excited) efffffsssssssssssssss-sEEEEEWWWWW RRREEEEFFFFFFFFFFFF.

Goodnight. Gonna give her the rest of the battery time, she really seemed to like to type.

December 3, 2009 - 10 pm

101.8 That is the way Juliana started today...are we still playing *that* game? They took blood, they took urine, and they took their sweet time giving her ibuprofen. By the time they came in to finally give her some fever reducer her bed was soaked from sweat and the cool rags on her head, wrists, and ankles. She had OT at 8 am and she was only mildly playing along. When it came time to brush her teeth she could pretty much do that, but she wasn't much interested in putting a shirt on over the shirt she already had on. Then she rested until 11:30. The Speech tech came in to give her an 'easy button'. You record one message, like "Wake up Mom, I need help" and she can push it anytime she wanted to. She wanted to for the next hour until, like a mom worn down by a persistent toddler; I found her a new toy: her white board. We played tic tac toe and she did pretty good putting O's in the boxes but scribbled the board away before I could win. I saw that Chris played thumb wars with her a few days ago so I thought I would try. She actually did it and she won by fighting dirty and digging her thumbnail into my finger. So, this is a meaner, rougher Juliana, eh? During speech, after confirming she knew the year and month, the therapist asked her if she knew the date. Juli hesitated until the therapist said, "well, yesterday was the 2nd…" to which Juliana didn't wait for the yes/no question that was forming and instead put up 3 fingers. "Great Juli, then what will be tomorrow's—"Four fingers before the end of the question. Well alrighty then.

Then they came in with the results of the blood test. All counts are good and the infection is going away. The fevers must be coming from the brain. They introduced a beta blocker to regulate her heart rate and temperature. I think that was the best answer of all possibilities but only time will tell.

Then in PT, her therapist got Juli on the mat to work on her sitting posture and balance. She very nearly sat alone holding herself up. It was great to see. Then he took her to the parallel bars and pulled her up to standing. She did great, held strong and eventually attempted to take a step. Her leg was as shaky as a slinky but she was trying so hard! She got the left foot ahead but the right foot was a much harder sell. She sat down took a break and rested. The next attempt did not include a second step with the right foot but instead a step backward with the left. Then when he transferred her back to the chair she had to turn and she took shuffle steps to position herself. A few hours later when I was getting her out of bed, I was able to stand her up, and maneuver her to the chair without the seat pivot we had been taught. She even helped me by scooting with her feet. If you assess the days as a whole, you can tell she is getting so much stronger, you just have to overlook the individual minutes.

Since her dad and Chris both felt that Juliana was getting a little depressed we thought she needed some mother-daughter time for us to just talk. And although she does communicate, obviously it is hard for us to really know what she is thinking with only yes and no to go on. But somehow in that chat I discovered that she is concerned about her eye. And although we are as well, I did my very best to convince her that it was going to be ok. We all know that Juliana is a beautiful girl. She is also a bright girl and she has seen a mirror so she knows she looks different and it surely feels different to her. I told her it's too soon to worry about that and she just needs to keep working on what she can control. But we are seeing a change in her. It's an awareness accompanied by a slight sadness maybe? Now when she doesn't respond to a question we know that it's because she doesn't want to, not because she can't.

And suddenly we are all aware that we have entered the next chapter.

December 4, 2009 - 5:45 pm

Well I have had some time to think, and time for many of you to respond to me and, first of all, thank you all for being my conscience, my memory and my perspective. You see, I indicated to you some time ago that I was mourning the loss of my perfect life. Well how naïve am I to not have remembered that Juliana would feel that loss as well? As she is stumbling into awareness, one of their exercises is to call her attention to the date. Every time they do it I cringe and silently hope she doesn't fully realize it because, for those of you that don't know it, Juli and Chris were to be married in 8 days. So is it unreasonable to think that she might understand what this accident has cost her? I think we might be on to something. So Chris and I will both have separate conversations with her to assure her (if that is possible) that her wedding plans are in place and ready to be executed when she is ready. Although our conversations will be coming at it from different angles, our approach will be the same: 'you haven't lost anything, everything is in place and ready, and you just need to let us know when it's time'. Who knows? It might even inspire her to work harder.

Speaking of hard work let me tell you that Juliana has had a job since her 15th birthday, sometimes more than one. At the time of her accident she was a cocktail waitress, a babysitter, a nanny and a housekeeper. She slept very little because she worked so much. But check this out... today was awesome. Standing is getting easier for her each time. Each time she gets in and out of bed she is expected to stand and maneuver and she DOES it. She sat, stood, tried to step, kept her frame straight and got even steadier. The PT said it is so rewarding to see her improve so much every day. During speech the therapist told her, "We know you can't use your voice yet but try to move your mouth along with me..." And together they 'sang' the ABCs all the way the through to the verse. You could see her mouth all the letters and the words. It was a great day of accomplishments. Tonight we are bringing her a keyboard her friend Jay loaned her. Let her snap away on that for a while. Tomorrow I am going to bring her purse and let her rummage through it. If any of you have seen her purse you know it would be the perfect accessory for 'Let's Make a Deal'. The girl carries her life in that purse so I am going to plop that bowling bag on her lap and see what she does. This is so exciting. I can't even believe how great she is doing. Not much structured therapy on the weekend so it's all us. Bring it on, we can handle that.

December 5, 2009 - 10 pm

Last night Juli had a great visit with friends, responding quite a bit to their questions and appearing to engage in their conversation. At one point she was asked if she played guitar and gave a thumbs down of course but added to that a pat on Chris's chest as if to indicate, 'that's ok because he does'. Shortly after that she grabbed Chris's shirt and pulled on his arm to let him know she was trying to get a hug. You know how girls are about guys who play guitars….apparently the attraction transcends brain injury.

So Chris and I both had our talk with Juli about the wedding and it's all good. She agreed that she does not want to roll down the aisle so she will wait until she can walk. Considering that yesterday she took a couple of assisted steps, I better get back to dieting and looking for my mother of the bride dress! Ok, so I may be a bit ahead of myself but she is definitely getting stronger every day. Tomorrow she should get her ankle splints so that will secure her ankles as she starts to walk again. We have been fearful of her turning an ankle while in therapy which would surely be a delay in rehabilitation. It seems this rehab game is really a matter of dodging the obstacles. And from the stories I have heard from other families, we have been fortunate. I won't list the things that haven't happened to us because; I am just superstitious enough to not want to put it out there. In any case, we are in a good spot right now: Her fever is gone, infection is being treated, medications seem to be working, not too many, and not too few and her food seems to be staying down. And when I told Juli all of that and concluded with, 'that's a reason to smile', she did. It was the small smile of someone forced to 'take one for the team' but she was able to execute and that is good enough for me.

The purse idea was amusing for a few minutes. She dug right in there, pulled out a blush brush and started applying her makeup! Now you might be amazed at her putting on makeup but I was shocked she found what she was looking for in that purse! Now THAT is an accomplishment! Then she pulled out her little Vaseline jar that she uses for lip gloss and stuck her very small index finger (I never realized how tiny her hands were) and put some on her lips. She kept the straps of the purse on her arm for a while, even when she tired of rummaging through it.

So now that we know she will walk and talk, our last unknown is her vision in her right eye. I still have no indication that she can see out of that eye yet. I tried the suggestion to cover the left eye, open the right eye and try to elicit a blinking reflex but I got no response. So we just don't know what the future holds for that eye. But then again, haven't we learned that we just don't know what the future holds at all? As I tell Juli every day, I will take her anyway she comes. That's part of my contract.

December 6, 2009 - 4 pm

Another day, another fever (101.7) another antibiotic...I swear this place is doing as much harm as it is good! Nah, not really. But apparently she has somehow contracted a superbug, as is common in hospitals and the choices of antibiotics are getting fewer. She is allergic to 2 strains and has been on, by my count, 6 others. I think the way this game is played is you just have to expect the progress to exceed the setbacks. Thankfully so far, the good guys are winning.

PT went well today, she keeps doing the same things; she is just doing them more independently and better. So, sitting, standing, attempting a step, all very hard work for her. In fact, her PT had her stretching in a way that would make me ache too. If you have ever watched a therapy session such as this, you feel like you physically participate. I am often as ready for a nap afterward as she is. The most impressive part of the whole therapy experience is the effort that she is putting into each session. The girl wants to get better. She wants to come home. As proof of this I told her, "When you come home you know you get a 'dishes week'. Do you still want to come home?" Big thumbs up. (For those of you familiar with the drama surrounding 'dishes week' in our family that is really saying something).

It's changing of the guard time up here at RIC so unless Chris or her dad call me with something new and exciting, this is the last you will hear from me until tomorrow evening. Going home to be with my other children. Before I left, she gifted me with a very small, very pretty smile and a warm hug. Now, just like 'thumbs up', not all hugs are created equal. Today's hug included a few pats on the back and a rub which, for those who have received one of those recognize the action is accompanied by affection and it feels good all over. I love you too Juli. See you tomorrow.

December 7, 2009 - 12:30 am

Well...you are hearing from me again so you know what that means? You got it. New AND exciting. Well after a nurse scraped the inside of Juliana's injured right eye with the ointment tube and really hurting her, Chris wanted to make sure it wasn't scratched or bleeding. And while he was examining her eye, he asked her if she could point at his face. She did. Hmmmm.... coincidence? Perhaps. So he asked her to point at his hand, which would need to be a little more deliberate and she did. Thus ending two months of speculation on Juliana's injured eye: She can see out of both eyes! So hopefully it's just a matter of regaining strength in her little tiny eyelid muscles so she can completely open her right eye. We will definitely know more after the visit to the Neuro Opthamologist on Thursday. I love being woken up for the fun stuff. Much better than the wake up I got when this all started. Never mind... Lets not go back there.

December 7, 2009 - 11:30 pm

Well, we got another week added to our stay here at RIC. Our new discharge date is December 21. I guess they will continue to only commit to a week at a time so we still don't know if she will be here on Christmas. Delaney asked Santa for 'Juli to come home' but I had to tell her if she doesn't get that for Christmas, it will because it is better for Juli to stay where she is a little longer.

She had a good day today although the swallow test has been delayed until next Wednesday. They said that there won't be any doctors here this Wednesday. Huh? There are 18 floors here and no doctors? I am sure I must have misunderstood that. That is unfortunate because I know Juli really wants to get started drinking and then eating. Before we took her to the gym for Physical Therapy, we were trying to keep her hair back because even with her ponytail, there are always escapees that get in the way. So Chris put his hat on her, cocked to the side. She looked so darn cute I had to take her to the mirror to see. She didn't flinch away from her reflection like she had been doing. Even SHE thought she looked cute. When we got in the gym Joe, her PT said she was the coolest patient on the floor. No doubt Joe. She did so well during her session. She stood today for probably a total of 15 minutes broken into three 5 minute segments. During one of the standing sessions she was standing completely on her own and she wasn't struggling either. No one was holding her up. She was leaning slightly on the table in front of her for her balance but that was it. We had her reaching to the front and sides, taking colored cones and stacking them then moving back to center. She did it as if it were effortless, almost, tedious. "Well" Joe said. "I guess tomorrow we will have to challenge you a little more!" We didn't even have to tell her what to do after the first time she just kept grabbing the cones, stacking them up and moving on down the line. Then moving herself back to center. 'Check' she seemed to be saying. 'Now give me something hard'. She had her eye open the whole time too. Her doctor came in to "see her in action" and she was pleasantly surprised by Juli's activity and alertness. She still only opened her right eye a little bit but her left eye was wide open and beautiful.

The rest of the night was a different kind of awesome. It felt more like old times than ever before. She was awake and alert and we were really visiting with each other. She patted the bed next to her for me to climb in, which of course I did. She rubbed my knee as I sat cross legged on her bed with her upright looking at me while I just told her all kinds of secrets she promised (thumbs up) not to tell. She told me she didn't want me to ever leave (ok so I stacked the deck on that question) but she held my hand a lot and gave me a little smile and rubbed my hand. I read to her a little from the journal I have kept for her and asked her periodically if she wanted me to keep reading. She gave me a thumbs up until the fifth page when she took the notebook and closed it. I asked her to mouth letters, numbers and words with minimal success but she was able to mouth 'mom' when I coached her through it.

All in all it was a successful day for Juli and what I refer to as a 'good mommy night'.

December 8, 2009 - 11:30 pm

Remember in early October when I would explain that days might go by where nothing new happened? We found each little activity to be a small deposit on the million dollar recovery. Now it seems as if the improvements are by the handful. I am not sure what this looks like from your vantage point, especially since some of the updates include the same things: 'she stood today', and then 'she stood again today'. I need you to understand that each day that she does the same thing is progress. But she is doing more than that because she is doing the same thing...BETTER. So let me see if I can describe today as it was described to me. She started therapy early today at 7:30. We typically don't see the best results from her in the early sessions and today was only slightly different: She still didn't do her best, but she did better than she normally does at 7:30 sessions. She washed her face, brushed her hair, brushed her teeth and helped to dress herself. She wasn't exactly happy to do it, but she did participate with some mild encouragement. That is another thing that is different. Our encouragement used to need to be about the ability, now it is about the intention. She is capable of so much more each day that our effort is spent on breaking through what she wants to do to get to what she is capable of doing. A mind is an interesting place. A 'mind of its own' is a powerful place.

She was also taught some sign language. I haven't seen the signs myself yet so I can't convey them to you but I would guess they taught her official signs for words and not a newly invented vocabulary. Let me get back to you on that. But one thing I can tell you now is whatever they taught her very briefly early in the day she was able to easily and quickly recall later in the day. They are both excited and impressed by her memory. All of that is good but what happened in PT once again proved to be better. As she was being positioned at the parallel bars for her standing and walking practice she decided to start 'get ahead of the teacher' and before being asked or assisted, Juliana stood up! Both Chris and her PT Joe were shocked but quickly jumped into action by helping and supporting her and making sure she was in a secure position. (Sounds a little like opening the door for a lady after she started walking through it herself.) She followed that up with taking steps the entire length of the parallel mat, about 8 feet or so. Her PT felt she was ready for the mechanical 'sling walker'. There is an official name for the apparatus but in lieu of that, I call it as I see it. They put her in the sling to focus on the walking action and remove the balance and weight. After spending a few minutes adjusting to the rhythm of the machine, she started to get the hang of it. Since she had braces on her ankles that were not made for her, they were a little larger and harder to step over but she got better each step as she put one foot in front of the other. She completely wore herself out. As the session ended Chris in all his excitement told Juliana she did great and that she must be pretty pleased with herself today to which she responded with fervent thumbs down followed by a middle finger up. Well! I guess she expects better of herself (or perhaps expects better questions from Chris?). Well either way, today was awesome and thank God, tomorrow is another day. One day she will realize what we already have...having a 'tomorrow' is her greatest accomplishment.

December 9, 2009 - 10 pm

Pinching, hitting, pouting, ignoring...Anyone have a 2 year old out there who can relate? I had what Oprah calls an 'Aha moment' when I realized that those behaviors are not only age and attitude related. Sometimes they are a result of the limited ability to communicate. Juli is getting better at getting her point across. Better that is unless you are the one getting hit or pinched. I actually had to reprimand her twice today! I was pleased to know that even with my 23 year old, I still got it. I pulled out that mommy voice and she stopped immediately. And just like when you try it out on your little ones, you just aren't sure if they are going to listen, until they do. I told Juli a hundred times that this whole parenting thing is on the job training and she is my experimental child. At least on those situations I have plenty of experience this time around.

Juli was reluctant to participate in her first Speech therapy today and there was a certain amount of concern in the room. During her second therapy there was a lot of stretching and complaining going on. That is where the hitting started. Juli made sure her OT knew she did not appreciate all of the stretching she was doing. Immediately after that her PT session started with Juli being fitted with her new leg splints. They will secure her ankles during weight bearing exercises but they won't likely make that orthotics popular in Juli's eyes. Fitted with her new equipment, Juli did her parallel bar routine then the sling walker aka 'light gait' (the official name). That is where the pinching started. It took poor Joe by complete surprise...the first time. After the third time I had to actually go in her ear and tell her that behavior was completely uncalled for and she had better stop it this instant. That is when the pouting began. She clearly didn't like it but she straightened up after that so it was all good. Throughout the session you could see she was physically stronger but she was still a little on the reluctant side. Right after PT she went to another session of Speech. That was when the ignoring started. By that time Juli was completely exhausted and Juli was just not acknowledging her at all. Then suddenly the therapist noticed Juli's engagement ring (she just recently started wearing it again after a month of 'asking'). "Wow, that is a gorgeous ring, Juli." Juliana immediately did her automatic splay of her hand and a wave of the fingers. She is very proud of her ring and her engagement. It was a very clever, if not accidental, ice breaker. The rest of the session went smoothly. Juli drank juice, had some applesauce and answered questions that were a little tricky: Is a foot bigger than an inch? Is your neck above your chin? Are there four quarters in a dollar? She hesitated but got them all right. She mouthed a bit of Happy Birthday and other random words that she asked her to try, including a very obvious, "Chris". Then the Therapist told her a bit about herself, where she was from and about her wedding and her son. Then began quizzing Juliana on what she had just heard. Again, she got all the questions right. At the end, they were friends and Juli even gifted her with an "I Love You" hand sign. I think she tried to give thank you but got a little over zealous. Tomorrow we take a field trip to see the Ophthalmologist. No pun intended. Wish us luck and hope she doesn't try to poke HIS eyes out.

December 10, 2009 - 7:45 pm

Today we had our appointment at Northwestern to see the Neuro Ophthalmologist. The intent was no longer to find out if Juli can see, they can't tell that by looking at her anyway. They can only know what she sees by what she *can prove* she can see. Our intention was to find out if anything can be done to improve her ability to open her right eye and use it. Well let me tell you, the experience was eye opening in a couple of ways. (Shameless pun intended). You see this was our first experience back in circulation. We were no longer under the protection of a hospital with staff, no longer one of many patients that all had similar issues and were understood. We were 'the mom with a daughter in a wheelchair'. The building we were in was an office building with people dressed nicely and walking quickly to their destination. Those passing us by either avoided looking at us, or looked at us with pity. I wonder which one I was in my former life. I don't blame any of them; I just have to acknowledge now that I am no longer one of them. A friend of mine recently told me that I have been given an opportunity to see the world with a little more clarity. Today was expanding upon that. This was an experience not about me or Juliana but how 'being different' feels, a clarity I never thought I needed... until now. I can learn to deal with it as her advocate. That will be easy because I will have something to protect. Juliana getting used to that position is a huge unknown and suddenly I am a little more fearful of whatever comes next. For the first time in my life I don't want to plan and I think I prefer blissful ignorance of what comes next.

Once in the office even the doctor and his resident were uncomfortable and unsure. They asked me what medical problems she had.

Blink...blink....duh.....blink.

I was thinking...'How do I answer that?' "Well, she has limited use of her right side, she is currently unable to verbalize and she doesn't open her right eye." Weird silence "Anything else?" he asks. I am thinking, 'Well do you mean other than she spent 6 weeks in a technical coma and eats her food through a tube?' Instead I say, "No, that's it." They also didn't know how to communicate with someone who appears to be sleeping and talks with her hands. I of course was her translator but by this point I was also her protector and my heart was breaking for what she was going through all over again. For the exam I had to push her body forward awkwardly so her head could press against the head brace and her chin could rest on the bracket. This whole thing required all of my limbs and was a very hard position for her to maintain. She only tolerated it for a few minutes before she tried to peel me off of her. What made it worse was the doctor kept saying, "I can't examine you if you don't stay still. You have to look into the blue light." Then they were trying to get her to follow a light and a red colored cap and they whizzed it by her so fast that I knew the exercise was pointless. They typed into their notes, 'Patient unable to follow objects.' I didn't bother correcting them. Maybe I should have but it didn't seem to matter. Their analysis would not determine if my daughter would see normally again any more than the original doctors saying 'she probably won't live' could make her die. So it was uneventful in factuality. They can't tell us anything we haven't heard already: Time will tell. They must all read from the same book. The one thing that we got out of it is a referral to an ocular plastic surgeon. Since Juli's bottom eyelid is turned inward her eyelashes are resting on her cornea and that is causing irritation (I imagine so). They think she might need a slight procedure to correct that. Appointment is set for December 29th.

Back in our newly appreciated comfort zone of the Brain Injury floor, Juli was once again ready to behave like a superstar and walk the parallel bars faster and easier than the day before. Although this was not a group we ever wanted to be a part of, I understand much better why we work so hard to get the staff to love Juliana...we have the need to belong.

December 11, 2009 - 11:45 pm

Juliana had a great PT session where she walked holding the parallel bars three lengths of the path. That is a distance in total of about 25-30 feet. Each day her steps get a little faster and a little more automatic. She even completed 4 steps (2 with each leg) without assistance with her legs. That may not sound like much but to us it is equivalent to Neil Armstrong's "One small step for man...". She still needed support on her lower back and a reminder to move her hands along the bar as well, but the footwork was all Juli. During OT we practiced transferring her from the wheelchair to... ahem...another seat in the bathroom. I will not elaborate more than to say, this exercise was successful. Later, as the Speech Therapist walked in, Juli was thumbing through a People magazine. The therapist was shocked as this surprisingly normal behavior. You see, her mannerisms seem so...regular and typical. They really have from the beginning when she covered her mouth to cough. Anyway, that session started with drinking juice, and moved on to eating applesauce. It's very subtle but she also does that better than she did just a week ago. She brings the cup right to her mouth, opens and then closes her mouth around the cup and completes the action without spilling. Again, it might seem minor, but that is what we are trying to achieve... making all those seemingly minor things happen again. (Remember when we were counting the blinks of her eyes?) And anything today that is better than yesterday is, well, better. The therapist told her that she was certainly the most ladylike patient on the unit because she routinely wiped her mouth after every sip of juice, then put the napkin under her leg for safe keeping. It was quite cute. At one point her dad said, "Juli, you missed a spot right here (pointing to her upper lip) and I know you don't want me to wipe it." To which Juliana took her rag and tossed it sideways to him as if to say, 'fine, go ahead'. It was random, it was cute, and it was funny... You had to be there. When quizzed on the sign language she had been taught, she recalled all of it and responded accordingly to all questions. In saying goodbye to the therapist she gave an 'I Love You' sign with her hands which made the therapist happy enough to steal a hug. See what a little food and drink will get you, speech lady? They are all really impressed with her progress and it is comforting to have her be evaluated as doing so well. This is all great 'feel good' stuff. All positive and forward in her current world of 'rehabilitation after a life threatening car accident'. The disclaimer that I must constantly put out here is this: She is a very long way from where she started and I often see in visitors eyes that the updates make them believe something different, something MORE than what they see for themselves. I 'guess' I apologize but it feels so big and important to me and I am only able to recount the days from my perspective. I am neither a doctor nor a politician. I am a mom talking about what happened to my daughter from my vantage point. So, to me, it was a good day and she is making excellent progress. And if I had to calculate the point she started as zero dollars and her complete recovery the one million dollar mark, we probably have 15% of our goal. (You do the math). I think that is wonderful and I am very grateful. But I also recognize that Juliana is miles away, many months or years away, more than ¾ of "a million dollars" away from her destination. It's ok because I am taking the journey regardless. Again...job description...

December 12, 2009

Today was to be Chris and Juliana's wedding day. Grab a box of Kleenex and check out the video Chris had made in honor of this day. You can find it on www.YouTube.com called "What Has Become of Me".

December 13, 2009 - 11 pm

Juli didn't sleep much last night or all day yesterday in fact, which is odd for her. She generally naps throughout the day. She really had a great day though. Her visit with Delaney and Mackenzie went so well. Mackenzie gave her the white board and told her to write whatever she wanted. I took a picture of what she wrote, and will upload it shortly. She seemed so completely aware of them were and who they are TO HER that it made me cry. I haven't cried in her presence since...well maybe not ever during this situation but if so and have forgotten, surely not in many weeks. It was the way she stroked their hair and moved it over their shoulders and reached out to pull them into a hug. It was so "Juli the nanny" holding them that I just couldn't take it. She knew them and missed them. It was powerful. I know once she can be around that emotional tug on a regular basis there will be healing powers exponentially greater than we have today. She also had a great PT day yesterday walking with the parallel bars four times, faster and more accurate still. Her writing is getting clearer too. Chris had asked her to write his name, he had to ask her to move her hand over a little after each letter so she didn't overlap them. She understood and complied. Then I asked her to write my name, curious to see if she would write Mommy or Janet. Guess which one she wrote? I will leave that to the end. The Speech Therapist asked her if she wanted to work on 'drinking' or 'writing' and to write on the white board her preference. She wrote 'drinking' very clearly (I could have told her that). Then she asked her if she wanted cranberry or orange juice and made her write the answer. Which do you think she chose? Answer at the end again....hmmm, this is getting fun. So the clever little speech therapist got what she wanted, both writing and drinking practice and Juli got her cup of juice. Chris brought Juli some flowers though I don't think she was aware of the missed occasion or even the date. I have been wrong before though and it could explain her moodiness throughout the rest of the night and consequent lack of sleep. She watched the video of Chris 'song, (minus the intro of course..."tooooo soon") and followed it through to the end. However, when it got to the part with the segment from her engagement, (a video clip she has voluntarily watched many times while at RIC mind you), she shoved the laptop off her lap. For the next couple of hours she didn't seem to want to communicate at all. We tried to encourage her to tell us was wrong and she finally tried to write something and Sarah and I tried to decipher but we failed our portion of the charades team. She was again overlapping her letters, though she knew distinctly what she was trying to write. She even circled it for emphasis but we still couldn't figure it out. She was getting very frustrated with us and actually wanted me to leave. Its ok, I am a mom, and therefore used to periodically not being liked. We eventually decided to divert her attention by playing thumb wars (she won) arm wrestling (she won again) and tic tac toe. Guess who won that? Answer at the end. By the end of the night she gave me the 'I Love You' sign, let me polish her nails, did her signature pose with Sarah and let me sit on her bed to hang out and read. I fell asleep with my head on her bed and realized at 12:45 am that she was still blinking her long eyelashes, wide awake. Hmmmm. Today, of course, she fixed all that by sleeping the day away. Let's hope we aren't establishing a backward pattern again. For her short time awake she pushed her wheelchair around with her feet, going backward and did some very effective standing and balancing. She also took a moment to scare Cheyenne by writing her a message on the white board...'Help.' It was a little freaky for a minute until I realized she just wanted to go to the bathroom. Nuff said.

Oh yeah...1. Janet; 2. Orange; 3. She cheated.

December 14, 2009 - 8:30 pm

Juli had a good and tiring day. She wasn't ready to participate in Speech early today so her therapist agreed to come back later. Sounds very nice and accommodating but we are noticing that Juliana is learning to play possum you see, she is able to 'fake sleep' because her right eye isn't open. All she has to do is shut her left eye and she gets a bit of a 'pass' for a while. She does this in all the uncomfortable moments as well, like around other people (or when she is in the bathroom...shhhh). Think about when you were a kid and you thought if you closed your eyes that made you invisible. A lot of the brain injury recovery process mirrors development from infancy through early childhood so it's not that surprising. She continued her drinking juice and added tastes of pudding as part of her preparation for her swallow study on Wednesday. I am not sure who is looking more forward to Juli eating again; Juli or all of us. Then in PT she took a walk. She simply stood, had Chris on one arm and her PT on the other and they just walked. She still is unsteady and slow but, to quote her dad, "Every day she gets better and better." Her recent blood tests came back and her seizure levels are a bit low (what is a seizure level anyway??) so they are going to do another EEG just to be sure she is getting the right amount of valporic acid to prevent seizures. Honestly I have been seeing some strange additional tensing and toning that concerns me so I would rather she did get checked out. For that we get to travel back over to Northwestern on Thursday. Oh joy, here we go again. The blood tests also indicate her liver function is a little high, (those two levels need to talk) and that might be attributed to her recent onslaught of antibiotics so they will take her blood again in a few days and adjust something after that. She also needs to go for another CT scan since it has been a month since her shunt was put in. A month already, wow. I can't believe how long, how detailed and how complicated these last couple of months have been. And finally the doctor got the notes from the Ophthalmologist visit and the short story is, vision loss is likely based on the nerve damage they were able to detect but only time will tell.

Well its shower night for Juli and hopefully shortly after that, collapse night for me as my sleep deprived brain is suffering its own emotional toll. All of my balancing of responsibility and holding it all together is starting to choke me. For all of the support this situation has generated, it is also equally isolating as the legend is growing greater than the people living through it. And more unnerving, even when you are trying to do the right thing, perhaps the only thing that you can do, for some people, it might never be right at all. As they say…"No good deed goes unpunished".

December 15, 2009 - 11:30 pm

It's Tuesday, and that means its 'Juli and Chris Day'. That is what Juli calls it. It was formerly known as 'Juli and Erica Day' but as the girls grew and went their separate ways, Juli's time was focused on Chris. On her 18th birthday she drew flowers on her foot with Chris's name intertwined in the vine, walked into a tattoo parlor, pointed to her foot and said, "make it permanent". I would like to say I was angry and begged her not to do it, but the truth is I tried to talk her out of it for a minute, then paid the bill. I have pretty much been 'Juli and Chris' fans from the day I met him, though I teased him mercilessly. There was never any doubt that we loved that boy and wanted him to remain in our family. Yeah, I know, you guys all love him too. But I loved him because Juli loved him so much. She told everyone that he was going to be her 'last first kiss'. And although that didn't end up being the case (because they did the Ross and Rachel "on a break" thing…ahem) he was what she wanted all along. And she always tried to make sure she protected time for their relationship. She planned Tuesday's as her day to not be scheduled at Starbucks and Chris did the same. Smart kids. Relationships take care and feeding. Juli is also very particular about her food. If she chose to eat something, she enjoyed it and ceremoniously included it in all of her most special moments. I have often seen her assemble the 'perfect bite' for someone to taste some of what she had purchased or prepared. When we were planning her wedding she said "I only care about three things and the rest, you take care of: My dress, the music and the food." Of course once I started planning anything else, suddenly she cared very much. Last night I wrote on the white board "Talk" and "Eat" and told her to circle which one she wanted to be able to do more. She took the marker and drew large circles over and over around the word "Eat". Yep, that's my girl. My cousin Charles once joked that our family crest should include a knife and fork. So true... Well, lucky Juli tomorrow is the Swallow Study where they x-ray the path that liquid and soft foods take as she swallows. They need to ensure they are going down the right path and she is not silently aspirating. I am very confident that she will pass this test easily. She never coughs or gags or in any way seems to have difficulty when she is given her juice and pudding. After she passes this test, she will be cleared for some amount of food, though we don't know what or the consistency. Stay tuned for that. Today's big news was Juliana's improved vocalizing. According to one report (I was not here for this) Juliana hummed. She had done this before but today her dad asked her to open her mouth and hum loudly. She opened her mouth and said "Hmmmm" which was nearly officially...her first word. I want to call it, but I am waiting for a real word. I have been telling her for weeks as I hold up one finger then two fingers respectively: "Walking and talking by Christmas." She knows what I am going to say and when I ask "What are you going to do before Christmas." She holds up her fingers the same way. Today she had her second experience moving the hand pedal machine. The first time was very difficult for her because her right arm is still quite tight and contracted so stretching and using that arm is difficult. Today she did it with a lot less effort. During PT her therapist decided to try a walker. She didn't move it much but it was her first day for that so there is room to improve. Tonight while we practiced she stood up easily, remained standing on her own steam. I held her to keep her steady but I hardly had to do any of that either. Then I asked her if she wanted to freak out the nurses. I stood by the wall as she scooted her wheelchair with her feet backward right into view of the center nurses' station. I asked Juli if that was fun. She shook her head no. Where has her sense of humor gone? Then I helped her move her chair forward with her feet. I had to do most of that work but she did get the hang of it after a while. Then when I was getting her back into bed I spent a few minutes having her stand again, trying to tire her out and she had her arms around me like we were dancing. I said, "well at least you aren't pinching me like you did to Joe (her PT)." Yeah, you guessed it, she pinched me. "Hey, what's up with that?" I said "Good thing you don't have much of a reach." Suddenly, she DID and started pinching me all over. I laughed so hard and she started rubbing me where she pinched. Found her sense of humor.

Happy 'Juli and Chris Day' everyone.

December 16, 2009 - 7 pm

Juliana is coming home!

Monday, December 21st she will be released into our care….GULP…We are so excited (I think) and really think it's the best (we hope). We are totally ready (Oh God, are we???) and everyone is very confident (terrified) and just thrilled that she will be in familiar surroundings (oh lordy I think I am going to faint!) Seriously, yeah, it's good, it's ALL good, really, I mean, its progress, right….? Breathe, breathe, breeeeeeeeeathe.

It's the next step and we have been preparing for this for almost 3 months. But even so, even after nine months of carrying a baby, aren't you a little nervous to bring them home the first time? Yeah well, so am I. I know that we have a strong support system for Juliana. In fact that is one of the reasons (so they say) that she is heading home 'so soon'. They said that we were extremely supportive and eagerly learned everything we needed to know in order to take care of her. So how about that? I thought that was required of us. I didn't know that not everyone does what we did. Oh well, yeah us. So that is the biggest news of the day but we have more, oh yes we do. She had her swallow study and did quite well in terms of safety of swallowing. No problem there. She is still a little 'inefficient' in getting the food to the back of her throat although I tell you, she likes food. Why not savor it a moment? Anyway, she will be treated a little more aggressively in speech the next few days where they give her more types of food so that we can hopefully advance to getting some of her nutrients by eating. Since we can't count on that enough yet, it's just considered, 'pleasure feeding'. Ummmm…hello…does no one else consider all food they eat pleasure feeding?? Whatever. Anyway, that is moving along very well. During PT today her therapist told her to walk as fast as she could to the end. So, with him holding her steady on her right side, guided her to the end of the course which was nearly normal walking speed. (Insert slight mother's exaggeration but it was impressively fast). After that he had he step up onto a stair with both feet a couple of times and she did very well at that. Then it was on to the bike pedals which she had previously been coached and begged and prodded to do 15 painful rotations. Well today she did 5 full minutes like it was easy enough to sleep through. She could have gone longer but WE were bored! Then, as if that wasn't all spectacular enough…wait for it….wait a liiiiiiiittle more….she said, "Mommy". Oh yeah! She said it, she did it, she said it, uh huhhh. She said it a couple of times and I was so excited I ran out to the nurses' station and told our new bff's, all the 10th floor staff. That was her dad's accomplishment as well because he is there every day working on humming and vocalizing with her and that was the result. He could have asked her to say daddy you know but he gave knew that mommy would be easier with the way she is breathing out the words. Just a few minutes ago when I put her on the phone with Mackenzie she tried to say something but I am not sure if it was 'Hello' or an attempt at "I Love You.' Who cares, right? It's all coming on strong now. I think she is just so darn happy they gave her food. (Might be projecting a little of my own food obsessions on her)

We spent most of the afternoon planning all of the details of her discharge to home and trying to coordinate her doctor's appointments. When Juli goes home she will attend day rehab where they pick her up three days a week for a half of a day and bring her back home. We won't be in attendance all day like we are now so it will be all up to Juli to pull this one off and I guess we have to let the chips fall where they may. It might just do her good to not have us hovering for once. We will of course continue what we learned in helping her with PT, OT and Speech to get the maximum results. In addition we will likely have people we know from these fields come by to try their magic on her as well. They have us set up for a whole bunch of things way up here in Chicago because that is who RIC is affiliated with and not necessarily because they are as fabulous as the therapists here. So I am asking you, our FB friends, if you know good doctors in the south suburbs that you would recommend, in any of these specialties, please send me an email through FB.

I am looking for a good adult Primary Care doctor, a Neurologist, a Neuro Ophthalmologist, and an Ocular Plastic Surgeon.

Next up, planning the logistics of getting her from place to place. Apparently neither of our cars are juuuuuuust right for getting her home and then wherever else we might take her. Her chair is too big for the car and the van is too big for Juli and neither of them offer restraints sufficient for someone who can't sit up on her own for extended periods of time. Working on it still but may need to rent an accessible van for a while.

Heading over to Northwestern for a late night CT scan appt.

What a good, awesome, blessed and wicked cool day.

December 17, 2009 - 11 pm

Well we are ready. I know yesterday I was a little panicked but today I am a little eager. I am seeing this through a little more perspective and if looking at pictures of home is stimulation and therapy, she is about to be flooded with it. As soon as she comes in the door, all that familiarity will be all around her. Now instead of an hour of OT learning to live in her former life, she will have doses of it throughout her whole day. Instead of PT being a specific hour which we hope she is rested and willing enough to participate in, it will be moments sprinkled throughout the day where she moves because there is purpose, not request. Besides, she is getting less willing to comply with them each day. She tasted the food they gave her then pushed it aside. I have eaten that cafeteria food for a month now and I wanted to push it aside at the lift of the lid. So it really is all good and as long as we have no additional health issues, we should be headed in the right direction. She is starting to add to her communication. She said Thank you and Water and is able to shrug and hand gesture more frequently. Speaking of hand gesture, I owe you a story...So while at Christ hospital for our second stint, Juli was being poked and prodded and stuck with needles and was getting very annoyed. So Chris told Juli, "If someone does something that you don't like, you need to let them know. Flip them off." It seemed a little funny, just at the notion that she might do it. A few days later when she actually did do it, it was hysterical. Now that she does it to EVERYONE, it is far less funny. She even reached behind her back to give her therapist the finger. So if you know anything about brain injuries, especially frontal brain injuries, one thing that is compromised is their ability to control some of their behavior. The fact that she is hitting, pinching and flipping people off is to be expected....and should be temporary. Thank goodness because although Juliana will fight for anyone that she loves, she is never aggressive to anyone. I am hoping I can use the "You are going to teach your sisters bad things" card. I will keep you posted on that.

On a separate note, I have ended my hospital vigil and spent my final night at RIC last night. I am going to spend the weekend away from Juli, and attempt to prepare for the next step (and Christmas). I will continue to update but, fair is fair, the information will be coming from the rest of Team Juli as they continue to push Juli to learn as well as protect the staff from her.

December 18, 2009 - 4 pm

I have been asked by some of you "what can I do for you?" And some of you have reached out and offered prayers, emails, food, gifts...all pieces of yourself for the purpose of our family and my daughter's healing I have all that I truly need (and probably far more than I deserve). I have been gifted with so much lately and so has Juliana and we are so fortunate to have your support. Many of you are aware that earlier this year my brother Joe was diagnosed with Leukemia. If you know him, you love him, if you don't, you should. He has long been my hero and for very good reason. He is generous to a fault and to say he is "magnanimous" would be an understatement. His diagnosis hit our family hard as we couldn't believe anything that tragic could possibly really happen. However, with his family and friend's support, much like in Juliana's case, he was able to brave the battle. Although he has been slowly improving for a couple of months now, we did not get a chance to celebrate his recovery because shortly after he found out he was officially in remission, Juliana had her tragic accident. Well on January 9th we are finally going to celebrate the health and recovery of my brother in a spectacular night of fun and festivities. I would like to ask all of you to join my family, along with Juliana, at this wonderful event filled with entertainment, magic and some special guests. We will all celebrate the blessing of Joe's ongoing recovery efforts. Details for this event are on the **@All Odds on Joe, Celebrating Joe's Road to Recovery** Facebook page which indicates where you can get tickets, although tickets are also available at the door. I look forward to seeing you there as I plan to do my best to support my brother and take all of this support I have been given and pay if forward. Hope to see you there.

December 20, 2009 - 11 pm

It's getting dicey folks. You see we are at 11 hours and counting and now we are getting spooked on the medical aspect. She is experiencing muscle spasms and pain that keeps her up at night. They are adding a muscle relaxer to her ever increasing medicine list. I can't imagine that her body knows if it is coming or going. If her brain wasn't scrambled before, it sure is now! Not to mention, now she is getting the shakes from the new anti-seizure medicine. All of this 'unknown' right when it's time for her to be released? I just hope that when we discuss all the discharge plans tomorrow they have a clear back up plan for us otherwise we are not budging. Ok, not really but that would definitely take the homecoming in a whole new direction. I guess it's just another reminder that this roller coaster is not over yet and to stay on our toes. First order of business is to get her to her new doctors and start where we are leaving off. I am going to pick up all of her meds in the morning and probably need a trailer to bring them all home. Juli seems to be excited about coming home and that keeps us excited. I keep visualizing tomorrow and it doesn't look like anything familiar to me. Although she has come through that door a million times I can't imagine what this next time will mean to her. In fact, will the car ride home, where she is sitting upright, (yes we solved that problem) be difficult for her? I know the likelihood of her remembering the accident is slim but couldn't she subconsciously have a memory of what she went through? Then when she comes home, her role as 'daughter/sister' instead of 'patient' defines her. Our hope is that those memories will come flooding in and have healing properties all its own. My role will be redefined as I am suddenly present for all my kids and my husband, who have done without me for the bulk of the last three months. Will I come back and be able to juggle it all? Will I be able to be the nurse/doctor/aid/psychologist and be a wife/mother/housekeeper/worker as well? Now don't get me wrong. I am in NO way doing anything alone and this load will surely be shared by many. So before I hear a revolt among other Team Juli members that I am taking too much of the credit, I am simply stating my fears from my perspective of my position in this next phase. I just know that when there is a question of what to do next, the heads will turn toward me to decide. It's the responsibility we all accept as parents I just don't know if I am qualified to do it. I have wondered many times if I am a 'good enough mom' to handle all this. I never got the answer, nor did I get to give the role back. I will stop now, it's just fear talking. The next you will hear from me will be to tell you Juli is home and adjusting: Watch for that.

December 21, no its December 22, 2009 - 12:30 am

Phew....phewwwwwwww......

Juli is home. Her release was a little delayed while the doctors reviewed all of the latest blood work, EEG and CT scan. Her liver enzymes are trending down (good thing), her sodium is a little low (not so good) but her EEG shows NO 'epileptiform activity' (aka, no seizures) So...we have another difference in opinion. It seems the doctor who came in to say, 'those are seizures' when seeing Juliana that day for 5 minutes was really diagnosing only what he saw that moment. However, if she had been having seizures, especially in the frequency she was tensing up, she would not be progressing as much as she has. So now we are back to the muscle tension that we see being attributed to spasticity. That is a normal reaction to a brain injury. Not a desirable one, but not so terrible either, now that we are pretty confident we know what we are dealing with. The tremors she was experiencing seems to be a side effect of one of the meds she was on, so, it is being removed from her regimen. Enough medical talk, Juli's return home has been a very good one. She was happy to be home and seemed to be very comfortable right away. She was surrounded by family and general commotion, as is common in our busy house anyway and she seemed to be just fine with it. She pet the cat, avoided the dog, watched Mackenzie flit about....all very normal activities for her. She still doesn't have a very big interest in TV which is odd for her but she has so much to process, I guess I should be glad that TV isn't what she is using to rejuvenate her brain. Her bed is not nearly as comfortable, nor as convenient as the good hospital bed at RIC. Neither is the nursing care. We are realizing quickly how much the staff there did! We are also realizing how uncoordinated and unorganized we are. In spite of tendency toward spreadsheets and planning, we still are scrambling a bit. I am sure we will get there; I just know it will be a lot of work. Now that we are home, sharing that work will be easier. Anyone who visits might just get pulled into nursing duty. We ate fish and potatoes for dinner and Juli liked the bite or two she had but she still has to have small quantities. When she was coughing a bit, we had to stop trying. She still enjoys liquids so Chris may try her with coffee tomorrow... just a sip. Starting Wednesday she will go to day rehab where they will continue what RIC started. Not sure if they will be as good, but it's the next step so we will gladly take it. Juli found a way to get my attention by tapping her ring on the metal rails of the bed and is doing it right now so I will sign off and go see what she needs. Gotta get up for work in 4 hours so, goodnight!

December 23, 2009 - 7 am

Being home is definitely good for my daughter. The sights and sounds, the behaviors and expectations...it's all very familiar. When the dogs bark, Juli moves her curtain to see who is coming in. When the cat jumps on her lap she pets him the way you pet a cat: straight down through the tail. It is great for the family, though it is completely exhausting, I just don't know if it is because we are new to this or if it really is just very hard. Either way, it is the best hard work I have ever done. Nothing else compares. I would say the rest of the team agrees as well. We are starting to establish a routine. Yesterday Chris had a great day with Juli, helping her walk from the bathroom door to the toilet and back again, twice. Then later in the day she indicated that she wanted to go upstairs to the kitchen. He helped her to WALK up those 6 stairs. I knew that once she had a purpose to her 'therapy', she would more willingly participate. She indicated she wanted to go out on the deck, so Chris wheeled her out there, and then back in a moment later. (She was cold but, duh, she needed a coat...boys) She was trying to tell us something while in the kitchen and so we gave her the white board. We have to remind her to write slowly and not put the letters on top of each other. Once she got that, her message was clear: "I'm Hungry". (See, told ya.) We gave her a few small tastes of pasta that was surprisingly delivered to us (thanks Vickie and Tess!) and she ate it but only had a few bites. (Don't worry, it didn't go to waste. It is true; the best meals are the ones someone else makes for you). Speaking of that, thank you to all of you who have sent over food and cookies. You know the way to THIS girl's heart is through the feeding of her family's stomach so she doesn't have to! My family appreciates it too though I am SURE it is no reflection on my fabulous cooking....ahem...

The things Juli is able to communicate through writing to us is really our best indication that she is more put together than she might appear. For example, my brother came over on Monday and that is a special occasion because with his severe cat allergies, he can only come if he takes precautions. He usually has a couple of Pantothenic Acid pills we get from the health food store that will help him tolerate our cat for a while; but with the Leukemia, he was advised not to introduce anything other than 'as prescribed'. So anyway, as he came in I asked Juli to say "Hi to Uncle Joe". I expected a wave but since she had the white board already and she started writing. She wrote "Allergic". Now think about that. She had to recall that he had allergies and then consider the fact that his being there could stir those allergies. I have no doubt she will return to us. My goal is to live to see it! We are also learning now that we each have a niche and will work toward focusing on that. Chris is all about the therapy. He tries such creative and interesting things with her that she thinks they are just playing and hanging out. He also compliments her on every effort and says that he loves her even more for how hard she is trying. Since sometimes therapy takes a certain amount of strength to assist her, he really does better with that so, have at it. My back is shot now anyway. I on the other hand tend to gravitate toward the planning, organizing and coordination aspects. So the doctor's appointments, medical supplies, care giver schedules, etc., that is where I focus. I am kind of Juli's 'Food and Drug Administration'. It's much better when we divide and conquer. Of course we aren't both here all the time so there is the need to do the other's job and it's a good thing we both learned both aspects. Last night was her first shower at home. (Don't worry, I won't get personal here). Let me tell you, to say it was a logistical challenge would be an extreme understatement. We were ultimately successful but if I would have executed a project at work with that much 'making it up as I go along' I would be out of work. You see, even planning it all out in advance doesn't always do the job. It's just a very physical activity with the added element of risk. No worries Juli fans, she was not harmed in the taking of the shower. In fact, she probably didn't even know it was hard. Boy do I have a lot of things to tell her one day. Speaking of that, she dug her nails into me so hard last night she broke my skin. All those years of fostering respect and insisting on the kids treating each other and their parents respectfully and one little TBI and it all goes out the window. She was glaring at me and I told her the same thing I told a tantrum throwing toddler of mine many years ago, (you know who you are and my comments are still true today). "I don't care if you don't like me, I love you anyway." (Now excuse me while I bandage my wounds and pretend like I didn't feel a thing).

Ok, "miles to go" today so more information later.

December 24, 2009 - 9 am

Yesterday was our first day of day rehab and it was a mixed bag. First of all the actual therapy was mostly evaluation because they had to determine where she is in her healing. She was certainly the lowest functioning person there but that doesn't bother us at all. That just means that she is their biggest challenge and will win their hearts just like she has won the hearts of them at the previous locations. Getting her there was the first obstacle to overcome. You know what it's like the first time you take a newborn anywhere? Well, consider if your newborn was the size of a grown woman. I thought I planned the day well. I adjusted all of her food and medication schedule and even typed two different agendas for "Therapy Days" and "Non Therapy Days". I am sure a few people who know me are laughing about this, knowing that I do tend to 'over plan' the unplannable (is that a word?) Anyway, things were going well, her dad came over to take care of Juli while I worked and then eventually to help get her ready for therapy. I set aside 15 minutes to get Juli to the bathroom and ready just prior to her meds then the quick trip out the door in the medivan. 15 minutes.

Hahahahahahaha

5 minutes into the 15, the van showed up, 'wanting to be early'. I was trying to rush getting Juli dressed, which never would have worked before but this time it was physically not possible. The braces and shoes she wears make a very hard object to dress around. (Why not take them off you say?) Well that is harder so once they are on, which had only been for moments, we leave them on for the duration of her therapy. Let me cut to the chase: Her dad had to carry her up the stairs, the coat had to be thrown over her because we could not rush opening up her arm to get her arm through, and then her dad had to carry her outside to her wheelchair. I thought that we might just

be too old for this stress until I saw how the whole thing affected Juli. I have no idea if our stress caused hers (which I would have thought was true with a baby) or if perhaps her poor sleep for two nights was the real culprit, but during our hours at rehab she shook from head to toe. They were a bit concerned, as I was. I had heard about her 'tremors' from Chris and her dad but had not experienced this extensive shaking. The nurse there took her blood pressure, it was 154/100, and her heart rate was 119...hmmm. We gave her some time to relax, laid her down on the mat (raised padded table) and she slept for about 5 minutes. While sleeping they took it again and it did not go down. She finished her PT eval and then we met her OT. She continued shaking and they took her BP again. 180/120. We all got very concerned so they moved us to a dark quiet room (which would make ME more anxious) and her speech therapist came in there to meet her. Once the speech questions started happening, she seemed to mostly stop her shaking. She seems to be calmer when she has a way to divert her attention and something to concentrate on. She did very well in speech and answered all questions accurately, including a short-term memory test, which the speech therapist was sure she wouldn't be able to pass. They set their goals and planned for her next sessions. Then they took her BP again, sure it was much lower. It was 148/100. High BP was not something we ever had to deal with other than the time her ICP was elevated in the first week at Christ (lets NEVER do that again) and then one other time when we discovered she didn't have water that whole day and had been dehydrat– Wait a minute...in our rush to get to therapy, we had to cut corners. We skipped her water flush (the 350 ml of water given through her G Tube after her 325 ml of liquid food). Maybe, hopefully, that was the cause. I called the doctor when we got home and she thought we might be right. Let's not repeat that mistake. No medication was going to be prescribed, just bring her back to the doctor today to have her BP taken. What? Back to the doctor for BP? Really? I am no doctor nor even a nurse but I can take a BP. I did it last night and again this morning and she is right as rain. Ok, now stop reading about us, get back to your busy holiday and enjoy it. I am going to use the entire day to get ready to go to my sister's with my whole family. My goal is to get better at all of the traveling with Juli and to really just love my kids. Juliana, Adam, Dylan, Cheyenne, Delaney and Mackenzie... you ROCK and I love you!

Merry Christmas Eve.

December 25, 2009 - 4 pm

Merry Christmas everyone and thank you for your Christmas wishes. This whole experience has been about giving and sharing and faith and healing so in a way, it's all been Yuletide for me. We had our first social outing yesterday which was a whole day in the making. We planned to leave the house at 5 pm and didn't make it until 5:45. Not all that unusual for us so I was pretty impressed! We spent the whole day giving Juliana the beauty treatment she has been working toward for 3 months. We gave her a facial, did her eyebrows and gave her hair a much needed trim. Then we got her dressed and did her makeup. She looked lovely. She gave thumbs up for how each of us looked but gave a 'so-so' to how she looked, also not that unusual. We got her and all her equipment and entourage out the door and down the road a mile where we unloaded her equipment and entourage and proceeded to have a nearly routine and normal Christmas Eve. It made it all worth it. We even stayed until after midnight and then made the trek home. Everyone in the family pitched in, willingly and lovingly. How awesome is my family? I can't even express how lucky I am. We gave an exercise to our kids to write a brief statement on what this year meant to them. They all groaned at the idea of homework on Christmas but laughed and got down to work. The results were worth it. I will cherish them and save them always. In exchange for their entry they selected a gift card from the gift tree. Next year we will have a different question but will continue making it introspective. I just don't want to lose the deep family connection and our spiritual momentum when next year, Juli is healed. I want all this to be ultimately worth it because we have not just been changed, but changed forever and changed for good. So far, it's true. Juli is still not convinced of her recovery and it becomes more apparent with her responses to some things we ask her. That's ok. We will be her strength and confidence while she doubts. That won't deter us, will it? I didn't think so. (So, sappy moment coming.) Once again, I am extremely grateful for all of you who read and follow Juli's progress. We started this to let those who are interested know what is going on but quickly realized this is a way to continuously perpetuate the prayer and thought for Juliana. I want that girl whole. I am confident that with all that you each put into the universe and send to God each day on her behalf is working in her favor. So, since you show up, so do I, even today. This is a team effort and for the record, I count us ALL as "Team Juli".

So, good work and Merry Christmas team.

December 26, 2009 - 8 pm

I can see it is going to be a little more challenging to diligently update you on Juliana's progress but I can assure you in this case, no news = good news. Today was as close to normal as I can remember. We are getting into a better groove and what was at first monumentally difficult has become just something we do. It helps to believe (and essentially KNOW) that this is all temporary. I completely respect the effort required of any parent who must do what we are doing every day of their life. I know that many are out there and I am humbled by what they are able to accomplish.

Juliana is able to gradually increase her food and drink intake. We are trying to simulate real life with something offered whenever we are eating. Just yesterday Juli had turkey with gravy, sweet potatoes and cheesecake. She is also more frequently vocalizing and attempting words. She said, "Dylan", "Medina", and "I Love You". The words are faint and lacking normal clarity but a distinguishing ear in close proximity would understand. She indicated to Dylan that she knows she is going to get better and that she is trying hard to do so. Every day that passes by has more and more of her awake time where we can have fully functioning conversations with her where she understands absolutely everything. It does not appear that she has forgotten anything and responds appropriately almost all the time. Granted, we have to be clever in our request for response since she isn't really able to speak so we have to leave a lot of questions with a hand gesture for an answer. A friend (thanks Cathy) gave us some sign language DVDs and we are currently working on learning those with her. She tries very hard to do her stretches and listens to our suggestions to combat the tremors. She also seems to understand what has happened to her and we have discussed it in detail with her as well. Some may think that is a foolish thing to do but it has always been my way to be open with the kids giving them more information rather than less. Right or wrong, it is what they have come to expect. I know the previous Juli appreciated that, I can only assume the new Juli will too unless I learn otherwise. In this case I feel if she knows how far she has come she will appreciate it the same as we do. Without that information she might only understand where she was before the accident and be depressed. It's a dangerous perspective... I know. I used to avoid coming home due to 'former Juli influence' all over the house. Coming home for good would have been even more painful if it wasn't so incredibly busy and exhausting. It's all settled into us just being grateful at the progress and increasing normalcy. Today she sat on the couch (for the first time) for hours with us and at one point pulled me over for a hug. When she was eating leftovers with me I said, "Juli, I am doing a lot for you, right?" She gave her very subtle nod. "I want you to promise me 2 things then." Blink. "I want to be there when you have your babies and you have to take care of ME when I am old." She gave me a thumbs up. Then I said, "It's only a deal when you shake on it." She quickly stuck out her hand, shook mine hard then pulled me to her in another big, long and lifetime memorable hug.

It's a wonderful life.

December 27, 2009 - 10 pm

"The frontal lobes are considered our emotional control center and home to our personality." That is one of the locations of Juliana's injury and the source of her sporadic outbursts of anger and violence. Now mind you her capacity for either at this point is minimal but it is obvious. It started with the occasional pinching and hitting of the therapists and now is sometimes directed at us. It's hard to know when it's coming either so a random pinch might first appear to be a loving embrace. We need to learn more to know if this is a temporary situation, permanently increasing situation or somewhere in between. More than likely we will hear that 'they just don't know'. In the meantime we are all learning to duck and weave. She also has moments of tenderness like when she hit Chris in the nose then pulled him toward her for a kiss. Other than that we had another normal and happy day. Juli had a few visitors and they flowed in and out. It looks like Sundays will be Juli's day for company. She ate some food, cookies and drank lots of water and juice. She still needs to get better at taking a smaller amount of liquid so she doesn't spill but there is no more choking or coughing. She tried to say "Yes" and "Coffee" today. Still very faint and hard to decipher but if you know what you are looking for, you can tell. Tomorrow is therapy where we will ask about her braces to see if they can do something to make them less painful. I also plan to call the medical supply place to see if they have a more comfortable option in hospital beds. If not, we will likely look elsewhere. Tuesday is our big appointment at the ocular plastic surgeon. I say its 'big' because of my expectations, not really anything based in reality. Wait, the ophthalmologist did say he may be able to perform a procedure in the office to adjust her lower eyelid. We really want to know if he can help her open her eye. If he can't help her and has no recourse I am not sure what to expect next.

Thank you all for the cards for Juli. I didn't open any of them but will instead let her do it very soon. I just want her to get a little bit more aware. Also some of you have asked if we read her the wall posts and although we have read them to her sometimes, we haven't read them all. I am trying to find a way to print them all so that I can keep it all for her. Working on that; it's just that opening 'older posts' takes longer each page you go back.

Gotta go….I hear her down there now boxing Chris and Dylan and now the girls are getting into it. They all seem to really enjoy Juli's new confidence in her strength and try to playfully turn her anger around. I will let you know how that turns out. I can only find it mildly amusing. It's all a little too 'Three Stooges' for my tastes.

December 29, 2009 - 4 am

Cheyenne: "Juli, here, take the phone and call someone."

Juliana: 1-3-1-2-3-5-2-0-0…

Cheyenne: "OH my God" (screams) …"Mommy!"

Me: "What's wrong?!"

Cheyenne: "You have GOT to see this…."

Somethings are just second nature I guess and although we have tried that little experiment before she was never accurate enough in her aim and vision for us to know if she hit her target or not. This time, she was accurate. That was my cell number.

We also tested her on the vision in her right eye again. The last time was weeks ago and since she is more aware all the time, we wanted to just confirm for ourselves again. Cheye held her hand over Juli's left eye and Chris opened her right eye and asked her to point to him then me and she did. Then he asked her to hold up the same number of fingers that he was holding up. She did each time. He asked her to put up one finger if he was frowning and 2 fingers if he was sticking his tongue out. She put up 2 fingers. Then we asked her to grab the blue ball (in a string of other colors). She didn't attempt to grab any. She can do this easily with her left but perhaps deciphering colors is harder, or not possible with her right eye. It's a small price to pay. Today is the appointment with the Ocular Plastic Surgeon. I know I have told you that several times but I am just really excited. There has to be something they can do, right? If he can't, we will get a second opinion and third if necessary. We wheeled Juli to the computer last night and showed her Facebook. We tried to login to her page to see if she remembered her password and she was trying to recall, but couldn't. We can try again another time. I clicked around at her friends pages to show her how many had a picture with her. After a while it was a game: "Juli, who do you think Sarah has on her profile picture with her?" Juli pointed to herself. Cheye whispered (in a 'Cheye-can't-whisper' way) "Juli, it's like you are famous." We showed her the wall posts and some of the emails. She tried to type to Mary LiFonti but she got distracted by whatever was bothering her on her leg. That happens sometimes. Complete awareness peppered with confusion. Yesterday was therapy. It was eventful, in a very inconvenient way. The medivan that came to get her stopped running in our driveway and Donnie had to give him a jump. Then on the way back, it broke down, with the lift halfway so Juli was basically in a van with an open door until a new car showed up. On the ride home, she threw up. We tried the 'ginger in her food' trick for the way there; I guess we will have to try it before she leaves the place too. (I will have to remind Chris to give her some before today's car ride.) She was very sleepy during therapy and not very helpful. We can't seem to get her sleep just right, even when we give her the Trazadone, though she is sleeping soundly right now. As Chris says, "She's a tricky girl." They evaluated her leg braces and said that they confirmed they needed adjusting and were contacting someone about that. They are ordering her a brace for her arm to gradually open it up by gentle progression. They put a small brace between her thumb and forefinger to open up her hand. Sometimes she tolerates it easily, other times she fights it. This is not going to be easy but we will get her back into place. We were shown techniques for stimulating her mouth for maximum participation in feeding and speaking. Basically, provide oral care to get her moving her jaw and stimulating her taste buds. Well, gotta go…it's time to get Juli's morning meds and food going before I am off to work. I will let you know later how the appointment went. Promise.

December 30, 2009 - 7 am

At the doctors' appointment yesterday he examined her eyes a bit and found that there is no infection in the eye, and that is good. Then he tried to roll the eyelid out and it kept springing back. He did that about three times then determined he would need to perform a surgery. Although I went in with the expectation that he might have to do some procedure or another, I thought, 'if we tried something with her only a few times then gave up when she didn't do it, or it didn't happen, she wouldn't be doing anything." Is it possible that if we do it ourselves the eyelid will turn out and stay out on its own? Maybe we should give that a try before we commit to a surgery. Once again, I just don't know. The surgery doesn't sound too involved but he would need to put her in a twilight sleep and cut under her eye, turn out the lid and stitch it across. She will have a slight scar under her eye and there is a 90% chance this will work. Only 90? Oh, ok. He can't do anything about the upper eyelid which is called a "droopy eye". I did a little poking around on the internet on treatments for droopy eye and they are all treatments for what CAUSED the droopy eye. Makes sense but does us no good since the treatment for a TBI is 'wait and see'. I guess I have seen too many makeover shows because I figured the plastic surgeon would surely be the one to have the creative solution. And to top it off, the answer is always to wait. I have learned a lot about patience in these last three months and mostly I learned I don't like to wait. Sorry, I wish I could be more evolved than that and say that I am accepting but sometimes I am just…not. Almost every accomplishment and advance she has made was a result of time passing. Well, you know that. You are here every day too. All of the medical interventions were different ways to 'stop the bleeding' so to speak. The medical process for treatment is: just try to keep the effects of the TBI under control: swelling, infection, toning, etc. Medically they have done well to maintain her health but it all comes back to letting her brain heal itself. That's a lot of trust and faith. So, yes, I was a little disappointed, mostly because I expected too much. Add to that the fact that the office is downtown at Northwestern and Juliana gets carsick all the time….it was not a pleasant experience. She was a trooper though, holding the bucket to her mouth all the way home. We do have some anti- nausea medicine that we will start giving her before she gets in the car. Hopefully that will help. Back at home I explained to Juliana what the doctor wants to do, showed her a mirror and tried to explain what he could fix and what would he couldn't and what would take time to fix itself. Then I asked her if she wanted the surgery. She gave a quick, emphatic thumbs up. Of course she does. I am not yet convinced. I will look today for others in that specialty who might be able to give us a second opinion.

Juli had a pretty good night after that doing simple things like throwing a ball with her sisters (now there's a sentence I never thought I would write) and moving her wheelchair backward by herself. Cheye took her to the computer again and tried to get her to recall her password to Facebook but she couldn't do it yet. Stimulation wise I think we are making progress. She participates more normally every day, though again, it is only pennies at a time. She continues to vocalize a tiny bit more as well but it is almost too little to notice…pennies. As far as becoming more ambulatory we haven't made any additional progress there yet. Maybe next week in therapy. Time will tell.

December 31, 2009 - 8 am

Now that I am nurse, therapist, social worker, administrator (and let's not forget, mom) for Juli, I need more hours in the day! Even with others here to share the work, I am scattered and overwhelmed with so much to juggle. Don't get me wrong, we are all managing, just hanging on to the notion that this is all temporary. If only time would stand still for just a moment so I can catch up with all that I need to complete…I remember in my former life being SO busy. I had no time for anything to be added to my schedule then when Juli had her accident, I changed my life to follow her and now I don't even recall what happened to all those things I 'had' to do. Now, in this new world I am busy every moment again, yet, I rarely leave my house. I am glad we have a beautiful view of the outside but it almost looks like a picture, not real. Juli is sleeping now, an activity that she picks and chooses. I know she has a lot of adjusting because, well, "she does have a TBI and there is a lot of commotion". (TBI =Traumatic Brain Injury) That is the phrase that Chris and I use to explain all that we find unexplainable about Juli's condition du jour. Yesterday she had visitor after visitor and we were both exhausted by the evening. She complained of a headache with a pain level of 8 (1-10) and for the first time since she has been home, asked for pain medicine. If you have ever been to this crazy house, you would understand that most days pre-accident ended the same way!

She usually turns down the offer for medicine but asks for us to massage her neck instead. Gloria got her a neck massaging machine for Christmas and Juli likes that but just like everything else, only in small doses. She indicated that the pain is where her shunt is. I do not like the sound of that, though I don't know what is normal and what I should be alarmed about.

That is the hardest part of having her home. We are making choices along the way that can affect her without the benefit of daily medical advice. To us she appears to be doing well medically but we aren't checking her blood daily for signs of infection or chemical levels. Ignorance is our safety net but it only works when she is stable and all is right. When something seems off, it is a bed of nails. So today I will work on getting her a primary care doctor. Thank you to everyone who sent me referrals. We have been offered so many resources from this group. I have not been keeping good enough track of who offered what, so I am trying to go back and capture all of the emails and wall posts (but that is another block of time I will have to invent).

I would like to reconnect with those of you who offered your special services for therapy once Juli returned home. I will have to put together a schedule to fit with her therapy, doctor and visitors so if you are one of the people who emailed me to say that you would like to come by, please email me again. I will save it all this time, I promise.

For now, this day signals the end of a year of tragedy and miracles for our family. It's really incredible when I think about how far we have come, even if it is a journey we didn't want to take. The celebration and benefit on the 9th of January for my brother will be signifying the new year of possibilities and I am really excited to bring Juliana there to join in that sentiment as well. Thank you to all of you who said you will be attending. I look forward to meeting you there next Saturday.

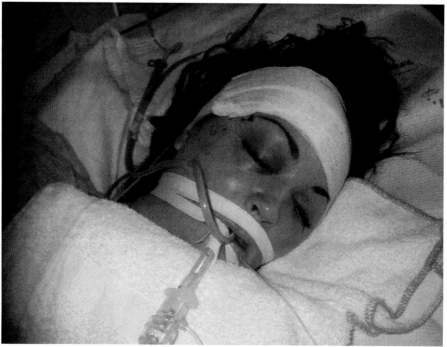

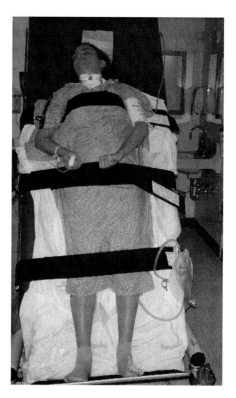

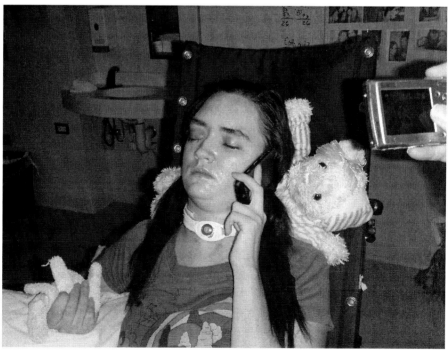

New Year's Day 2010 - 3 pm

Even though I totally expected to be doing something else this year, my New Year's resolution is to skip past all the 'might have beens' and move on to what is and what will be. Maybe not worded quite like that, but that is the gist of it. We had dinner at the table last night and Juliana had her share of the softer stuff and a LOT of juice. We had a pleasant night and an equally pleasant morning. She doesn't seem to be complaining of a headache anymore though I am looking feverishly for just the right doctor. Thank you all for your suggestions, I called some yesterday but they either weren't available or would not take Juli or were not quite right. So I see that I have to choose an Internist who specializes or has experience with TBIs. Also preferred would be to be associated with either a University Hospital or Christ Hospital. It's a lot to take in and sort through that I am really now wondering why they would let us come home without one. She seems to be doing just fine though. She does get shaky sometimes but it passes as she concentrates on doing anything else. She also gets sleepy while sitting sometimes and then her head droops down, (remember English class in high school? Yeah, that kind of head drooping.) But for the most part her alertness continues to improve. Today she walked across the room with help on both sides and she did pretty well. It has been a while since she really got that kind of physical therapy since she went from three hours every day to only 2 days since she has been home. That just means we have more to do with her at home on our own. We also noticed her leg braces were causing her blisters and bruises so they asked us to stop using them unless she needed to put weight on her legs. The day rehab will contact someone to see if they can have her braces evaluated and adjusted but the time lag we have to deal with now is disappointing compared to the immediate response we got as an inpatient. Waiting for 2 weeks to get new braces? Waiting 3 weeks to be seen by a doctor? I wonder how much of the "long process" is attributed to the idling built into the system. We are trying not to have her progress stall so whatever is available to us, we do. Yesterday again Christine Gialamas (LOVE her) came by and worked with Juli on speech and words, etc. We hope to have a friend who is an OT spend some time with her too. For our part, it is far more 'left of center' but we do whatever we can to stimulate her brain and make her muscles function. For example, last night when Juli was balling up her lemon sized fist to punch Chris, he put a boxing glove on her and taught her 3 different styles of punching, then gave her a series of punches to throw: "3 jabs, 2 uppercuts, 1 left hook". She really seemed to have fun with that and we secretly got a little memory exercise under her belt. Add to that some fun hand-eye coordination exercises and everyone is happy. Today when Chris was playing the guitar, we gave Juli a drumstick and the drum and asked her to tap in beat with the song. I have no idea what type of therapy that constitutes, music therapy I guess, but we don't like to have a single moment where she is not participating in something. We have lots of creative options for communication now too. I like that she has alternatives to speaking, sort of, but on the other hand I want to get her talking and am afraid if she has too many crutches she will not learn to speak. I don't think I am being impatient because if she can do it sometimes, why not do it MORE times?

January 2, 2010 - 10:30 pm

3 months gone by...

I started reading backward the updates from the beginning and had to stop. It was like someone else was writing it and living it. We are in SUCH a different place now. I won't deny that the unknowns still worry us a bit but what is different today than 3 months ago, or 2 months ago or even 1 month ago, was the clear vision of the future. It gets closer every day. There are no questions about the past that Juli can't answer, short term or long term. There is no lack of understanding of the world or the situation. She does fade in and out of concentration but usually it can be related to being tired. She is getting more comfortable with the constant commotion at the house and has just become part of it. She plays with Mackenzie and even tried to pull out her loose tooth last night. Her shaky hand scared Mackenzie away though. She kicks Miley (the dog). She never really liked her; combine that with her new aggressive behavior and ...there you go...kick the dog. We are pushing her more with talking and mouthing words. In fact, we decided that January is the month for talking. We are still pushing her to walk but talking is the target. Since she is mentally there, if she can talk to us we can make the rest happen easier. While waiting for that to happen we surely have been making use of hand gestures to communicate. We also want to get her to eat more foods. Her stomach tube is a constant concern of ours because a few times a day, she decides to tug on it. We do our best to distract her from it because telling her NOT to pull on it only increases her fierce need TO pull on it. The clip and the valve on the tube are also loose and we didn't get any extras from the hospital so I have to order them. You would think out of all of the supplies they ordered for us that would have been one of them. So anyway, every meal time we try to offer her the soft version of whatever we are eating. Sometimes she likes it and sometimes she doesn't. I am no Betty Crocker though so thank you to all of our guardian kitchen angels that have been bringing over food. It feels like every night I have the least amount of time to cook or prepare, someone gifts us with wonderful food. We will find a way to thank all of you; I just haven't figured it out yet. Next week Juli starts her appointments with new doctors. I still haven't landed on a primary care doc for her but not for lack of trying. We have just narrowed our list by a few because, by the doctor's own admission, they weren't a good fit. Fair enough, we have more numbers to dial on Monday. We continue to do our thing with her eye trying to stimulate the dormant and injured nerves and remind the lower lid to turn out. Juli does not like us messing with her eye but ultimately tolerates it. I wish you could all see her and how she continues to improve daily then you would know why I am so grateful for the outpouring of support. If you have ever doubted the power of prayer and positive thinking I certainly hope you don't anymore. We are all living and breathing this miracle together. It still is a phenomenon to me how so many people have reached out to tell me that their life and outlook is better as a result of our beautiful daughter. And even though I am physically much more worn out than when we were at the hospitals, it is SO much better to have her home and see her coming back to life with her family around her. In addition to seeing her flourish I get to see my other children and my husband grow into people that I am so incredibly proud of. How is it that after 3 of the worst months of my life I can't stop seeing the beauty in my life? I will tell you how: your love and support. I look forward to seeing some of you next Saturday at my brother's celebration so thank you to those who told me that they will be attending.

January 3, 2010 - 10:45 pm

Today Juli helped me make pancakes. Maybe it was the mixer moving in her hand or maybe it was eating those few bites of my delicious pancakes or maybe it was the quarter cup of Starbucks and quarter cup of Dunkin Donuts coffee but Juli was more....Juli today. You have to really see it to know or to notice but she was trying so hard to talk to us all day. She was mouthing words and using her hand gestures to go with it. The trick now is to figure it out before she gets frustrated and gives up. Today I felt like she was ahead of us. It's one thing when we are asking her to say something and then watching her say it. We know what we are expecting. The same thing is true with her writing. It's easier to know what you are dealing with when you set the rules but when you are trying to figure it out...that is a whole different ballgame. You have to read differently and listen differently. It took me between 5 and 10 minutes to understand what she was saying when I knew she was saying "Move me or move my..." I kept thinking she wanted me to exercise her arm or adjust her legs or take her to the bathroom. Finally I guessed, "Move you over toward Max?" She gave a big thumbs up, I wheeled her over by Max and she gave him a big long hug. I guess sometimes it's just that simple. She had a lot of visitors again today and kept the momentum going almost the entire time. She dozed off a few times but mostly, she hung with the crowd. We did have a very unfortunate incident with the dog that had everyone a little rattled but when that dust settled Juli was more alert than ever. Of course she is deeply sleeping now (otherwise I wouldn't be here writing to you) but she was alert and participating until the end of the night. In fact, when Chris got here after work she seemed happy to see him until he told her she had to get her braces on and practice walking. I don't know if her aversion is to the braces or the walking but she was not interested. In fact, she was so mad she made me take off her engagement ring and nearly threw it until I gave it to Chris to put back on the chain around his neck. She has done that before. More of the temper she doesn't understand and can't get under control yet. But Chris took her aggression and made her throw measured punches in a sequence. That suited her and it was fun for us. I took some pictures and uploaded one for you to see. Oh and when I was looking in the folder I have of pictures marked "Juli's recovery" I came across one taken on October 3rd. I uploaded that too, just as a frame of reference for how far she has come. Anyway, when it was time for her to do her 'family room walk' Chris challenged her to do the length faster than she had done it the day before. "How long did it take you yesterday Juliana?" Allison had timed her but no one could recall how long it took her. Well, no one but Juli...3 fingers, 3 fingers, fingers in the shape of a zero. Ah yes, Allison did say she did it in 3:30...

"So Juli, you can't do it faster than that, can you?" Chris challenged the still angry girlfriend.

Thumbs up.

"I bet you can't do it faster, or am I full of shit?"

2 fingers indicating she thought his second comment was accurate.

"Well, let's do it then."

...: 58 seconds later...2 fingers in his face.

In addition to getting fast, the girl is getting feisty.

January 4, 2010 - 11 pm

For whatever reason, some night Juli just doesn't sleep. When I last left you she was sleeping soundly, and I was so ready to hit my pillow. But no sooner had I crawled into bed than Cheyenne came to get me to say that Juli was wide awake and restless. That was the way the rest of the night went. Luckily I was only planning to sleep until 4 am when I get up to start her morning routine before I head to work. So, no sleep for Juli or me. Something tells me it was going to be harder for Juli than me. She still got carsick on her way to therapy but progressed to slight vomiting on the ride to therapy and dry heaves on the way home. Because she was so tired at therapy, Chris said that she wasn't participating much. Then it was on to OT and Juli did not like that one bit. She was stretched and pulled and braced back into place, like it or not. Although we liked the OT, I am thinking Juli did not. Then onto Speech and the therapist started working on little tricks to get her to vocalize. When she came home she had a fun afternoon with all her siblings...it just occurred to me they were all there....damn, missed a rare photo op. Anyway, all of us girls started to pile on Juli's bed at her request. We just got a little silly and it felt so goooooood. I asked her if I could just take a little nap at the bottom of her bed. She gave me the hand gesture to indicate, 'sure, go ahead'. Next thing you know I am getting toes in my nose and tapping and tickling on my leg. I am glad she still knows how to lighten up. She ate soup with crackers, pudding, applesauce and drank a lot of her new favorite drink: V8 Splash. (If anyone of you tell her that we got her to drink vegetables, I will deny it). I also started my list of things to ask the doctor when we see him and NO we still don't have a primary doctor. Tomorrow I am hoping the list I have narrowed down to will solve that drama.

Well folks I am really really sleepy. Not even going to proofread this but things are going so well, it doesn't matter what I say anyway. Right before Mackenzie went to bed she kissed Juli goodnight and said, "Juli looks so… normal." Yes Mackenzie, we are definitely getting there.

January 5, 2010 - 11:30 pm

On Tuesday's therapy at RIC in Homewood, their doctor is in. After hearing what he had to say, I feel like we are back to the beginning. Not the beginning of Juli's progress, but the beginning of trying to get another medical professional to SEE her. We finally found a primary care doctor (recommended from a Facebook family member so, thank you). We see him tomorrow night so we will continue with the introductions. But today it was a little frustrating but not as much as it was the first several times it happened. We are used to people underestimating her…Sigh…

Doc said "According to the last EEG, she is still experiencing seizures."

Chris said, "Her doctor at RIC said she doesn't appear to be having seizures." ('No epileptiform activity was recorded' to quote the report)

Doc said, "The report I saw indicated seizures."

…Moving on….

Doc said, "Does she still have the wires in her mouth?"

Chris said, "Wires from her retainer?"

Doc said, "No from when they wired her jaw."

Chris said, "Doc, they never wired her jaw."

Blink…blink

Chris said, "Her mom has a binder with all of all of her medical information. Do you want me to bring that?"

Doc said, "No, that's ok, we have it all on our computer."

Doh!

Doc said, "She is not yet able to follow a sequence of commands."

Chris said, "If I ask her to throw a jab-jab-uppercut-cross-jab-uppercut-uppercut and she does it, would that count as a sequence of commands?"

Doc said, "Yes, it would."

Smiling Chris said, "Good, I will work on that."

They fitted Juli for new arm braces and discussed Botox for her muscle contracture in her right arm. They stressed again the importance of stretching her arm to get the maximum healing for her. They took blood to check to see if she still needs the saline flush after her food in the G tube. Since we still have 30 bottles of it, I would be ok to keep using it. The speech therapist gave us more ways to elicit sound out of her by having her focus on bearing down in one way or another. She tries so hard and sometimes is successful. You know how sometimes you go to blow up a balloon and no matter how hard to push your lips around that balloon the only thing you get is a cheek cramp? That is what happens to Juli sometimes as she tries SO hard to get the sound to come out. But she definitely does it a little more each day. And this afternoon when drinking from a cup she spilled a lot less than she did yesterday. Practice, practice, practice. She is eating everything we have her try and is getting better at the mechanics of eating too. Once she gets a significant quantity by mouth I assume we will be advised to reduce the amount of Juli's food through her G tube. I want that to happen badly.

I said, "Juli our next goal is to have you talking and eating by the end of January." Thumbs up. That is my new cheer and Juli's new 'two finger goal'. To determine if the caloric intake is appropriate they want us to write down everything she eats.

I think I am going to need a bigger binder.

January 6, 2010 - 11:40 pm

My friend Carrie told me of a quote she has on her wall: "Life is not about waiting for the storm to pass. Life is about learning to dance in the rain." How cool is THAT? I wish I could take the credit for that one but even though I can't say I wrote it, I can say that I have tried to dance the last 3 months away. It still floors me to know that the worst thing in my life happened a few months ago and yet, SO many things have happened that are joyful. The fact that many of those things are 'starting over' for Juli, the progress never feels sad, just...forward. Today is no exception. In my opinion, we had at least a $1000 day. When I look at the other big steps that she has taken: following commands, opening her eyes, coming out of the coma, getting rid of her trach, taking a step, drinking, eating...each of those was not an event, but instead a process. Today we went really far into another process because today Juliana started talking. You are probably thinking, 'Wait, you told us she said words before.' Well she did. But today for reasons completely of her own (though I think it was the Fannie May chocolate) she was able to speak MANY words and phrases. She even tried to talk on the phone. She said all of her sibling's names and when I was so excited I could hardly stand still I said, "I have to call someone and have her talk to them. Jules, who should we call?" Juli very clearly said, "Aunt Lori". So I called Lori and let Juliana say "Hi Aunt Lori" all by herself., Lori cried, I cried, (Juli didn't cry she just talked) I don't know if I was stunned but I wasn't really believing what I was hearing. It was like she just "figured it out". As the night went on I was less stunned because she kept doing it. Now the reality check... Her spoken word is much like her written word: Hard to understand unless you know what she is intending to convey. So if you ask her to "say Mommy" and she then says a two syllable word where the vowels are obvious, you understand her. But when she wants to talk or write to tell you something you have to figure out... well, it's a race to the finish to see who gets frustrated and quits first. Now for those of you coming to the benefit this Saturday, don't expect Juliana to necessarily talk. Anywhere outside of our house she is definitely more reserved. Anyway, just a little side note.

Juli also ate a lot of real food today, which I cooked and prepared although my other kids might debate the 'real' part. Juli was able to eat everything and wanted more without having chewing or swallowing difficulty.

So the two goals for January of eating and talking seem SO within reach that I think I might have to have backup goals ready to go. At the orthodontist the wire from her permanent retainer was filed down so it wasn't sticking out anymore. He said she won't need new braces but instead would just need a new retainer but not just yet. It was actually a little strangely nice to see a doctor we had been to prior to her accident. And considering he put braces on four of my kids, we'd been there a LOT. This afternoon and evening we also started down our own path of recovery with some of the Team Juli Angels, TJAs. That is what I am calling the group of supporters who are offering their professional services to us just because they are generous of spirit and loving people and want to help. With the TJAs we are able to augment what the rehab center is able to do and what we are doing at home. They come to our house and do what they do to help my daughter heal. And how cool is THAT? I tell you, this whole community of 'For Juliana' supporters are going to drag her back to health if it has to be done kicking and screaming (and pinching, scratching, punching…). Bring it Juli, we will just keep dancing.

January 8, 2010 - 11:50 pm

As Juli gets more 'Juli', she also gets more aware of how much 'Juli' she is not yet. I want to be happy about her progress but sometimes it's just sad. She has beautiful big brown eyes with long lashes but when she looks in the mirror she doesn't even see them because one eye is closed. You can tell that she is aware of her condition and is self-conscious of the personal needs that have to be taken care of by others. Sure we keep the private things to just me and Chris but even so, she doesn't want Chris to do it. She is starting to reject his help and the aggression that we saw is getting a bit rougher. In fact, we all have cuts and bruises courtesy of our angel. I have been told this phase will pass. I am ready to weather the storm because she is after all my daughter. But think about it…she has to become something close to who she was to be Chris's fiancé. That is not to say he wouldn't accept changes that are coming but we used to joke about how Juli might change and now we fear the looming possibility. We know it's far too soon to draw conclusions on how her behavior today may or may not affect their relationship in the future but… well…hasn't it already? The question is, will it be for better or worse? Her anger often includes rejection and Chris is her most common target. So the similarities I have seen between people recovering from a TBI with raising a child would put her akin to a petulant toddler. One moment loving and kind, showing off what they have just learned to do and the next throwing a tantrum and demanding their way. Funny thing is, Juliana was never that kind of toddler. She was practically born a big sister. She was only 15 months and 9 days old when Adam was born so, yeah, she WAS practically born a big sister. Tantrum throwing and demanding her way just didn't happen.

But the good news is definitely how much she is starting to talk. Just in the last few days her voice went from sounds to sentences. It is a remarkable transition to witness. Today at therapy she did not do well in PT at all. She was basically forcing herself to sit back down when they stood her up. She sailed through speech therapy where she excelled at saying all the names of the people in her family. We have been told that is to be expected. Not all progress will occur at the same pace.

She is sleeping soundly so this house is going to sleep as well. I know I say that a lot but sleep is a hotter commodity than currency here at our house so I will take what I can get.

Big day tomorrow: Juliana's first big outing at my brother's benefit. Hope to see you guys there!

January 10, 2010 - 1 pm

Oh what a night! To get Juli ready to go to the benefit took 4 and 4: People and hours that is. It was a combination of timing of food, medicine, clothing, sleep, hair, makeup and as if that weren't enough...attitude. You see, as it turns out, Juliana did NOT want to go. In fact, as we were about to leave, after taking pictures that she seemed to enjoy (will post the new pictures tomorrow, maybe even a video, they are FABULOUS) she grabbed my arm and pleaded with me in a way that I could totally understand as, 'please Mom, don't make me go.' I told her that it would be ok and that she needed to be there to support her Uncle Joe. She clutched the wall and stuck out her foot as if that could really stop us from taking her. Now you might think that it is very insensitive of me to really understand her hesitance and then make her go anyway but have any of you parents out there ever made your children do something they didn't want to do because they SHOULD? Well that is what I was thinking. She didn't need to stay home for any medical limitation. In fact, if she was aware enough to be worried about how people might perceive her then, forgive me, but it's time for her to face it. She has always been insecure though she never really had a reason. The anxiety I am sure she felt tonight was all of that old fear compounded with the new fear of how her physical limitations will be perceived. Well you know what? I played the mean mommy and threw her into the deep end. At first the party was overwhelming for both of us because the logistics were challenging. Her ankles turn and her shoes weren't secure. (Stupid me trying to get her cute shoes) Then trying to get her in the car in the snow while I wore heels, even more stupid. Luckily I brought in a backup before I tried anything unsafe. Then as soon as we got her in the car she tried to take off her seat belt and open the car door. Cheyenne tried to get her secured in the car and Juliana hit her so hard that Cheyenne said, "She just hit me harder than any girl I ever got in a fight with." Um...yeah, I will deal with that later... So anyway... the ride there was a combination of distraction and illusion. She wanted out of that car so bad! Well, ok, so here is the TBI life...it wasn't just simple avoidance she was after, she does this rebellion and escape attempt EVERY time she gets in the car now and it's almost like just one more way she latches on to something and won't let go. Fast forward...we made it to the benefit and into the room. The band was playing and people were saying hello and it was just too much all at once. We sat there a while then I took her downstairs for some quiet. She relaxed a bit then she agreed to go back to the party. We started back into the room when Chris showed up. She seemed so happy to see him! She hugged him and held him like he was her lifeline. They chatted a few minutes then she rejoined the party. Ultimately she relaxed and enjoyed herself even clapping for the magicians and especially Chris's performance. She appeared to be enjoying herself. She had so many people come up to talk to her and hug her and I think the attention really made her feel more comfortable in her own new flawed skin. Maybe it was my imagination but I can tell you that in the hallway with her friends at the end of the night, she was still a member of their group. Phew! It was a good night all around. We can forget about the fact that she gouged new holes in my arm on the way home because I restrained her from taking off her seatbelt..."Juli, I am your mother and it is STILL my job to keep you safe so fight me all you want, I will not let you take off that seat belt." She didn't relent at all but I felt better knowing I said what I had to. Who knows what will matter and what won't in the end? All I know is we got that first big public event out of the way and she lived through it. Maybe this whole situation will yield a more secure young lady. Yeah, let's add that to the stack of value add we have already accumulated.

January 10, 2010 - 9 pm

So how many times have you thought that a hangover was more than just alcohol? Couldn't you have sworn that the headache, bloodshot eyes and exhaustion were surely due to the late night, loud music, commotion and not just what you drank? Well Juli woke up with all the signs of a hangover and she didn't drink a drop of alcohol. There is your proof for the next time. I also asked her why she tried to get out of the car last night. She rubbed her stomach to indicate she didn't feel well. It made sense to us...for a moment... but then realized that the missing logic was in the fact that falling out of a speeding car doesn't usually cure nausea. She didn't throw up in either direction by the way. She spent the day lounging around on the couch and we focused on talking and eating and some stretching of her ankles. She talks more and more but we have to work on the clarity because she is still hard to understand. We did some 'Friends' trivia and she got most of the answers right even though the questions were very obscure. I wasn't really testing her memory because I know it is pretty darn good but it was a great exercise in talking and she did really well. We are focusing on enunciating and volume. She also had lots of food today so I sure hope we are getting closer to eliminating that G-tube because it is a pain to monitor and manage. That will be a really big win. We are a little concerned about how weak her legs are and that her mobility seems to have declined since her inpatient stay at RIC. I feel we lost ground on that front once she came home either because therapy went from every day to once a week for the first two weeks due to a holiday and only 2 times the next week due to her other appointments. And now since her legs, specifically her ankles, seem to be getting weaker, that makes it hard to have her walk at all. We did a few passes through the living room tonight but she really hates to put any weight on her right leg. I hope they will tell us at rehab tomorrow if we should be mustering through it to make her stronger or if there is a problem that needs correcting. With Juli's increasing anger outbursts we are confused on how to handle it as well. It feels a little like we are heading into a forest of strange and sometimes scary creatures but we don't really know where we are going and what we will encounter. Any hug may result in a scratch without warning. Any touch might end in a pinch and it's sometimes very random. You can see the anger unfold though if you look at her. I explain to her in her moments of calm that she gets so angry because the part of her brain that was injured was the part that controls her emotions. I told her today that we forgive her because she has a TBI. Later in the evening when she was throwing her lemon handed punches at Chris I said, "Juli, you know why you are angry, right?" She paused a minute and then said, "My TBI?" Yes Juliana, you got it. Just another thing we will have to deal with until it is over.

January 11, 2010 - 11 pm

(Text from Chris at 1:36 pm): 'Juliana kicked so much ass in PT it's not even awesome...it's terrifying.'

(Rambling from Chris as he sits next to me): "What was terrifying about it was, when it was the most she had ever done, and I thought she would quit, she just kept going. I was feeling it FOR her and I kept thinking, 'this has got to be enough', and she kept going. She did new and amazing exercises, walked 20 feet with very little help and just freakin amazed me! And that is not including trying to punch out the PT. She threw in some punches and kicks too. She was just a talking fool in Speech today too. She tolerated having her arm bent but at one point was refusing to sit up straight. I knew she could do it so I egged her on to where she had to do a serious sit up to try to punch me in the stomach. (Random entry coming) And she saw a baby, and smiled. (End) I was totally relieved to drop her off and go to work though because I was exhausted. Especially since neither of us slept last night. She was definitely using her right hand more. She was reaching down to the floor and that was cool but you can definitely tell that her vision is JACKED UP. She is reaching but it's totally obvious that she can't see." (He just peered over and noticed I was writing everything he was saying...spewed some additional profanity and wondered if you guys will think he is on something. He is...pure adrenaline at this point.) He is not saying anything now. "He is done" he said to tell you.

I wait

Still waiting (he'll talk)

"No I won't" (told ya)

Yeah, it gets this silly sometimes from lack of sleep, intense muscle spasms (that's me) and just getting through the day.

Good night

January 12, 2010 - 6:45 pm

Before I tell you about Juli's Nadia Comaneci day, I have to tell you that the food angels arrived AGAIN!! The other day it was Donna Blazkowski and today it was Pat Westergren. You guys are just TOO good to us. I remember a few years ago the Blazkowskis put together a huge candy and treat basket for my son Dylan when he had mono as a junior. It was so sweet. And Pat Westergren has been sending Juliana a card at least every week since she got in her accident, sometimes more frequently. In addition to that, we have had food from Sherry Hall, Paula Mitchell, Dawn Slattery, Eva Mancusi, Maida

Ramirez, Gia Wilson, Lori Rago, Toula Spencer, Vickie and Tess Pappas, Mike and Amy (soon to be) Cahill, and SO many others drop off food just to take the burden of cooking off of me. I don't know how we got so lucky to have people around us that are so kind and generous but this family is truly inspired by it (and probably glad to not have me cook…don't go there).

So we implemented a new routine to hopefully take some of the exhaustion away: We gave up the night shift. That's right, Dylan, Cheyenne, and Adam are now the night crew sleeping downstairs and keeping Juli safe and sometimes company in the middle of the night. I think it will eventually help us all get a little more routine and rest in our life.

Waiting for the therapy to start today Chris was testing Juli's ability to follow a sequence of commands: "Can you jab me twice, touch my nose, slap my cheek, poke my chest then give me a hug?" As he was asking her she dozed off. The girl does have a TBI you know. He reclined her and took a ten minute break to catch up on texts.

Then Juli woke up, yawned big and…jabbed him twice, touched his nose, slapped his cheek, poked his chest and pulled him in for a hug…DOH!

During PT she walked even further and faster than yesterday. The apparatus they use is a support walker and she can do it with less help all the time. Chris took a video and will try to upload it with video technical assistance of course. Perfect 10. During OT they encouraged her to use her right arm and, well she did. She used her right arm and hand to clean a white board…with a rag of course (I know all you OCD moms were freaking thinking she had an arm full of dry erase dust). She tried to do it with her left arm until Chris held it back and then her determination to do what they asked forced her to push her right arm into action. Well what do you know…the gig is up, the girl can use the arm after all. Another 10.

Then in Speech, once again, she was a talking fooooool. They are working on enunciating, thank goodness. I was afraid she would just keep getting more mad if we couldn't understand her and turn into the incredible hulk or something. We all agree that she is 'freakishly strong' now. And to think we used to just JOKE that she would come out of the coma with a super power. That's three 10s.

I know I have said this before but it is MORE true now than it ever has been: Juli is really REALLY here. The OT was asking her where she went to school and she told them "Oak Forest" and her therapist said, "Oh, my Uncle works there." Juliana said, "Really? Who is he?" I think my daughter just had a legitimate verbal conversation. Then tonight Cheyenne was telling me about an internet hoax that Jacob (from New Moon) died. Juliana asked, "Really?" It's pretty darn cute. (He didn't by the way) Then when her dad called tonight we could ALL hear her say very clearly, "I love you too." Our goal was to have her be talking by the end of January then I amended it to be 'easily understood' by the end of January. Now I am thinking that maybe we should shoot for singing!

Wait…be right back…

Need ANOTHER new goal cuz she JUST sang with us!

We sang…"Lean on me, when you're not strong, and I'll be your friend, I'll help you carry on. Cuz, it won't be long, til I'm gonna need…"

Pause…"take it away Juli"

Then softly, but still on key…

"…Somebody …to lean on."

January 14, 2010 - 8:15 am

I started to update so many times and never got the time to do it and then depending on what time I wrote it, the story would have been different because yesterday was alternately positive and overwhelming. Well, that's pretty much every day now. Nothing is bad or wrong or sad, it's just….I don't know…it's a lot.

This ride that was once a roller coaster is now less up and down and more like…teacups. You know that teacup ride where you sit in a car shaped like a teacup and it spins in its own space on an arm of other spinning teacups while the arms spin around other arms of teacups? You remember that ride that you went on with your kids even though it makes you really sick, simply because no one else will ride with them? I always got stuck as the one to go with them until they were big enough to ride alone. I feel like I am back there. I am pretty sure I can last until the ride ends but while it's spinning; it feels like I will lose it at any time. Juli is doing well, progressing pennies, (sometimes dollars actually) at a time. Jennifer, (our Dietician by trade but Team Juli Angel by fate) is helping us work toward removal of the feeding tube by the end of the month. That is a BIG positive. That means an additional degree of normalcy and less area of maintenance and infection. Also, while Juli eats more by mouth, she gets the exercise needed to further enunciate her words and speak more clearly. I think that will help her feel more normal too.

Juli is in far better control of her mind and her actions every day but she hasn't yet had the actual realization that she has a role to play in making herself well. For example, talking will improve with practice. What else has she got to do all day but practice talking? (Seems simple to me.) But unless someone is there asking her or pushing her, she stays silent. I try to be available all the time or have someone pushing her all the time but no one's life, including my own, suddenly became completely wide open waiting for Juli to need us. I don't actually know how that sounds to someone who has a full night's sleep but I suspect I will find out in a series of emails or posts. Also, her right arm needs to be exercised. This is also something she can do herself and rarely does without coaching. I guess the subliminal progress you should note is that we never expected her to actually participate until now and so, the fact that she can, and should, is actually remarkable. WE knew she would get here but, well, 'the others' didn't. In any case, this brings us to yet another phase, the one where her will must be engaged in order for her recovery to progress. We can only do so much for our kids before they have to help themselves. As a mother who is a TOTAL enabler, this is a very hard thing to accept. I tend not to let things go, and really don't see where my role ends in any of their lives, much less someone in Juli's condition. My dad used to say, "Do it right the first time and you won't have to do it over." I used to quote that when I was pointing out that raising the first child correctly has a trickle-down effect on the others (doesn't always work by the way, my logic was flawed) Now I see that quote much more as a self-criticism and it becomes more personal. You see, I am a total enabler. If only I had expected them all to fly on their own, I wouldn't have to teach her now how to push herself forward, she would just do it. But today, at this point I would settle for her sleeping all night. That does happen approximately every third night, perhaps out of pure exhaustion and running out of steam so tonight she should sleep. We did start trading off the night shift so that Chris and I could sleep but they still have to come get me when she gets especially agitated. That would be last night. So, let's just see what today brings, for all of us.

January 16, 2010 - 3 pm

Bet you thought I forgot about you! Well I haven't. I think about updating you all the time (and started this yesterday) but I have so little time to sit at the computer anymore that it is just very difficult to juggle it all. I just keep telling myself this is all temporary and thankfully each day is a confirmation that it is. In the past few days Juli had a wonderfully relaxing facial and foot massage, a kick box lesson and visits from lots of friends. Her communication is improving and her anger seems to be manageable. She even told me that she wouldn't be mean to me, Mackenzie or Delaney anymore. We'll see about that. She does continue to be the hardest on Chris. Throughout the course of this situation we talked about the many ways this could play out and we recognized that Chris might have to stop being a caretaker for Juli in order to return to being her boyfriend. We were avoiding that since then that would just leave me as the caretaker but it is getting to that point because she is increasingly resistant to his help. He feels terrible stepping away at all, like he might be letting her down, me down, the 'cause' down but the goal is still the same, Juliana's recovery, so we will do what is necessary to reach that goal. To that end, Juli has goals of her own. For example, the other morning I told her she needed to bring her right hand to her right leg. It might sound simple but straightening out her right arm and hand is a challenge as well as lifting her right leg. She had to work hard to do it, but by evening she did it. The end of January is our goal for removal of the feeding tube and also being able to understand her talking. She gets clearer every day and that helps us all. Her long term goal at the moment is to go to New York over Memorial weekend for Tess and Matt's wedding. I think that is totally doable and that is what she needs to believe as well. In the meantime we will break down all the tasks to get from here to there and knock them out one at a time. I do wonder though…how long *can* someone actually go without sleep? Especially someone with a brain injury that supposedly NEEDS sleep to heal. It seems that she sleeps every third night, but even then, not the whole night. I don't know how she is functioning; I just know that I am exhausted. The plan to have someone else sleep by her so I could get some sleep was flawed. Since Juli started talking, she decided to call 'Mom' as well as rattle the side rails of her bed. So the dutiful night shift follows my instructions of 'wake me up if she needs me' which means I spend most of the night downstairs half-awake anyway. So I know if I am this tired with a little sleep, Juli can't possibly be able to heal with NO sleep. We gave her melatonin last night trying to offer a natural sleep solution and that didn't help at all. We have asked the therapists at RIC about muscle relaxers, especially since she complains of the muscle aches and toning and they are checking with the rehab physician. My concern is that we are working toward getting away from medications and then we ask to add another one. I am out of ideas on that one. In the meantime, life goes on. Dylan is going back to Hawaii next week reducing my live in assistants but reinforcing our commitment to returning to normal. Mackenzie was student of the month which was a great indication to me that she is also doing just fine, in spite of the circumstances. It's all going to be fine, if I don't fall asleep and miss it all.

January 17, 2010 - 9:45 pm

Guess who slept last night? ALL of us! Juli said this morning that she feels good. (Duh, me too). Good thing she slept well because we were a little worried because we had an incident last night that taught us all a lesson on safety. Juliana was in her wheelchair reaching to the floor for the napkin she dropped. Yeah, you see it coming…she reached forward and fell out of her chair to the floor on her right side. Cheye and I quickly scooped her up and assessed the damages, which appeared to be nothing more than rapid heart rate. She may develop bruises but so far, so good. She promised that she won't take her seatbelt off again and she would try to be careful not to lean so far. And we promised to not take our eyes off her. Next stage, here we come. Then this morning when I was getting her breakfast ready I buckled her seatbelt only for her to promptly take it off…sigh…the ride is still bumpy.

Today we focused on talking. I am having a hard time understanding her still and I can do it better than most. Not bragging, just time spent listening. I try to get her to open her mouth wider and use her mouth muscles to articulate the words but it's still a challenge to understand her. By the end of the month, that is when she will speak clearly. I keep saying that but we are flying by the seat of our pants on how to actually make that happen. The cool thing is that she talks, and not just one word, simple answers. For example, when I asked her what she wanted to drink, she pointed to the cup in front of her. I kept saying, "Tell me what you want." She kept pointing. It was a stalemate and I was determined to win. I was holding out for her to say something, 'cup', or 'juice' or 'Sprite'…anything. Then finally she got tired of pointing and gave in: "I want the only thing on that table, there in the red cup."

Well alrighty then.

We got another visit from a friend using their experience in OT to help us out. A little electrical stimulation and some stretches and, bada bing, bada boom, extra OT. Juli cooperated for a while then started clawing away. She was planning to go to her dad's house for dinner tonight but while waiting for Chris to pick her up she was getting more and more sleepy. When he got there she was barely awake. She told him, "Pick me up." He said, "You want me to carry you?" "Yes" she said. So he did. (See latest picture.)

At her dads she ate a full meal and visited with everyone then came home exhausted and went right to bed. I would love to say that as of now she is still fast asleep but, no, in spite of being completely tired and fully medicated, she is now totally awake and ready to get out of bed...sigh...here we go again.

January 20, 2010 - 7:15 am

Shhhh.....don't anyone move. The house is sleeping and I am awake so I have a moment, maybe not much more, to update you on Juliana's past couple of days. I don't intend to reduce the updates to every couple of days but unless I get my fondest wish of being the only person in the world to never need to sleep, I may not have time for more than that. Funny thing is, depending on when I update you could get a whole different story since this is also very mood dependent. Right now I am somewhere in the middle. You see Dylan left this morning and last night's goodbyes were very different than his first sendoff. We are all a little wiser now, and a little more appreciative of the fragility of life. Juli was upset at his leaving which made him upset as well. It's the right thing though, life must go on. On the bright side, we got more visits from food angels! Michelle Zurisk, Eva Mancusi and Dawn Slattery each made us dinner AGAIN! The cool thing is now that Juliana eats everything we eat she gets to eat good cooking as well. What a bonus. In the early days at Christ hospital and RML, I started each day with whatever breakfast foods Gloria brought us. It was such a treat to see what she had in the bag each day for us.

So here is where we are right now: We went to the neurologist, hoping to adjust some medications to get the right combination for her pain, discomfort, alertness and lack of sleep. I don't want to be too optimistic but if last night was any indication, we might have just found it. A lot will hinge on how alert she is through the day today but she slept peacefully all night with her hand open. For those of you who have seen her, and the OTs that have participated, you know this is a big deal. The doc started her on Baclofen which is a muscle relaxer used for spasticity of muscles. That is the good news since she has so much muscle toning that it is causing her pain as well. The bad news is that it is a generalized medication so it works on all muscles, not just the ones contracting so she may be less awake (good at night, not good during the day) and less able to control her muscles. And of course, whatever effects we see early on may be temporary as she adjusts. We will see how this plays out. I will give her three nights on this new med and then probably remove the sleep agent she is taking and see if the Baclofen alone will help her sleep and be comfortable. The goal had been to reduce her meds so this was a little disappointing at first. Just one more thing I had to get past my own preconceived ideas. Other than that, Juli is still appearing to be medically stable. We also had our appointment with her neurosurgeon (who spent 10 seconds pressing on the site of her shunt and declared the operation a success...see ya in a year). Ok, that's good as well. Today we go to the endocrinologist to have her hormone levels evaluated. It seems the pituitary gland may have been impacted and hormone replacement might be needed. Then we have no more doctor appointments on the radar until we schedule her eye surgery, which reminds me, I have to do that today. That is with the exception of the appointment to remove her feeding tube. I will talk to the dietician today about when I can schedule that. Her therapies are progressing nicely as well (if you don't count the vomiting on the way). She doesn't enjoy the work she has to do and routinely tries to hit someone (which they said is a phase that she MAY come out of ...gulp) but she is getting stronger and more capable. She told me the other night that she wants most to be able to talk better so we have a full court press on making that happen. Then she wants to work on walking. Well she gets the bonus plan because we are working on it all, every day. If we can master the juggling act of her pain and sleep we might just be able to move a little faster. In the effort to have her talk better we of course make her repeat herself when something is hard to understand. And here is the odd brain injury element here. She said that she was mad at me, Chris and Cheyenne because "you are all liars." I asked her what we lied about and she said "you know what I am trying to say but you act like you don't." Hmmm...mental note: don't patronize her by appearing to not know, just tell her to say it again.

Then Cheyenne said, "Well then you lie to us too."

"How?" Juliana says.

"By shrugging when you just don't want to answer." Cheyenne explains.

Juliana replied but here is the funny thing: Her voice is so small and muffled that you expect very little communication from her: small words, small phrases to simple thoughts. That is completely incorrect when you factor in that she is mentally all there. So Juliana responded saying, "Well I shrug EVENTUALLY, when you can't understand me." I smiled and told her she was so cute. She rolled her eyes in frustration. One minute she is an adult and the next, a child. This is the damndest thing.

So by all charts and plans, Juli is moving along fabulously. They even increased her therapy to four hours a day and we are working toward 6 hours) All of your prayers and support have been put to good use as she climbs out of the wreck, figuratively and a little bit literally as well. And if only all of that goodness could make me miss the girl she was a little bit less, I would just be happy all the time. She is here and she is healing and completely understanding. But she is changed and as much as I can appreciate who she is becoming, with her quirky shrugging and her random statements, I can't help but want the girl that she was, back. She was my friend and my confidant and the child that had been through it all with me and understood me. She was the first payoff for having kids young: we were sharing our lives and our adulthood. I have heard many stories of recovery that all leave me positive and hopeful that she will have her life back. But they all have a similar undercurrent as well...the person is changed. Anywhere from dramatically to subtly so I don't know how much of her former self will return. For now I will be grateful that she is mentally intact in spite of an injury forcing the contrary. That is a lot to be grateful for so I hope I am not coming across as ungrateful. But as her family and friends have attested to, Juliana had a phenomenal personality and the light around her was tangible. I need to see laughter and singing and interrupting to know that the same girl or a close facsimile will emerge. Until then, forgive me, but I do sometimes still miss her.

January 21, 2010 - 4:30 pm

Final doctor appointment of the week finished THANK GOODNESS! It is such an event taking Juliana anywhere. Friends of mine have people in their life in wheelchairs or with special needs and I know they have to carry extra everything around with them and I feel for them. It's like taking out a newborn…that's really big. Let me tell you something…this is NOT a handicap accessible world. Did I make it everywhere, around every corner and into every office? Did I get her into the bathroom and out of the car and up the ramps? Sure I ultimately managed but it was about as graceful as eating a pomegranate in handcuffs. No, I have never done that, I am just imagining. Yeah, I stood out like a sore thumb. And you actually kind of feel like a bother to the rest of society having doors open for you, people waiting for you to gather yourself and your belongings out of their bustling way. I no longer look at people who might be looking at me. I don't have the energy to spare. Now my focus is on juggling the wheelchair, the bags, and the binder of documentation, the puke bucket and spare towels. I barely see the ground in front of me much less the people around me but it sure would be nice if doctors really made house calls because office visits are really inconvenient for the sick and disabled. Of course this is not an event I attempt alone. Juli needs her own handler, and when we go to the doctor, I am more of her administrator so I bring a handler. Every trip is another experience of 'Ms. TBI's Wild Ride' between the grabbing for the door handle, the window or the puke bucket; you just can't take your eyes off of her. Someone tell me… Are we almost to the almost?? I am getting frustrated trying to talk to her as well though we might be able to blame it on a blooming sinus infection. It seems the more I need her to speak clearly, the less clearly she speaks. Don't discount the notion of defiance because THAT is the darndest thing…she is resisting many of our efforts to help her. I know it is the nature of her injury and I know that she isn't really aware of how difficult she is making it but it adds to the mental exhaustion. Then she will say something to make us think she is depressed and suddenly sympathy for me vanishes and I see her as a little girl lost. I knew that being a mom meant I was the 'last stop' and regardless of how much or how little others contributed I had to round it all out but I have definitely hit my capacity for what I can handle. And I miss Dylan already dammit.

Bad time to update I guess. Things are fine, really friends. It's just a juggling act and I am very uncoordinated.

January 23, 2010 - 9 pm

So here is the deal with recovery: you can't count an accomplishment or improvement until it stands the test of time. After 5 consecutive nights of sleeping all night long, I can say with some confidence that we might have turned that corner. Of course when you round a bend there are other things you might not have expected to be waiting for you but sleeping through is a corner going UP the hill, so be happy for that.

Our new questions are about tradeoffs. Juliana's muscle spasticity can be helped by muscle relaxers. However, if we give her the muscle relaxers to improve her arm flexibility during therapy, she is too lethargic to participate in speech therapy. So we have to determine which result is more important. And speech is not really the only casualty. Her ability to really do anything is altered because, well, a body has a lot of muscles! We haven't decided yet, we need more days under our belt but I am thinking the next course of action will be to keep giving them to her for a few more days to see if she levels out and if not, just remove the one during the daytime.

Juli is eating a lot more now and a lot more independently. In fact, the brownies that Dawn Slattery sent over were Juli's obsession for about an hour as she kept asking for more. She said to me at one point, "you don't have to stand there holding the brownie, you can just give it to me." (That took about 15 minutes to decipher I might add) but, Ummmm, me give up control of a brownie?? Yeah, I don't think so. Today she asked me if she could just feed herself. I was planning on letting her more after we got the tube out because right now I need to make sure she can consume enough calories to sustain a regular diet. So I made a deal with her. "Juli, I will let you feed yourself but I still have to make sure you get enough in your mouth so if you can't do it well enough yet, I will still help you, deal?"

"Sure" she said.

She barely missed a drop. What WAS I worrying about? So, maybe that is two corners today. A minor concern we have is with her diet changing from all liquids to solids of varying types and textures is making sure 'everything is working right'. Since I know she will likely read this someday I will pre-serve her modesty and leave it at that.

Juli also seemed to have come to an understanding with Chris. I don't recall if I told you but she pretty much 'broke up' with Chris, as much as she could in her state anyway. The funny part about that is you can tell it was just out of pure annoyance with his intimate role in her care. So we did what we could to adjust his tasks so it was less personal care and more support and encouragement. Even though he was doing both all along, the former was something Juli was getting very adamant about wanting only mommy to handle. But gradually she has been warming back up to Chris and today told us girls at least that she still plans to marry him. (Thank God, you know how much MONEY I already spent on that wedding??) That might be three corners…

Last night she had a few friends over and her beloved cat Simba also. She had a really good time, as we all did.

Right now she is working on talking with Mackenzie and let me tell you that little Mackenzie is a tough teacher.

"Say, 'BUCKLE', Juli." Mackenzie told her

"buuuu-lll" Juli mumbled

"No, that's not right. Say 'BUCK-LE' " Mackenzie corrected with emphasis. Pause…sigh…"Bu-ckle" Juli said

Mackenzie smiled "Good, let's keep going….."

And they are.

January 26, 2010 - 5 am

Our trade-off options are taking on new meaning. Yesterday at therapy Juliana broke her toe. There was not a clear explanation of how or when and in fact there was some speculation if it was even broken but my untrained eye says 'yes'. It wiggled around like a loose tooth. It was slightly swollen, moderately red-on-its-way-to-bruised, and possibly painful. All of that sounds pretty non-committal, right? Well our resource is not always to be trusted: Juliana that is. Her recollection or participation is best described as 'in and out' so we are never really sure when she says something hurts if it really does. The rehab staff thinks the break happened because of her muscle toning causing poor foot position. The possible break is to her second toe on her left foot, her strong leg so that is where she is putting most of her weight. When Chris called me to tell me I asked to speak to the nurse there. Although she was in a hurry to leave for the day she took a moment to talk to me. How nice of her.

"Does this mean that we have to be concerned about other bones breaking?" I ask.

She said, "No, she is not likely low on calcium so I don't suspect she will have a problem with bones breaking."

Blink. "But she did." I stated.

"Well it's just her second toe, the very tip, I wouldn't even worry about it, it won't be a problem for therapy and it doesn't seem to hurt her." She said.

"But I want to understand WHY it happened so I can prevent it from happening again. If her muscle tone is so strong to break her bones, shouldn't we address the muscle tone? Can't she be approved for Botox?"

"The doctor has to determine if it is bad enough or if the muscle relaxers are working well enough." She said.

"If the muscle tone is causing her to break bones, I would say she needs it. I would like to prevent this from happening again" I stated.

Well let's see what the doctor here says tomorrow, maybe she will agree to give her the Botox injections because she does have a lot of muscle tone. Her bones are fine; you don't have to worry about them breaking. She is young and strong."

"But a bone DID break. If nothing 'happened' to break her bone and you think that muscle toning is responsible (which I am unconvinced about still) then we need to stop the muscle toning, right." I was getting a little agitated at this point.

"The doctor will determine if the medicine she is on now is working or not."

(Little voice in my head) 'Give up Janet…just focus on pushing for the Botox, let go of the logic.'

"The doctor was willing to give her the muscle relaxers as an interim step to try to correct this problem," she said.

I corrected, "This doctor did not prescribe the muscle relaxers, her neurologist did."

"Oh, you could have gotten them here."

"But we saw the doctor every week here and she DIDN'T prescribe them." I said.

"Well you should get all of your prescriptions rewritten here since we are managing your rehab care. Normally when they release you from RIC they only give you a month's supply then we write new prescriptions for what you need."

"Interesting. We have been coming here for 6 weeks and no one prescribed anything or even asked if our prescriptions were running out. I just assumed it was my responsibility and I guess it's a good thing because she would have been without everything for the last two weeks. We were told that the doctors here would handle everything but since she saw the doctor each week and she didn't prescribe anything, we worked with our own doctors." I explained.

"Well next time just tell us what you need," she said encouragingly as if we had reached an understanding.

"Ok, we need Botox." Sounds simple to me.

"The doctor will have to decide." I am wearing her down, I can feel it....

"So, if the doctor isn't 'ready' to go with Botox, can we take her somewhere else and just pay for it out of pocket?"

"Oh, you can pay for it out of pocket here." She says happily thinking she has offered me something encouraging.

Ok, now I am REALLY annoyed. "So, the doctor is willing to do it, doesn't object to doing it, she just has to decide if she is willing to bill the insurance or not, is that what I am hearing?"

Line silence.

"Let's just wait and talk to the doctor tomorrow."

To quote Joey Tribiani..."letitgo".

Do you know what they call the person who graduates at the bottom of their class in medical school?

Doctor.

Stay tuned...

January 27, 2010 - 9:30 pm

The doctor agrees that Juliana's right ankle and right hand would benefit from the Botox and is submitting to the insurance company right away! If they turn it down we will just pay out of pocket. It doesn't make any sense to wait until the insurance company who has never examined Juli, approves the treatment she needs. But even the Botox won't solve it all. They will put it in her hand and ankle but her arm has to do it the hard way. We were given another arm brace that uses pressure to pull the arm forward for a stretch but allows for her to fold her arm when she tones. As you can imagine, that accessory is not popular with Juli. She tolerates it, if we distract her, but even that has its limits. We also noticed a very subtle, almost untrustworthy, change. It appears as if Juliana's right eye is opening. Now you'll recall that it took a full month for Juli to open her left eye completely so it's not inconceivable that her right eye is beginning the slow ascent as well. I want to believe this is that process happening again but I just don't know yet. She has her eye surgery scheduled for February 15th and that is when her lower eyelid will be cut and folded outward so her eyelashes will no longer sit on her eye. Ewww....I know, you can say it; it grosses me out to type it. But who knows? Maybe her eye will miraculously heal like the rest of her.

In addition to that, it seems that we might have another little obstacle behind us: Her anger seems to be more appropriate now. She doesn't lash out irrationally and seems to be back in love with Chris, asking him to carry her and lay with her on the couch. When he isn't here she asks where he is and when he will return. Penny by penny....

We haven't even hit the 4 month mark, though we are close, and she is doing so much better. She is eating all the time now and the feeding tube is more for quick and easy caloric intake and some medicines. Thank goodness for our Team Juli Angel, dietician and friend, Jennifer Conway for helping us to reduce our dependency on it and get Juli eating all the right calories. If it weren't for her dedication to helping us with that goal, we would be on the plan from RIC... "That's the LAST thing you worry about. Some people have that in for 6 months." We don't want to be those people. And what is even cooler about having Jennifer help us with Juli's eating is that is the eating has catapulted Juli into talking all the time, even if we can't understand her. We understood her very well when she said, "I'm ready" in response to my request to "let me know when you are ready for dessert." Then she equally clearly said, "e - flan" to indicate what Michael was calling the dessert he brought over. Sometimes she's not so clear like when it took me twenty minutes tonight to figure out that she was telling me I was "being ridiculous". I laughed hysterically.

Our night was a visit to the doctor for pre-surgery tests as well as another adjustment, (which she also does not like...let's just say she cracked like Humpty Dumpty). The doctor also confirmed my earlier suspicions of a possible sinus infection. Though she wasn't showing any normal signs of cold or flu, she was complaining about just the right things to have the doc put her on an antibiotic. We came home to a fabulous dinner for 20 (I am not even joking) made by Maida's mom and delivered all the way from Plainfield by Michael. And even though Juliana had just finished throwing up her lunch in the car (sorry guys, hope you weren't eating) she was ready for a refill. That's my girl! After all that, an intentional shower for Juli and an accidental one for me, she finally fell asleep and I am ready to collapse...wait...not until I run to Walgreens for her prescription. Sigh...No rest for the wicked.

January 29, 2010 - 7 pm

Many times Chris and I discussed the possibility of Juliana not returning to her former self. I must have mentioned this to you guys at least once, right? Well, having watched Chris grow up these last 8 years as well as Juli, I have become invested in his happiness as well. We recognized that regardless of where she ends up in her recovery she will always be my daughter, but she has to progress to a certain point to become his wife. We all know this. It is the scary undercurrent of all of his frantic attempts to help her recover. I tried to give Chris the opportunity to walk away from all of this and in fact have asked him to in moments when things got tense. But so far, the boy is sticking around. He told me once, "You know, all I really planned for my future was music. Then it was music *and* Juliana. So it's not like I had this driving desire to be married with children that was all wrapped up in Juliana. So without her, that doesn't exist so don't worry about me, I am fine just to wait." (Yeah, it was pretty awesome for me to hear too) But you see now that this chapter of life has turned from death defying into painful rehabilitation, I am feeling comfort but Chris still cannot find peace in himself. He wants his music to mean something yet he isn't sure it matters anymore. He wants his future to mean something but he isn't sure what that is anymore either. I ache for him like he was my own. And I know that Gloria and Steve are sad to see their son struggle with this and want Chris to have his life back as well as Juli. To them I want to say that I love your son too and want that for him as well. Chris and his band have a show coming up next Tuesday night at Schubas in Chicago and he was nearly going to skip playing it. I think he needs to do it. He is afraid he might not feel at home on the stage anymore. I think he needs to do it. He thinks he won't feel right without Juliana in the audience. I think he needs to do it. He is a talent that needs to be appreciated and I would feel doubly sad if his talent was lost in this bump in the road.

Maybe we will see you at the show...

January 30, 2010 - 9:45 pm

Before I forget, Chris's show as Schubas is NEXT Tuesday.

What a bizarre day. Juliana started the day with a pretty severe stomach ache that had me ready to call the doctor. I was talking to myself as much as her when I said, "what could be causing this?" She shrugged and moaned and then started making unfamiliar hand gestures. Now this is not uncommon. No sooner do we develop cues for communicating when her speech is unclear than she changes them to something all her own. But this time the gesture was able to be deciphered. She was gesturing a pregnant belly. I asked her why she was doing that because it looked like she was saying she had a baby in her belly and she said, "I had it already." Naturally I was confused and a little tinge of concern was starting. "When did you have a baby Juli?" She mumbled, "I just did." (Getting weirder, I know) "Where did you have a baby?" I asked. "Right here" she told me. Now before I go on, think about what you would do: You have a daughter who has a brain injury but also has most of her faculties. She is aware of most things but occasionally confused. Discussing what could be a sensitive and heartbreaking subject, I thought of a different ways to respond and finally went with, "No Juli, you didn't have a baby. You must have had a dream. Was it a girl or a boy? Its ok, with all the medications you are on, it is understandable that you would be confused and not know it was a dream." She just blinked, looked sad and said very sheepishly, "oh". I feel like I just had to tell my daughter she LOST her baby and she looked like that is exactly what I DID say. We talked for a few minutes more while I reinforced that it must have been a dream and asked her to tell me about my dream grandchild, etc. She seemed to settle for that eventually but she was never totally convinced. Ok, so let me fast forward through the rest of the day. She was talking a lot and also very clear. It was nice to have a conversation where she didn't have to repeat her words five times and then be asked to spell it one letter at a time while writing it as well. She was practicing singing songs which I found was far more productive for getting her to pronounce words. She was so aware and engaging that I almost forgot the morning confusion. But then Allison stopped by and asked her what she did all day and she said, "I went to the hospital." (She didn't, I would have told you) And Allison said, "What? Why did you go to the hospital?" And do you know what she said? Sure you do, she said, "To have my baby" I told you it was bizarre. I reminded her that it was just a dream and if she did have a baby wouldn't the baby be here now? Wouldn't Chris be here too? Wouldn't she notice 'our' baby making a permanent dent in my arm? She was still not convinced but said that she wondered if she might be pregnant. I assured her that she had been tested and we were going to have to find another reason for her stomach ache. Poor kid. The line between reality and whatever is going on in her head is very blurred. We should be concerned with memory loss but instead she seems to have additional memories of things that didn't happen. I am not sure if this is normal, but I haven't seen normal in four months so I am not even sure I would recognize it. She did drop the subject as did I. Then just now as I was putting her in bed she groaned and held her stomach...here we go again.

Oh, it was a girl.

February 2, 2010 - 5 am

Back in 1990 when Juli and Adam were my only kids, their dad and I took a road trip to Gatlinburg. In an effort to make the ride bearable we packed games in separate bags for rotating to avoid boredom with the same things to play with. I also drew maps to stick on the backs of our seats for each of them to see where we were coming from, where we would stop along the way and where we were going. I thought, if I make this trip as much about the journey as the destination, then the vacation can begin when we pull out of the driveway. Now I admit that back then when I was...er....12 (ahem) I probably wasn't quite that evolved in my thinking but I did recognize that my life was forever more going to be about raising my kids. In spite of all of those preparations, including the color coded map I drew by hand (before Map-Quest my friends) I heard the inevitable, "Are we there yet?" That is when we came up with the saying, "We are almost to the almost." Since then that phrase has been used in our home hundreds of times to mean exactly that:

We aren't almost there, but we are close to being able to say we are almost there. It gives a kind of comfort of its own, like a '1/3 of the way so I can still hang on because there is an end in sight' mentality. It's also the next thing that I have been waiting for in this journey.

Four months ago today Juliana had her accident and I think we are 'Almost to the Almost'.

Yesterday she walked 20 meters holding the walker without stopping. The therapist has to secure her right leg so it doesn't buckle but it requires less support to do so. She answers nearly every question correctly that is posed to her in an attempt to test her mental capacity. She attempts and succeeds at every difficult task to extend her extremely painfully constricted right hand. And her right eye is about 1/4 of the way open. We have settled into a routine where none of this feels sad or bad, at least not from our perspective. Even the glimmers of Juliana's depression seem to have given way to just tolerance and perseverance. Now our conversations regularly include what we will do 'once she is better' and she has lots of ideas. She has restaurants planned as well as vacation spots. Let me tell you, I plan to hit them all. She talks about the kids she will have (I think she is now saying four...Doh!) and that she wants to try out for American Idol one more time. Sometimes I look at her and feel guilty but not for what you might think. Guilty because I am....happy. Not happy for the accident but happy for the change in me, the change in my perspective and the opportunity that I was given to still have my daughter's recovery to live through. We still have many months ahead of us before she is able to walk on her own and fully care for herself but if we overlook the pockets of strange thoughts (which to be fair, she always had her own way of looking at things that was just slightly left of center) then it's truly all good. I suspect it may have gotten more comfortable for me than other members of Team Juli because I am in my comfort zone: at my home with my kids doing it my way. The control freak in me is, well, under control so I have a balance that Chris and others have yet to completely find.

The good news is, they too are 'almost to the almost'.

February 4, 2010 - 4 pm

Food fairies are everywhere! Paula Leuder and Dawn Slattery are among the latest making sure my family eats. It is a blessing to have all of you in our circle. That is the good news. The bad news, (or maybe bad is too strong?) is that once again I spoke too soon. I might have gotten a little too optimistic about where we are and the state of Juliana's mood. We have had a couple of days of odd comments and quiet behavior that indicate to us that she is in fact, rather depressed. I can certainly imagine. For as much work and drama as this is on all of us, we have hours or days where we have the option to resume our lives. For Juliana, who is aware enough to know where she is, and intact enough to know where she isn't, well, 'resuming' is a thing of the future. I believe this will all be a distant memory someday and am looking for that fast forward button as we speak. Not for myself, I can accept the pace for the greater good. I am locked and loaded and ready to do battle as long as it takes (don't remind me of that when I get down) but for Juli I want this to go fast I want, (who am I kidding, I have ALWAYS wanted) to take away the bad, quickly and painlessly. What parent wouldn't?

I am not quite sure how to solve this one. I mean, we certainly flood her with the positives: telling her how well she is doing, how fortunate she is and how her hard work is paying off but I don't think it is sinking in. I ask her what she specifically wants to get better, hoping to have a tangible problem to solve (I am actually from Mars) and she says 'Talking' so we spend time working on that. The changes are coming but they are so gradual it is like watching hair grow. So if it often feels to me like the days are running in place, I bet it does for her even more so. I think she is also a bit bored as well and I am not sure how to solve that in ways that we aren't already. She has visitors, her favorite music and TV shows. All her favorite foods and her pets even visit. She spends a lot of time eating and the rest in therapy or sleeping. There isn't much else she can do but she is really in a funk. I asked her today to promise to give us 3 more months to prove to her that she will get better. If after 3 months she still is where she is now, I would …well…I just don't know what I would do but I had to say something, didn't I?? She is talking the tiniest bit more clear and she is eating more as I said, but I think she needs an accomplishment, an independent achievement that would make her feel like she is moving forward. I try to will it, wish it, organize it right into her life but it's all happening at its own pace and outside of my control. She walks a little tiny bit stronger, her mind is a bit clearer, (if not a bit weirder), and yet it's just not enough cumulatively for her to accept as forward. We are also working with some amazing people to help address her various imbalances in the hopes that adjusting her physiologically will help her mentally as well. Tony Breitbach, you are a wonderful, organic genius who, for whatever reason, has decided to help little old us. Thank you for your time and expertise. So for all of the medical professionals who warned us that the road was long, and hard, and filled with ups and downs...they were right.

February 6, 2010 - 11 am

Well! I can see that you have very strong opinions about depression. Odd juxtaposition, don't you think? I mean, the hallmark for depression is the LACK of strong opinions, energy and interest and that very condition is igniting so many of you to comment in support of bolstering my little girl. It feels as if you can actually give her YOUR energy. Incredible really. Thank you all for that, once again. Juliana has been approved for the Botox injections. That means that next Tuesday she will look younger than Mackenzie, right? Ok so maybe this will be a little different application of the product. They will inject a portion into her right hand and a portion into her right foot. The expectation is that we will gradually see her hand open and she will be able to use her right hand. What no one has been able to explain to me is what will make her hand STOP contracting? Is it healing of the brain that will help stop the spasticity? I suspect the answer is the same one size fits all that we have gotten for every other problem: Time. I also had a very good chat with the Clinical Manager at RIC in Homewood and they will start doing a couple of things to help Juli cope with her situation. Now that she is communicating effectively and is extremely aware she has begun seeing the counselor there. After evaluating her they agree that Juli would benefit from antidepressants. I was really hoping to not go down that road but I understand that this is chemical warfare as much as beat the clock so... bring on the drugs...! Beginning the end of February Juli will start going to physical therapy 5 hours a day. By then the Botox will have had a chance to kick in, the eye surgery will be behind her and the antidepressants will have had a chance to start working. Sounds like a plan, right? Somewhere in the middle of this we will also be introducing new vitamins and supplements and maybe even decreasing her sleep medication. Phew! As much as I like to work on all fronts at the same time, I am getting a little motion sick myself. There is so much to consider all at once. Too much change, too many moving parts and I think we might need to slow it down just a bit. But nagging in the back of my mind is the dreaded 'plateau'. Sometimes I wonder if this is as good as it will get but that thought is fleeting and of course we assure Juli that she will get darn close to back to normal. I really believe it but I have to remind myself also how far she's come. Her sadness is so clear now that I wonder how I even missed it or thought it was gone for a short time. The counselor said that in some ways it is a good thing because that is an indicator of her level of awareness. I asked her if she wanted to have a day out that didn't include therapy and she said yes but she wasn't interested in any of the options I gave her. We will keep working on it but so far her only yes answers were to restaurants, and that we might be able to accommodate. I asked her if she was interested in going back to Holsteins if they end up having the benefit they talked about and she actually said she would go. Hmmm, how about that? I was surprised at first then a little nervous because she might not be ready for that kind of an outing just yet. Maybe late March? So for you planners, if Juliana is invited, maybe give her another month or so? Her birthday is March 26th so...well...timing is everything. Also, for the eye trackers out there, Juli's right eye is just the tiniest smidge open more. I am terrible at fractions but if I said 1/4 open last time, its, well, open more...3/8 perhaps? Well, I am listening to songs Juli and Chris recorded and I am getting a little misty eyed, hearing her voice again, so I am going to end this update before I rewrite it from my sadder perspective.

February 8, 2010 - 5 am

Remember in October and November when the changes to Juliana's condition were so slight that only the most discerning eye could see them? I feel that way again these days. We find ourselves trying to daily convince Juli she is getting better and you would think that just the fact that she is aware enough that we can HAVE that conversation would be convincing enough for her, but it's not. I used every analogy on her that I used on you guys: from the 'million dollars in pennies' to 'watching hair grow'. Nothing seems to assure her that this is not forever. I did get her to accept that we are 'almost to the almost' with some amount of consolation. She asked us the other day to take her off of the 'brain medicine'. I asked her why (though I feared the answer would be along the same lines as her desire to give up trying to heal) and she said, "Because it makes me imagine things". I sympathized with her and tried to tell her that recognizing that she is imagining is a good thing. The anger she was feeling is gone but perhaps it is replaced by depression, confusion and mild hallucinations? We are going to ask the doctor if this is a side effect of the injury or one of the many medications she is taking. Wanna bet they don't know for sure? Not that I expect them to KNOW, I just really wish they did. (Of course, I am googling all of the meds for my own investigation as well.) This is like a complex math problem sometimes. Finding the right balance of this medicine to counteract that symptom which might cause other things to get out of whack. I remember watching my brother go through similar trade-offs as he was fighting Leukemia and his wife was trying everything to fight the fires as they flared up. The lack of control over the situation is frustrating for everyone and I feel like I am letting Juli down by not getting to the root of her problems. Make no mistake, she is healing and improving but in that healing she is also feeling and expressing what she was not able to feel and express before: pain, discomfort, sadness, frustration, and concern. We are all trying to keep focused on the goodness in her ability to express.

We are also pushing Juliana to look and behave more like her old self, even if it is contrived. For example, although she technically can feed herself, in the interest of efficiency, we do it for her (bad Mommy, I know). Just like when you first allow a child to feed themselves, it can be very messy. We have been so focused on food quantity and quality; we neglected to help her do it herself. That is what we are trying to do now, help her to feed herself without making a big mess. She wants to go to restaurants and out to eat with friends so reclaiming her table manners is a step toward that. We are also handing her a mirror several times a day and asking her to smile. It looks familiar but forced and when we compliment her, she feel compelled to remind us the smile is fake. Regardless if the outward expression is forced, she does still show a sense of humor and throws in some funny and teasing comments once in a while. When the kids were getting into the difficult years and moodiness was an issue, I would tell them this little trick I learned: even when you are sad, make your face smile. You will feel silly doing so and the silliness will help you smile authentically. (Try it just once and see if it doesn't help a tiny bit). Plus there is something physically therapeutic about smiling that helps you feel better. Heck, I should know…I faked my way through the first

2 months of this ordeal by putting on a smile and, bada bing, bada boom, I really DO feel better. I can only hope that my pushing her to smile and talk and eat and behave like the old Juli isn't just for me and my comfort. Moms do that sometimes so I want to be careful that whatever we encourage from Juli is really in her best interest. I had a very insightful conversation with my girl Christine G and she forced a few light bulbs on. (Yeah, I heard ya lady, I am creating a lesson plan, really I am!) Wow! You know I just have to stop there and just appreciate all that I just told you....Do you SEE all she can do? Do you know how FAR she has come? I am just so grateful that we are here and able to tell you all of this! In fact, yesterday when we logged on her Facebook she said she wanted to put a status out there. She said, "People are going to freak out when they see me logged on." Since her vision is skewed, Cheyenne offered to type in whatever she wanted to post. After a few morbid suggestions from her that we quickly shot down (don't ask) she said, "ok, write, 'Juliana is on the mend' ". And that's what you will see on her page today.

Let's just go with that for a while.

February 9, 2010 - 4 pm

Once again, another hot topic with the support crowd!

So to be perfectly clear, the medication that Juliana is taking, (or being GIVEN to be more precise) are all doctor prescribed and mom approved. And I can assure you that I take nothing at face value with blind trust, not even in the doctors so when they say she 'needs' a medicine. I question it, research it and ask for advice from friends, family and strangers. But if you have been reading along, you already know that much about me. In fact, anyone who knows me recognizes that I question everything. If my dad where alive....boy the stories he would tell! Do we think we are making all the right choices? We are never 100% certain of that but we are sure that each decision is the best one we can make at the time. Ok, so the real question is whether or not to continue giving her the nuero-stimulators. The rest of the medicine is damage control: Anti-seizure, sleep aid, muscle relaxer and anti-depressants. I wish she needed none of the above but they all serve a valuable purpose for now. She does get quite a selection of vitamin supplements but those all get a group thumbs up. She doesn't take any pain medicine, other than the occasional ibuprofen, so all is right in the pharmaceutical world except for the Ritalin and Amantadine.   There is proof that introducing those medications to the comatose and minimally conscious patient does jump start the brain.   Even if I didn't believe the articles I read, I saw the proof myself in Juliana.   However there are some conflicting reports if the medication continues to work on someone once they are completely conscious.   That is why we are considering removing those medications, but timing is really important.   You see, we can't change, (or rather, I choose to accept good advice NOT to change) more than one thing at a time.   It is too hard to know what is working and what isn't, and where a particular reaction is coming from.   We planned to reduce or try removing the Ritalin once everything else stopped moving.   But that hasn't happened yet since so much has been changing for the last 4 weeks: we added muscle relaxer, then increased it, then added an antibiotic, then increased her sleep medication, added an anti-depressant and now she has had Botox to be followed early next week by surgery on her eye.   Any one or all of those things could change her body chemistry and outlook.   So I have decided not to remove those first stabilizing medications...yet.   Ultimately to get her off of all medications and onto all natural supplements and healthy habits is the goal.   But just like the other goals, it will take time to get there.

Can I just be grateful for a moment that everyone cares enough to comment?

Damn, Juliana is one lucky lady.

Juliana had her Botox today and I texted Chris, wanting him to ask Juliana if her hand and foot looked younger and he sent me this text: "Omg, she chuckled! She told me to tell you 'yes'." That's the first chuckle out of that girl in 4 months and 8 days. Good luck tonight Chris and The Able Body. Juliana and I will be thinking of you while you are onstage, hoping you only figuratively break a leg. Just get up there and do your thing!

February 11, 2010 - 10 pm

What is it about medical specialists that prevent them from acknowledging anything outside of their specialty? There is an arrogance that it so inappropriate you really want to take them down a peg, except of course, you need them for precisely the reason they are arrogant. We took Juli to her pre-op appointment and the ocular plastic surgeon and I noticed he had a pamphlet in his room on Ptosis and the surgical procedure that he could do to raise the upper eyelid. Well! That sounded like a topic worth bringing up since I really want that to be corrected if possible. He sounded insulted that I even asked the question. "No, I already told you that there is nothing that can be done. Hasn't the Ophthalmologist already told you this is a nerve problem?" he said. Take a breath, regroup...Then I said "Well we have never been told that this ISN'T a muscular problem. In fact, I don't know that the muscles in her eye were ever examined." He missed the sarcasm and he looked just as appalled that I would continue to ask but I went on. "What about the bone above her eye? Is that something you could repair?" He spun around to look at me and said, "I don't even know why you are asking me that. That is the neurologist's call and they said that brain matter was protruding so why would you want that to be repaired?" He thought I was an idiot, maybe I was but he was rude. "Well DOCTOR, I am ASKING because I don't have a glossary of which question goes to which doctor and for that matter we haven't had an MRI ever or an EEG lately or a CT Scan in months so maybe this would no longer be a problem? I don't know, I just thought you might know since every doctor seems to tell us the piece we ask about needs to be addressed with someone else." I was fuming but I kept quiet after that, even when he decided to give us advice on her car sickness which I doubt had anything to do with her eyelid. Whatever. He made me really angry and I thought about taking Juli out of there at that moment but then just put it on the list of one more aggravation I was going to have to take on the chin for the greater good. He came highly recommended so I was going to have to rely on that. My dad used to say, "It's nice to be liked, but it's not necessary." I guess that works for all people in authority, not just parents. He did try to test her vision in her right eye and we are still finding disappointing results. Now that she can talk, we can check her vision with more feedback and right now it doesn't seem that she can see out of her right eye in spite of earlier (possibly) false positives. When we asked her how she was able to see the number of fingers we had up before she said, "I was guessing." Gee, thanks for playing along.

As we wait for the effects of the Botox to kick in we still have to stretch her arm and leg to help defeat the muscle contractions. It's probably my imagination but she does seem the slightest bit more flexible already. She even kept her arm brace on for 3 hours before asking for it to be removed. Her speech is improving too and her desire to communicate is increasing. She also is eating all of her food by mouth now since no food is off limits. We even started giving her all of her medicine orally so the G Tube is next to go. In fact, Juli asked me tonight when she could get rid of the tube. I told her that we would pin Jennifer, our Dietician to a date on her next visit. So Jennifer, if you are reading…start your calculator and lets set a date because Juli wants her stomach back!

February 14, 2010 - 5 pm

Happy Valentine's Day! Juliana got the sweetest visit from Chris right before he left for work and she was very happy to see him. She wanted me to thank all of you for the cards you sent to show you are thinking of her. She was especially fond of the chocolate (which has become her drug in the past few days). I honestly did not know she liked chocolate this much! It's her 'thing to obsess on' I guess. Its 5 days post Botox and we haven't seen a significant change in her arm or leg but perhaps, just like every other change that occurred, it is slight. We are still accumulating our million in pennies. Her talking continues to improve as she tries to enunciate each syllable but as soon as she gets tired or winded, she trails off to squeaks and no one can understand her. I know she is improving but, greedy me, I want it faster. She has been saying sorry a bit lately for little things, and in general showing awareness of other people's feelings. I understand that as the brain matures you gradually learn empathy as you recognize your impact on others around you. She is at that stage of re-maturing. Today she apologized for always waking me up. I told her, "that's ok Juli; I was just lying there waiting for you to."

"Ok," she said, "but you need your beauty rest".

Ya gotta love the frankness of a TBI.

She has been smiling more and once in a while will claim it is real. She still doesn't seem happy but she accepts our description of improvement. She doubts that her future will be as bright as she originally planned it. In fact, she said to me yesterday that "this wrecked my relationship." I explained to her that I think it strengthened it. "Juli, remember all of the times that you and Chris fought about stupid unimportant things? It was because you didn't yet know what WAS important. Well, now you know." She looked at me for a moment then said, "I guess" But it's ok that she can't see yet how her life will be richer for enduring this, it's a 'retrospective kinda thing'. She has time to catch up. A good thing we noticed though... since we have backed her off one of the more 'suspicious meds' she seems to have stopped 'imagining things'. We are hoping that more of them can trail off as we pace ourselves slowly through to recovery.

The eye surgery scheduled for tomorrow has been postponed. With her upper eye opening ever so slightly we agreed to wait just a bit longer to see if her lower lid might heal enough on its own to not need the surgery. That might be naïve but a few extra weeks seemed a harmless risk. We are going to get a second opinion as well. When I called the rude doctor to break the news, he was not pleased and once again thought I was an idiot, this time for cancelling. That's ok, I am getting used to my decisions meeting objections. I figure as long as objections don't become obstacles, it's all good. My dad used to say, "If I get in a fight with a bear, you don't have to help me, just don't help the bear." Some days, 'absence of resistance' is as much as I can hope for. Other days total solidarity is the name of the game. We already know these days will be far behind us someday and she will fully recover. So I figure if we make well thought out choices for Juli we are also giving her the opportunity to look back at this journey and be proud of her accomplishments, (while hopefully not being embarrassed by what I communicate to you!) She has always been so self-conscious and aware of how she is perceived; I will be satisfied to not have to apologize to her for any of my choices, actions, or words.

February 15, 2010 - 3 pm

A day in the life of a typical 23 year old girl:

A quick breakfast, shower, makeup, dress for the day. A trip to the mall with your sister and boyfriend to buy an outfit for a big date on Friday and new shoes for every day wear. Then it's lunch at the mall food court before heading to an appointment at the beauty salon for a quick touch up. That is really what Juli would call, 'a good day'. That is exactly what she did today.

DON'T YOU JUST LOVE IT??!!!

I am so happy for that normalcy to be in her life today that I could cry. How many of you ARE that 23-year-old and do those things without thinking they are so special? How many of you are the parents of that 23-year-old who think she is wasting her day doing those things? I guess appreciation has everything to do with your vantage point.

Friday night Chris has a show and Juliana is going to attend. That means we will spend the week planning the logistics for making that happen. (Another thing that I previously took for granted.) This has continued to really test my 'planning' skills but at least I feel like they are really needed as opposed to building spreadsheets of preparation and cleaning duties before a big party. How irrelevant that seems to be now. So I am home (Bank Holiday, yeah!) waiting for Juli, Cheye and Chris to come home from their day to hear how they managed. Cheyenne will talk about the clothes, the food and the deals they should have taken. Chris will talk about how much Juliana ate, how she used her hand and leg, and some sweet comment Juli made about the clothes he chose. And Juli will look lovely, be rejuvenated and yet still tell me that her day was "Bad". That is until I remind her that she is supposed to consider the question 'How was your day' POST accident. Once she thinks about it that way, she will modify her answer and say, "OK, it was good."

Remember, it all depends on your vantage point.

February 18, 2010 - 10 pm

I had almost forgotten that the pendulum could still swing the other way. I stopped thinking about the fact that we weren't out of the woods yet. I had myself convinced that this whole situation was just slow and steady so the worst I ever got was impatient, never really worried anymore. That might have been premature.

Let me back up...

The kids went to the mall and it was very enjoyable and normal. They bought new outfits (but forgot the everyday shoes that I told them over and over to get but who listens to the mom?? But back to the story) Then they went to the beauty salon and came home in just enough time for Chris to go to work and Cheyenne to run to wherever she runs to...probably 'BDubs'. Anyway it gave me a chance to ask Juli how she enjoyed getting out and going somewhere of HER choosing and how she liked having a bit of her life back.

She said "Good. What's for dinner?'

Nice chatting with you Jules.

Speaking of dinner….more food angels! Liz Dampf and her mom stopped by with a very tasty and very large meal which we ate that very night for dinner. Juli actually ate so much she turned down the brownie…for about a half an hour.

The next day Chris attempted to take Juli to a movie. After a morning that including hair pulling and eventual apologies they went to Starbucks for lunch and coffee then to the theater to see "Wolfman".

They got Sprite and Nachos and made it all the way through the Previews before Juliana had to go to the bathroom. By the way, do you know that they don't have accommodations at the theater for a male to take a female to the bathroom? Chris and I talked about it ahead of time and he said, "Then I will just go in the women's with her". And he did.

Anyway, they got back to the movie which had already started and Juliana was restless and sleepy and not really paying attention. It took only a few minutes before she 'needed to go to the bathroom again' which is sometimes a code for, "get me out of here". Chris concluded that it's just too soon for that. It's really not surprising; she doesn't even pay that close of attention to American Idol.

Tuesday night she didn't sleep well. Not an 'up all night cage rattler' but still, she didn't completely sleep. That meant that Wednesday she was tired for most of the day. She had a massage in the morning and a visit with her Dietician in the afternoon. Which reminds me…we scheduled her G-Tube removal for next Thursday!! I was pushing for sooner but Jennifer thought it was wise to wait another week. I bet she wanted more than that but she saw the begging and pleading from both of us and agreed to be comfortable with next week. Let's hope that will still be possible.

I keep getting side tracked. So Wednesday night Juli didn't sleep well again. That means that again today, she was very tired. But her fatigue seems to be increasing and today I started getting a little worried. I googled everything I could think of and landed on possible shunt malfunction. Now I may be blowing it way out of proportion but I called the Neurologist anyway and he advised me to make an appointment. He didn't sound concerned but why would he based on my proportionately harmless complaint of: excuse me Doctor but, my daughter is sleepy, should I worry? She just seems…TOO sleepy. She can barely open her eyes, sleepy. I told Juli if she is like this tomorrow, she was not going to Chris's show. She said, "Ok" and then drifted off for her 2 minute nap. Yeah, you see where I am going? So I will re-evaluate tomorrow after what I hope will be a restful night. Chris is on couch duty tonight so I actually going to try to get some sleep of my own.

February 19, 2010 - 7 am

She slept all night.

You know I was never a worrier before all of this and now…geez…ok, so I guess I will see how she is today. Maybe she really was just tired. We may be at the show tonight after all!! Here are the details for tonight if you haven't seen them already: Sylvie's 1902 W Irving Park Rd (Ravenspark).

Show starts at 8, The Able Body goes on at 9. (21 and over)

February 22, 2010 - 5 am

So the show the other night went well for Chris but not as well for Juliana. She did go… but she didn't stay. All week long, (and all that day) she really wanted to go, looked great, and seemed happy the whole way there. Once she got there she said her feet hurt and it kind of went downhill from there. (I tend to not ask her or any of the kids for that matter, a question I am not willing to accept their answer to. For example, asking a 2 year old if they want to go to sleep is really pointless if it is bedtime and you are putting them to bed anyway.) So with that in mind, as I watched her out of the corner of my eye, when Juli got slightly uncomfortable at the show, I just let her talk with her friends as a distraction, hoping she would just tolerate whatever it was until the show ended. Too late…the questions started: "Do you want to leave?" And eventually the answer was "Yes". Then the 'Yes' was reinforced often enough that there was no choice but to honor her request and take her home…just as Chris was beginning to play. Big bummer. Juliana even said in the car ride home that she was disappointed she didn't stay. Yeah, me too (That's why sometimes you don't give kids or brain injured people choices). She would have been interested and distracted enough while he played that she would have suddenly wanted to stay, we just gave her an 'out' too quickly. She gets an idea in her head and you have to really work to distract her. She used to pull on her G Tube until we distracted her with something else. Now she asks to go to the bathroom every few minutes and often it's just for 'something to do'. If she is involved in an activity of any kind, or a visit she is enjoying, she doesn't even think about going to the bathroom. The power of suggestion is strong with her so we generally try not to suggest anything negative or depressing and certainly not something that we don't want her to do. Team Juli will just have to huddle and develop a game plan before the next outing because that was a very long drive for a very short stay.

We are now into planting positive thoughts. She has been given the task every time she stands up (which is every few minutes to take her to the bathroom) to smile and tell us one thing she is happy about. She doesn't even need to be reminded anymore; she just has that smile ready. Last night I said, 'Ok, what is your happy thought?" She said, "That I have you." *sob*

"Back atcha girlie."

We got dinner delivered to us again yesterday, thank you my lovely sister-in-law Toula. With so much on her plate as well, it's very touching that she still has time to feed my family. That is what this experience has taught me: Some people are just never too tired or too busy to just be there for you. I have a great family and my siblings rock in that department.

We started using an amplifier and microphone to help Juli hear herself and improve our ability to hear her as well. She is getting much louder and clearer but still, it helps. Mackenzie has taken over that little task and routinely 'interviews' Juli to get her to talk. She is a great little girl. Juli is always saying, "Ask me questions" or "Talk to me" and it struck us that she is willing and able to carry on a conversation but not initiate it. It's still part of what we had previously heard that as much as we want her to do what she can on her own, she isn't able to initiate the action. It's all odd. I would like to get more coaching on the specifics of her particular injury. Of course we do our own research of the areas of the brain affected but since the emphasis has been on treating her medically we haven't spent much time on understanding her and treating her behaviorally. That is where we find ourselves most perplexed of course. Her behavior is what we live with and try to decipher each day. Her reality is clearly skewed, yet, still based in reality. It throws us for a loop sometimes and we get lulled into thinking we are talking with a rational person when suddenly she will say something that reminds us that she is a long way from normal. It's like Tim Burton scripted this portion of her life. I also happen to hate the fact that "we just don't know" has become an acceptable answer in this field. I mean, what the HECK?

Just one more adventurous step through TBI Land.

February 24, 2010 - 10:30 pm

Yesterday at therapy we learned that in order to get the maximum benefit from the Botox procedure we have to increase the muscle stretches on Juli's arm and leg. In addition, the braces that Juliana has to wear on her legs, arm and wrist must be worn for most of the day. For those of you who have seen Juli while she has her braces on, you know this is going to be extremely unpopular. Chris explained to the therapists that she appears to be in so much pain when she has the braces on. Although we put them on for periods of time, doing so feels like abuse. They told him that in their opinion, NOT putting them on is abuse. Well. So they put together a schedule of alternating having the braces on and off so she gets some relief wearing each brace at least 3 hours a day. We can't put them all on at once and for the arm brace in particular, 3 hours straight would be torture. So that means many of her waking hours she is begging for mercy. I keep saying a soothing, "I know honey, I know" and she just gives me a sorrowful and truthful, "No you don't." We can distract her somewhat from trying to pull them off, usually by feeding her something so we try to schedule her brace time to coincide with her meal times. If she develops an eating disorder as a result of this unhealthy association we will just have to get her therapy and a gym membership later. I think the stretching is working though because inch by precious inch we are able to see her hand open just a touch more and with the slightest bit less pain. Her ankle appears easier to move into position and her arm definitely lengthens with greater ease. Her mind is there but then there are things that continue to be 'off'. She imagines the braces are on her when they aren't, she recalls things that just never happened and can go from adult to child in 5 seconds flat. I quizzed her on her sibling's middle names and who they were named after and she was correct on every one. Then I asked her for her own middle name and she drew a blank. How odd. She really couldn't recall it at all but then I said, "What was my name before I got married." She said correctly, "Spencer" then looked at me and said, "My middle name is Spencer." Guess that one just slipped through the Swiss cheese hole for a moment.

So, we are going to do what we can to get her through these next couple of months in the hope that this is like basic training. She could possibly make great strides with the aggressive stretching. Here's hoping so because sometimes … this pace is maddening. Living it every day, with most days seeming nearly the same as the one before it, you start to wonder if there really is a change. I mean, I know there is, there must be…her hair is definitely growing. I ask everyone who visits, 'so, now that you have seen her, do you think she is doing better or worse than your perception from what you read?' Most people say 'better' but I wonder if that is truthful or just to encourage me. (Ann, I need your honestly out here please. Any chance you are coming this way soon??) In the meantime as we survive the daily chaos, (another reality that any visitor can attest to) wonderful people like the Dampf's continue to help ease our workload by dropping off dinner. Then there are the wonderful Angels, Jennifer and Dena who continue to take their personal time to help Juliana in their own special ways. I am so ordinary yet still this extra help is offered to me. I have to come up with a huge payback…or pay forward. And as if that wasn't enough, Juliana's former place of employment, Holsteins is sponsoring a benefit for Juli on March 27th from 3-8 pm. Details can be found in the Facebook event 'For Juliana: Almost to Almost.'

Cute name guys, wish I'd thought of it.

Tomorrow is a big day for Team Juli as well. Juliana is getting her G-tube out! She is very excited about it and so am I. I wanted this badly for a long time now because I need to be able to have a tangible gain I can point to when Juliana thinks she isn't improving. I want her to see the scar for what it is: a challenge she has overcome.

February 28, 2010 - 9 pm

Well I know it has been 4 days since I posted any update and in some regards time is flying by, but in others it seems to have stood still. So sorry for the delay, I know you want to know how Juliana is doing. (I am also behind on my email, voicemail and paper mail!) Juliana did get her tube out as planned on Thursday. The doctor just gave it a tug and it popped right out. It looked like a little plunger. The incision barely even bled and closed up on its own. It didn't require a stitch and she doesn't even have a bandage on it anymore. In addition to having the tube taken out she also had an adjustment which she really does not like. To celebrate we went to Olympic Star for dinner since that was one of Juli's favorite late night haunts. She made a good attempt to feed herself but the Grecian salad was a little too optimistic. I was also once again reminded that 'handicap accessible'...isn't always. Navigating the hallway to the bathroom was difficult enough but the stall, although larger than normal was not big enough for her chair. I will spare you the compromises I made.

As instructed, we are putting the braces on Juliana for a majority of the day. She hates it of course and by extension, hates us. We try to explain to her that it is for her own good but she has a hard time accepting that while they are on. She does however rely on expectation setting so when we put them on her she immediately wants to know when they are coming off. That seems to help...some. The good news is regardless of how she feels about them, they are working. Her hand is more easily opened, her arm has greater extension and she is able to walk more often since her ankle is supported. In fact, when she has the leg braces on, instead of wheeling her to the bathroom or up the stairs, we walk. It's really quite an accomplishment but it's also pretty hard for her to do it. I said to her, "Come on Juli, as much as you hate these braces, aren't you happy when you are walking as well as you do?" She said, "Well, I'm happy when I'm done." I suppose that is all we can ask for right now. She said that the braces hurt her feet so there is an appointment set in three weeks for them to be evaluated and adjusted as necessary. That is one of the many downsides to day rehab: nothing happens quickly. I would love to say that I am as impressed with this day rehab as I was with the other facilities she has been to but sadly, I am not. They are supposed to be guiding us and setting examples (I guess...maybe I am expecting too much) but as soon as Juli expresses dislike for the braces, they cave in and either take them off or don't put them on. (Thanks for making US the bad guys.) No wonder Juli thinks that we are telling the therapists to put them on more often. There are several other examples that make me less than pleased here but I will address them with the facility directly.

Although her progress is evident in some ways, in other ways we have to look closer. She isn't talking any better than she had been and that is some-times very frustrating. But then if I turn on the radio and ask her to sing along...with complete abandon she makes a warbled attempt, remembering more words than I. Anyone who knows Juli knows that she may be able to spend a lifetime being less active but NOT less communicative so we need to increase the momentum in that direction. It just doesn't seem to be possible to advance on all fronts at the same time so maybe her energy and healing are going toward physical improvements? At least that is what I tell myself. Another subtle improvement is that she seems to be moving her head from side to side more fluidly and she has more eye control with the eye she can open. This might not be anything noteworthy but any step toward more normal movements and activity is change in my bank. And if you are tracking progress of her right eye, it is still mostly closed, occasionally 1/3 open and the bottom lid…well…some days it looks better, some days it looks the same. I have an appointment with another Neuro Ophthalmologist but not until early April. We continue to have to encourage Juli to be positive since she sees only the negative and on the top of her list is "being half blind". She wasn't at all comforted by my attempt to show her all that we can 'see' more clearly now as a result of her accident: how precious life is, how good people are, how strong we can be when tested, how much we can overcome. This road ahead is still long for all of us so I guess time will tell.

March 1, 2010 - 11:45 pm

Once again, I am proven wrong. Its ok, I am starting to like it, especially when I am feeling negative and she turns my perspective around. Juliana had, what Chris calls, "A rock star day." In other words, she had a very successful day at therapy. During her PT session they were noticing that her right leg was stronger and straighter than it had been and said, "You know what? I think we could try her on the treadmill."

And they did.

Her once wobbly legs moved with the pace of the belt, awkwardly at first as she tried to keep up, and then when the speed was adjusted, more comfortably, one leg after the other. She hated it and it was hard but she stuck with it the whole time. They assured her that the next time would be easier. She vowed there would be NO next time. Then during OT she was able to utilize the pulley to fully extend both of her arms over and over again using even her right hand to grip the handle. This exercise she said was easy so I am sure tomorrow they will up the ante. After a morning begging to not go to therapy, the day was probably the nightmare she expected. I keep telling her that I promise she will be grateful for all the hard work later. She remains unconvinced. Brain injuries will do that to you. She continued to practice her writing and her speaking and when she came home from therapy and I came home from work, I asked her how her day was. And with perfect volume and clarity she gave the answer I expected: "It was really, really terrible."

Let me rephrase the question…

"Juli, on a scale of 1-10 how well did the therapists say you did today?"

"10," she admitted. 'Terrible' sounds pretty wonderful to this mom. Tomorrow, Chris is planning to videotape Juli at therapy so we can share her progress with you.

We once again had a fabulous dinner prepared and delivered by the Dampfs and Juliana was very ready to eat after her hard work at therapy. I asked her if she wanted to eat in the family room (her makeshift bedroom) or the kitchen.

"I want to walk up the stairs," she told me.

"You have to have your braces on then," I said.

"Ok, "she said. "Do you promise to take them off?"

"Sure, right after dinner, we will come right back down and I will take them off." Let me just tell you, it took twice as long to get the braces on than it did for her to go up the stairs. She can walk the stairs better than across the floor! Here's how it works: She holds the handrail with her left hand and I stand behind her with my hands under her arms, just steadying her. She lifts her feet, stair over stair even, until she is at the top of the stairs. Its 6 steps and she does it pretty much without stopping. Then at the top of the stairs, someone is there to steady her while I get up there to help her the next few steps toward the table. Going downstairs is another story. We sit her on the floor and scoot her down, one step at a time until her feet touch and then she stands. It's so simple. It's something I will gladly give up but it works for now. It's also much easier than having the guys carry her chair up and down. And an additional bonus: she works so hard that she sleeps hard too. A great relief for whoever is on the couch that night. Tonight it's Chris and I am off to bed.

March 2, 2010 - 11:45 pm

5 months ago today….

I keep counting thinking it means something, but I can't decide if it is time lost or time earned. My thoughts still swing wildly from the past to the present. I look back at the pictures from the early days of October and can manage a sigh of relief. Then I look see pictures from our luau in August and feel sad. I think about how much Juliana has overcome in these last 5 months, the odds she has defied, and I am proud. But then I think about the shower and wedding that couldn't take place in 2009 and get mad. I look at this girl who is regaining expression, opinions and voice, and I am grateful. But then I remember her infectious laugh, smile and personality and I cry. I know she is coming back, but I also know that she will return differently, and as a result, life is going to forever be different as we learn to accept that a little more each day. (Ok, honestly it's more like 'some days more than others'). I am realistic and I know that anyone's life can change in a moment and I am no more deserving of healthy stable children than any other mom. But I still wanted it, arrogantly expected it probably. For those of you who knew Juli before the accident, you know that, having her gone in any capacity is a cavernous void. I can reflect fondly on that 6 week old baby who won the 'Pretty Baby Contest' in 1986 and grew up to be a beautiful young lady. But what leaves me empty is missing that same young lady who had matured into my best friend. The tradeoff is that I am wiser and more aware and have developed a new appreciation for the gifts in my life. The flip side to that is that although I may not have had this much clarity before October 2nd, my prior ignorance was less painful.

But here we are in the present and in this moment, Juliana had another phenomenal day. The therapists, doctor and nurse are all so happy with her progress that starting next week she is going to have therapy 6 hours a day. And as happy as they are with Juli, that is how annoyed they are with us. They are a little put off by the steps we have taken on our own, 'without their involvement' which includes working toward the tube removal and vitamin supplements to replace some drugs. They tried to insinuate that Chris is a 'middle man' and that the rehab doctor should be coordinating her care. By the end of the conversation we all agreed on one thing: Juliana is exceeding all of our expectations.

And here is the real advancement today. Instead of the treadmill, today they decided to take it a step further. Juliana walked with a CANE. I could hardly believe she had that much balance, that much stability, that much strength in her step but Chris took video that made me cry all over again. You have got to see it to believe it. Now she wasn't doing it without being held on her right and without instructions still to "pick up her leg, straighten her knee and pull her leg through again", (relearning to walk is also relearning the mechanics of it) but still she was able to do it with just a cane. Crazy.

Once again, I feel like the energy and encouragement is coming from our wonderful support system so when I wallow in 'it' for a moment or two, you keep watching for my lovely daughter to return to her life. Thank you to my brother Michael and his awesome fiancé Maida for sending us such a wonderful feast for dinner tonight. What a brat I am for complaining about anything, you know? It's really alllllll good.

With a cane?! It still blows my mind.

Happy 5 months everyone.

March 4, 2010 - 4 pm

Juliana asks every day how much longer it is until her birthday. She knows that her birthday is on March 26th and she has been asking to go to Hamada so we have been dangling that out there for her birthday dinner to encourage her to strive toward independence. Of course she could go there for dinner regardless of being able to accurately feed herself but we were hoping she would be inspired to improve as much as possible. But here is the strange and new thing about Juli: She doesn't seem to be as concerned with how people perceive her. I would love to just say, "Wow, this is a very positive change" but I am more inclined to think it is more likely related to an attribute of the TBI which has her perspective more closely aligned with a young child. I am not offering full disclosure of all of her limitations but I can tell you that she still occasionally drools, often misses her mouth with food and has been known to…gasp…burp without saying 'excuse me'. Details, details, details. Now you guys will lovingly say, "that's ok" and truly it is. But these are just some of the social particulars that have to be re-learned in this recovery… which again draws our attention to how this is similar to navigating from child to adult. Quite an education we are all getting together isn't it!? I am telling you all of this because if you attend the benefit on March 27th I want to prepare you for what you might encounter since Juliana is going to attend. She is actually eager go which is a little bit strange because I can tell you, the 'former Juli' would have been driven by insecurity and probably would have not wanted to attend. The question is… is she 'over it' or if she is unaware of her situation? Sometimes I think it's one then I think it's the other. Kind of ironic, isn't it? But she is a funny girl: Beautifully insecure. Her family, close friends and certainly Chris have struggled for years to help her feel comfortable in her own skin but her insecurity was debilitating on a daily basis. Is this news to some of you? Will Juli wish I hadn't shared this much? Perhaps. But if this experience will allow that part of her personality to mature, (a part that she always wanted to mature), maybe it is just one more reason this sort of thing happens: so that we grow and learn and become better for it. For those of you who believe in fate, destiny, karma, kismet, you will nod your heads at the correlation. You cynics will just find it cruel. I will plead the fifth and just get her through it.

March 6, 2010 - 9:45 pm

Because the Botox has worked so well for Juliana's arm and leg they are going to follow that up with a booster shot to her hand, fingers, and foot. Although that sounds a little painful, if you have seen the way she clenches her fingers and flexes her foot, you would agree Botox is a better alternative. Once we can get her hand open and more functional, she may be able to use a walker to get around, provided she has her ankle braces on. Her walking has improved so dramatically in the past few weeks that I hate to even remove her leg braces because with them on, we walk her to the bathroom, to the couch, to the recliner, to the stairs, etc. And once she has that freedom and a reason for wearing them, she tolerates them a little more. On Tuesday she has an appointment to have them reevaluated, and if necessary, adjusted. With her walking improving and her manual dexterity improving I am even more desperate to have her speech improve. It just seems like something that SHOULD be getting better faster. And although she is certainly more understandable than she was, she still often slips into mumbling and whispering. I try not to get frustrated but when the whole house has to get quiet in order to hear her repeat her whisper several times (and if you have ever been in this house you know that 'quiet' is a rare occurrence anyway) it can get tiring. The speech therapist said that we should be working on having her repeat short phrases and focus on the articulation. But short or long, one word or several, she isn't opening her mouth. Many people have told her that she should be a ventriloquist. And it's not that her mouth can't open...I have seen a whopper with room to spare make it through her jaws. In fact, we are noticing that she talks clearer with food IN her mouth. Crazy, huh? That's why it gets so especially frustrating because it seems like she could be doing better and she just chooses not to. Now I know that isn't the case but her articulation is so random. It seems the best motivation for her to speak more clearly is to offer to shorten the time she has her braces on. And then she CAN do it. So you see why this is so frustrating? (And can you tell I am fresh out of a failed conversation with her?) The Speech therapists' suggestion is to get Juli to sing. The phrases are short, memorable, and singing requires more breath control than just talking. And if none of that matters, at least we got to listen to music along the way. Today it was so nice outside that (thank you leg braces), I had her walk outside and sit on the deck for a while. We brought out the iPod and listened to a little bit of Miley Cyrus and a little bit of Wicked while the girls played with playdoh. Cool combination, eh? She does try to sing so that seems to be an exercise that might work. We will keep plugging away at it. She even dances a little if we ask her to. Taking direction without question AND dancing are both directly attributed to the brain injury because other than a little shimmy here or there, the girl was not willing to dance. Now there's a scenario I didn't consider: perhaps Juliana traded her voice to the sea witch for the ability to dance? Ok, getting tired and punchy, goodnight.

March 7, 2010 - 4:30 pm

A good friend reminded me that even though my life feels "all about Juli" right now that I still have 5 other kids. Ok, so I didn't really need reminding that I have 5 other kids, they remind me every day. But maybe I did need to remember that I can't sacrifice it all for this overwhelming recovery effort. So to that end (and oh so many others...) I made a bold move...I am going to visit Dylan in Hawaii. What a guilt trip I had to overcome to book that! The money, the time away, the abdicating of responsibility for Juli and Delaney and Mackenzie, the house, the dogs, the cat the fish (uh oh, um Chris...you remember you said, "No problem "on staying with Juli 24/7 while we are gone? Did I forget to remind you about the animal menagerie? Yeah, so, let's chat about that...) But seriously, I struggled with how to walk away from this situation, even if only for a short time. Then I remembered Juli saying that 'relief' is the best emotion. I expect that Hawaii will give me some of that as well. It should...its Hawaii! It's just that I miss Dylan an awful lot and, well, it IS Hawaii. Juliana is supportive of my going even if her initial response was, "Don't go, you'll die." (You see she has this very direct side to her now. It must be her difficulty in speaking; she doesn't want to waste words putting the sentiment into context.) But she patted me on the back and said, "Don't worry, I will be fine. I can drive myself to therapy." (Yeah... she also is not completely in touch with her own reality. Not to mention, even if she was able to drive, she would DEFINITELY be playing hooky.) "I HATE them!" she tells us as everyday she begs not to go to therapy. I bet her $100 that someday she will be grateful for them. She took that bet, sure that I will lose. We are trying to convince (manipulate) her into liking her leg braces. It's not totally working but I am proud to say it's not totally failing either. When it's time to go to the bathroom, instead of putting on regular shoes and wheeling her there, I put on the braces and she walks. It is an extra workout for me as well but...hey, I do have a Hawaiian vacation to get ready for so it's all good. I also got a little upset with her today and kind of lectured her about not talking better. I let her know that this is the one thing we can't get a medicine or a procedure, or a brace to fix. This one is all on her to work out and it really bothers me that she isn't trying harder. She paused then said sheepishly, "Tell me how to try harder." Awwww....ok so then I felt bad. I hate that 'after the lecture' feeling when they really seem affected. In any case, I gave her some pointers (again) and the rest of the day saw an ever so slight improvement. Let's see if this momentum can continue...stay tuned.

March 8, 2010 - 10 pm

Juliana had a fantastic day at therapy: She walked stronger and steadier and the therapist said it was her best day yet. They are very encouraged by her continued progress and one of them even said that Juli was their favorite patient. Aww shucks...

They had her stand for a bit in her stocking feet balancing without the braces. This is not only a good stretch but it seemed to give Juli hope that the time would come when she wouldn't need the braces. (At least that is what I tried to put in her head when we talked about it and she really seemed to think about that one and get the slightest bit happy.) Since she is now up to 6 hours of therapy a day, she had 3 hours of PT where they also had her walking up and down stairs. She read very well according to the therapist. But according to Juli, she was 'just guessing'. I don't know what to believe because she has been pretty confused on a few things lately. First of all, she insists she has the braces on when she doesn't. And because she is so certain, and we are telling her they aren't there, she thinks we are lying to her and is getting very angry with us. She is also adamant that I told her she did NOT have to go to therapy today. Who heard me say that?? Exactly. She must feel persecuted if she really thinks that we are all lying to her. And she gets SO angry! It's amazing how effective one open eye can be in conveying blind rage. I guess I should be more bothered by her anger but after 23 years of child raising, having one of them angry at me for one thing or another barely gets an 'honorable mention'. Chris on the other hand gets a little more wounded by her anger and I am again reminded that although he and I are side by side through this, we are experiencing totally different things. You see, I have already won the battle and have my daughter back. But for him, Juliana is miles away from being his wife. In fact, he will have to make some serious decisions in the next couple of months over what to do with the new tentative wedding date in December 2010 and the accompanying reservations. As rapidly as she is progressing, we are still uncertain of where she will be as the year goes on. She can't remember much of anything prior to coming home in December and frankly, I hope she forgets the last few months and some of the next few months too. As for me, I hope I NEVER do. Do you find that odd? When the pain was new and raw I just wanted to wake up and find that this was all a nightmare. Then when I couldn't deny it was happening, I just wanted to get through it without losing my daughter or my mind. But now that we have come farther this year then I could never have imagined, I wish to never forget. I figure, if I have to live it, I want to remember it.

Tomorrow is the Botox booster in her finger flexors and her heel. They are also supposed to adjust her AFOs (leg braces) so hopefully it will be another day of moving Juliana forward...even if she is kicking and screaming.

March 9, 2010 - 5 pm

No Botox today. ☹ The machine that allows the doctor to find the small muscles to inject is not working. It has been rescheduled for next Tuesday. That is the biggest difference in the Day Rehab...nothing happens right away. I assume the machine will be fixed before next Tuesday but the doctor is only in on Tuesday so...we wait. Her AFOs were adjusted and Chris thinks that they will be more comfortable for her. However, she is getting red marks on her feet so they think that she needs to wear them for less time. What? Excuse me? They also said that they think the pressure she is feeling in her feet is not due to her AFOs but her shoes. They asked that we get a bigger size. So check this out...she normally wears a 7 1/2, and yet the shoes they had us get to fit over her braces are a 9 wide. That is what we have been using for the last 3 ½ months. Now they want us to get a 10 wide! (I don't know about you but I am picturing Juli as one of those Barbies in the upright stand). She got good reports from all of her therapists who assure us that her reluctance to go to therapy is normal. After working in daycare for 14 years I know that even when kids didn't want to be there, the teachers they were left with could make them want to stay. I had hoped the same would be true with the therapists but I guess it's not the same with patients with TBIs. At least not this patient and not just yet. They may have found a way through to her though: They helped her make cookies. She had to reach to get the cookie sheet, get ingredients out of the refrigerator and then put the cookie dough on the pan, mostly using her right hand. Sounds like a good use of her time. We continue to try to find normal activities for her to engage in at home as well. The other day Chris had her standing at the sink in the kitchen to wash her hands. Yesterday we had a delicious dinner prepared and delivered AGAIN by the Dampfs. (Those brownie cupcakes were INCREDIBLE!!). A few days earlier Paula Mitchell also made us a wonderful meal. We are very fortunate to have so many people helping make our days a little bit easier and I have to tell you, it is so very much appreciated. We surely don't deserve all of the assistance you give us but we thank you for it. I have an awful lot of 'paying back' and 'paying forward' to do! So after dinner I walked Juli to the sink to also have her wash her hands there, upright. And while we were there... "Um, Juli, while you are here, do you mind washing the dishes?" (It's worth a shot) "Sure" she tells me.

" Aww, thank you but I am just kidding" ...sorta.

Soon enough my dear.

March 10, 2010 - 9:50 pm

Slow news day folks. Juli was pretty tired today which ended up working out well because my long bragged about streak of 'not getting sick' is broken as I spent the day with a sore throat and every joint and muscle aching. Now I just hope Juli doesn't catch…whatever I got. Today was her day to just relax since therapy is getting pretty intense so Cheyenne took good care of her and did her nails and made her lunch. She also got a chance to enjoy the warm weather a bit as she sat outside and listened to Delaney and Mackenzie sing and dance to their interesting iPod playlist. Tomorrow I am definitely going to get her a calendar though with great big boxes. That way she can keep track of which days are therapy and which aren't and how much longer it is until her birthday. She is definitely fixated on her birthday. Can't blame that on the injury though, birthdays have always been kind of a big deal, to her, to the family. I used to tell the kids that their birthday is really MY day. I did all the work, THEY just showed up (well its true!) Birthday attention was also elevated to new heights by my brother Joe who would often show up at midnight with a cake and to deliver a very loud rendition of Happy Birthday. (Some of you have experienced it.) Ok, out of steam. Going to try some cold and flu medicine and see if maybe a good night's sleep will knock out the aches and fever.

March 12, 2010 - 1 pm

I am home from work today still sick so you are getting an on the spot update. Chris just texted me from therapy saying they have discovered Juliana is beginning to see light in her right eye! I know, I know, we have been encouraged before but Juli did admit to us that the other times she was just guessing. I really don't know what to believe but here is the funny part: There are exercises we can do with a flashlight to strengthen the muscle to her eyeball. Sounds great, right? I have to ask though…if there was some-thing…ANYTHING we could have done up to this point, why didn't any of the experts tell us that? We sure asked an awful lot. The only advice they gave us was to 'come back'. So here is why I get so darn frustrated with this whole process. If the other doctors were right and there is nothing we can do, then the new doctors are wrong. That brings into question the credibility of everything they say to us now. But, if the new doctors are right then we question the previous doctors and are furious at potentially wasted time! I wish they would all stick with, "we have no idea, but…try this". And all of you out there reading this, take notes because I am sure there are just as many differing opinions on every aspect of health and healing. I am just glad that we took it upon ourselves to try some eye therapy, even if it wasn't suggested or even exactly like they are suggesting now. If it works (or maybe is the reason her eye is healing) then so be it. It would sure be nice to tell Juli, "See, you AREN"T going to be half blind after all." She still hates therapy and still spends a lot of energy trying to convince us she doesn't have to go. Unfortunately, she isn't convincing us by being totally independent but rather playing mind games. Pretty funny coming from someone with a brain injury. Try and follow her logic, it's scary. It really does make you wonder about the mind of an ultra-creative person and how they must be wired because we are witnessing Juliana's thought patterns develop and they are slightly skewed, yet she seems oddly intact. She could probably function in the real world with the way her brain is working and those unaware of her former self might not realize she is just left of center. It also explains quite a few people that I know ARE just left of center. If Chris gives me any other good info later I will update again. Right now, going to take advantage of this oddly silent house and try to nap off the rest of this ugly bug.

March 14, 2010 - 10 pm

Since I have acquired a shotgun medical degree, here is my tip of the day: When you have a cold and flu, standing outside in the cold and the rain for a St. Patrick's Day parade will not help you get better. It was a fun day out with my little girls early, my son later on but I thought a lot about last year's St. Patrick's day celebration at Holsteins where Juli was our waitress. (Remember, Carrie?) We had a blast and I was so proud of Juli for no real reason other than, she was my daughter. And just as she is seeing glimmers of light in her eye, she is also seeing it in her recovery. We are constantly trying to convince her that she is getting better but she keeps holding out for the big prize before she acknowledges any of it. I had to set her straight on that: "Juli! When you have a baby, they can't do ANYTHING for themselves but you still love it and appreciate it. And as they grow and progress and learn, you marvel in all of the little winnings, don't you? You love them when they feed themselves, even though it's messy because they are becoming more independent. Why is it so hard to accept that we are all happy with how YOU are progressing?? The messy baby is thrilled to death to get ¼ of their food in their mouth. They give that pasta- smashed face 'look at what I did' grin. Be THAT proud." I saw just the slightest hint that maybe she got it.

And while we wait for confirmation of her improved attitude, we watch for signs of spontaneous smiles and unsolicited gestures of love and affection. And yesterday we got a few of those. She asked Chris if she could once again wear her engagement ring. So he slid it off his chain and put it on her finger. Then she told me that she wanted to have a 'date night' with Chris and that Friday's would be good. Chris was happy and touched and started thinking of ideas. Then, in a quiet moment while we watched TV side by side she did something she has not done since the accident.

"Mom?" She called.

"Yes?" I said.

"I Love you"

Waaaaaaaaaaaaaaaaaa. (Couldn't help it, instant waterworks.)

She just looked at me concerned and puzzled and said, "But…I do."

Awwwwwwww. "I know honey."

So funny story…this morning I climbed into her bed as she asked to get up and I begged her for another few minutes.

"Talk to me a minute Juli."

"What should I say?" she asked

I thought about what might take her a little while to think about then said "Tell me a joke."

What followed was 30 minutes of communicating through sounds, spelling, writing, hand signals, smoke signals…you name it, just to complete what for you and me is a 2 minute thought. It was a brand new exhausting behavior with a happy ending. Here is the 'joke' she painfully (for both of us) told:

"What time did Shirley Temple go to the courthouse?" I was surprised by the question, the formation of a joke, the ability to respond to my request and the speed that she came up with it (yeah, the 30 minutes was on my part…It was like the kid in 'A Christmas Story' trying to find out the secret message from the Ovaltine decoder device)

So I gave the answer a respectable effort then finally said, "I don't know Juli, tell me."

"12:00" she said.

Hmmm….Huh? I don't get it.

"Juli, that's not really funny."

"I know." She admits

"But aren't jokes supposed to be funny?" I asked.

"It's from 'Friends'" she explains. "Chandler told it to Monica and Phoebe."

"Oh, I see... Did THEY think it was funny?" I had to know

"No" she said flatly.

"Oh" I said.

Then she made sure I was following along by telling me "that's the joke." Now THAT'S funny.

March 15, 2010 - 10:15 pm

Last night Juliana had a cookie monster moment….er...hour….hours actually.

You see, Paula Mitchell stopped by to offer her OT services (thank you!) and sent a plate of homemade delicious cookies with Sarah. Juliana could NOT get enough. She even begged and pleaded for more cookies just as she begs to leave therapy or have her braces taken off...hmmm... I wonder if the therapists bribed Juliana with cookies if she would be happier to be there? We have joked up to this point that food is a big motivator but it is more like an obsession. She eats anything we give her and seems to enjoy it all. She even said that going out to eat is what will make her feel most normal and make her the most happy. She even agreed to try sushi next Friday at Hamada. The other day we had an enchilada feast provided by Maida Ramirez's mom, Lina Pagan, and the whole family ate for two days. Then Gloria came over with some cheesecakes for dessert and we continued to eat. Today we had another meal prepared by the Dampfs who have now fed us several Mondays in a row. I have to tell you...you ~Food Angels~ have certainly struck a chord with our family, our daughter and (when the odd morsel falls to the floor) 'the food stalker', our beagle, Miley. Thank you all for such care and comfort because even though we will all likely have to diet and exercise when this is over, the food is certainly going a long way toward soothing far more than our stomachs during this time in our life. Has anyone else ever experienced such an outpouring of support? This is far too kind but certainly, certainly appreciated.

We are noticing a slight improvement in Juli's awareness as well. I am not sure I can describe what we are seeing but it's very good. She appears to be thinking deeper and reflecting further than she had been. It's a subtle change, made even harder to notice by her very soft voice, but instead of just answering our questions, she now seeks information. (I am not explaining this very well.) Here, let me give you an example and see if you can figure out how to describe it. The other night we were watching American Idol and after Andrew Garcia sang 'Genie in a bottle' I said, "It sounds creepy when he sings it." (Sorry Andrew fans). Because I was just talking to myself, but out loud, Juli would not normally (um...this 'new' normal that is) comment unless I addressed her directly and even then I would probably just get a passive "yeah". But instead she said, "Well, have you heard the original?" When she spoke, I was a little surprised for a minute like I suddenly realized there was someone in the room with me. She reflected upon my comment, interpreted why I might feel that way, then asked her own question as a way of understanding my thoughts. (Thinking twice removed??) If there are any experts on this topic out there, feel free to send me an email with your insights. So, I may not be able to define it but I know what I heard, saw, and felt and knew it was progress. Moving right along...

March 16, 2010 - 11:30 pm

No Botox for Juli AGAIN this week. I bet if the doctor needed the Botox, the machine would have been fixed by now. (Bitter much, Janet?) I don't understand why three weeks ago they said that the Botox booster was 'time sensitive' and needed to be given in a 'window of opportunity' but now that there are technical difficulties, waiting is 'no sweat'. Her hand is constricted and in pain. She had to just suffer through when we thought she had no choice and now that we know something can be done but...they don't have a battery?? When I go tomorrow, I plan to discuss that with them. I suspect they will wish for Chris to come back. I asked if we could go somewhere else for the Botox. "Yep, back downtown." (Well, I did ask).

On another note, since the social worker had indicated that the dosage Juliana was taking of her antidepressant was very low, Chris asked the doctor if she thought it should be increased. They discussed Juli's mood and her reluctance to be at therapy. She asked how Juli is at home and if her sleeping and eating were a problem. She asked if Juli participated in conversations and gatherings at home. After Chris told her how she sings, talks, dances and even cooperates with stretches even when it hurts they knew the dosage was just fine. What was concluded is that regardless if she hates being at therapy, she always participates and does what is asked of her, even when it hurts. So she verbalizes her dislike? I guess it doesn't matter as long as she executes, right? And since they all call her a 'rock star' I guess she can't be executing too poorly.

Tomorrow she is supposed to be fitted for a new wheelchair. The one they gave us when we left RIC was a loaner which would be replaced by one that is suited to her. While we have been waiting 3 months (and counting) for the one that she is supposed to use...her needs may have changed so I asked for her to be reevaluated. We happen to have acquired a small basic wheelchair from my father-in-law so that we have one that is more manageable. Of course, the therapists cringe that we use it at all. They said it 'isn't set up for her' and 'it won't promote proper posture or support'. To that I say, 'if it really is that important, why have they left us with an improperly fit loaner for 3 months??' Whooo, I am CRANKY tonight! It must be the 30 loads of laundry staring at me or the cough that just won't go away. Hopefully I sleep this mood off or tomorrow the therapists will have to count on the 'Luck of the Irish' to save their day.

March 18, 2010 - 5 pm

I went with Juliana to therapy yesterday and it was the first time I had been there in many weeks so I was really looking to learn some new tricks (as well as share my frustrations). I wasn't really able to read the riot act on the Botox because I barely got the words out when I was humbled by the fact that many patients there were in the same position and it just wasn't the doctors fault. (Duh, machinery repair wouldn't be now would it?) They had already been complaining to the appropriate people so much that they were getting hour by hour updates. Sorry.

So the experience was many things: tiring, inspiring, encouraging and disappointing. I asked her before we left to try and show off for me and I think she actually might have tried to do that. Her PT set a goal for her to walk 110 feet without stopping and expected that she might need to work up to that. She didn't share that goal with us but instead just got her started walking. By the time she finally tired out she had walked 112 feet without stopping just using a four pronged cane on her left and gentle balance support on her right. When asked ¾ of the way if she wanted to stop and take a break Juliana said "yes", but kept walking anyway without stopping. Literal and confusing…that's my girl. Then in OT she did quite a few difficult stretching and reaching exercises. She stood and held her balance during the balance exercise and sat and held her balance as well. Speech continues to be her biggest obstacle so I asked her Speech Therapist if she was at all concerned with Juliana's progress. She looked at me shocked and said, "I know you want her to be louder and clearer but I have to tell you, she is progressing MUCH faster than I would expect for someone with an injury this severe." Gee I want to be happy about that but sometimes even a positive report feels like bad news. It was really a long day for me so I know that Juli was tired! She also got fitted for a new wheelchair because the monster they sent us home with is really overkill now. Juli got to choose the color she wanted and picked a red one. It will look pretty slick and she already has plans to decorate it. It takes 3 months to get the one we ordered made but in the meantime we will get another loaner that is the same type as the one we will ultimately end up owning. (Pssst…by the time OUR new wheelchair comes in, THAT will be overkill as well but it will be pretty☺) The other slightly disappointing part of yesterday was that I realized I may have been preventing Juli from 'being all that she could be'. Ouch. I saw her stand up and sit down more on her own than I allow her. I saw her walk more effortlessly than I expected. I saw her use her right hand more purposefully than I required. So I came home yesterday a bit bruised and set my sights on being less of an 'Enabler'. That will be difficult because it's pretty much hard coded in me. But I tried to get the same results from her at home and was bothered to find it wasn't so easy. 'She's tired' I reasoned. I will try tomorrow. Well tomorrow came (today) and it was the same. She was not as independent as she had been at therapy. (Can you feel the rushing water? Yep that is a flood of guilt) So I had a mild meltdown today as I concluded that I am bad for my daughter and that we will all be in this situation forever. I suddenly felt so completely inadequate and incapable that I considered my options for other care. (Drama mama for juuuuuuust a while) Chris walked into my meltdown and listened to my overreaction (he is a very good listener) and said all the things that people say (and you don't want to hear) when you are feeling sorry for yourself and...voila! I felt much better. I will still try to 'do less' to achieve more but I will try not to take it quite as personally.

It's just sometimes, regardless of how 'fast' they say it is, living it reminds you that everything is relative, even speed.

28 days til Hawaii...

March 20, 2010 - 11:15 am

Things you might not know about Juliana:

She was born in England while her dad was in the Air Force and we were stationed there.

She went to work with me every day until she started Kindergarten (I taught preschool)

She used to hate her middle name.

She is double jointed.

She was the MidCrest Panther Homecoming Queen in 1995 then decided to never cheer again.

She can do the Chinese split.

She went on an International tour with Blue Lake Fine Arts camp choir.

She had many of the same grade school teachers as her dad and I.

She is the oldest of 10 kids.

She went to Fan Fair in Nashville twice.

She had a surprise party for her 16th birthday and also got a car.

She met Chris when she was 16.

She tattooed Chris's name on her foot on her 18th birthday.

She spent half a semester at SIU and was too homesick to stay.

She was the nanny for Delaney and Mackenzie for 4 years.

She lived with Chris since the summer of 2004.

She has a fierce impulse to protect and defend her family and friends.

She sits in the bathroom sink to apply her makeup.

She developed a severe allergic reaction while in Germany and was hospitalized.

She has hung out with Fall Out Boy.

She is Chris's number one fan.

She LOVES Oprah and Tyra.

She has 6 tattoos.

She was almost done with Beauty School.

Her favorite shows are 'So You Think You Can Dance' and 'American Idol'

Her favorite food is Mexican.

She always wants to have 'a bite' of someone else's food.

She always wants to share 'the perfect bite' of her food with someone else.

She is very close to her siblings.

She doesn't like to swim.

She doesn't like to dance.

She learned how to snow ski quickly and easily.

She has an incredible singing voice.

She has seen Wicked 7 times.

She believes her friends are 'the most interesting people ever'.

She believes her family are 'the strongest people ever'.

She wants to have 5 kids.

She is incredibly jealous

She is a wonderfully helpful and respectful daughter

She is a lot of fun to hang around with

She is an interesting conversationalist

She is very smart.

She is very tolerant of others.

She does not judge and accepts people for who they are.

She thinks that Chris will be a great husband and father.

She went back to her house last night for the first time since October 2nd, 2009.

March 22, 2010 - 10 pm

So Juli went back to the house she previously shared with Chris and her brother Adam. Since…'before'… Chris and Adam acquired two new room-mates, rearranged the studio, got rid of two cats and live like…bachelors. But somehow, even so, Juli felt she was home. And as different as it was, her bathroom was still littered with her curling iron, makeup, bobby pins and shampoos. Her clothes were still lying across her vanity and her pillows were still the same. The wheelchair didn't fit into any room so Chris had to either carry her 'like a princess' or make her walk from room to room, up and down stairs. They didn't have any food (at all man!) so Chris had to give her the morning medicines in water with a little crystal light. And in spite of all of that familiarity mixed with inconvenience, Chris said it felt so much better, so much closer to normal just having her home. He described a feeling of comfort and peace that made the obstacles seem almost like welcomed challenges. They will do that again, maybe make it the Friday night plan but it will depend on everything else that is going on that night because in spite of how much rest she gets throughout the day, she gets tired early and shuts off around 9. For the rest of the weekend it was not nearly as interesting. In fact, she did a lot of sleeping yesterday and today was rather quiet. I think she is probably getting the bug I am getting over, in spite of my feeble attempts not to breathe on her the last week. I really hope she is pumped with enough vitamins to fight it off before it becomes an issue because she has a busy week planned: Therapy on Monday, Therapy with Botox on Tuesday, Shopping at the mall Wednesday afternoon, Dentist appointment, beauty appointment and shopping on Friday followed by her birthday dinner at Hamada, then the benefit at Holsteins on Saturday. I am tired just typing it. She's sleeping now and my little daughters are calling me to come lie down with them, so goodnight everyone.

March 23, 2010 - 5 am

Yesterday Juli walked 144 feet with taking only one break. Her walking is really getting so much better. Her balance is what is preventing her from doing it alone but the mechanics are improving. In fact, we will likely have her walk into Hamada on Friday and Holsteins on Saturday. That is what she said she wanted to do so, why not? She is very excited to start her birthday week so I am excited for her. The sad part is that 'excited' looks very different today than it did pre-accident. Those of you that knew Juli before could attest to her exuberant and over the top personality. Normal often looked...radiant. So when I say that she is excited you may expect something familiar but we are not there yet. Smiles are still rare and usually only upon request, laughter is nonexistent and emotion is hard to notice. So the current 'excited' is..."Juli, are you excited?" With her response..."Yes I am". She still seems reluctant to believe this is not her permanent state and no amount of reassurance seems to work. Just yesterday when she once again said, "No I am NOT getting better." I said, "Has your hair grown in the last 6 months?" "Yes" she answered. "Well how do you know? Can you see it growing?" She shook her head 'no'. "Well it's just like that. Wait another 6 months Juli, you probably won't even remember this." "I hope." she said more to herself than to me. I really believe if her talking improved then her mood would as well. Then she could more actively engage in conversation as she once had. It is such a slooooooow process! I have heard from so many people that this just takes time and you have to wait it out and since we really have no other choice, we wait. I recall other times of drama in my life that seemed to be so important at the time...like when I eloped at 18 with Juli's dad. I could swear that the drama surrounding that would never go away and that would define my life forever. But now my siblings simply ADORE me (come on you know I am your favorite) and I look back and hardly believe it was even an issue. I really believe that a few years from now, (maybe a few more than a few), this will be something that Juli can say 'happened' to her but it will not define her. I am not naive enough to think there will be no lasting residuals but I am also completely confident that she will have all that life has to offer...and more for she will have gained a valuable perspective, appreciation and wisdom that otherwise she may not. I explained to her yesterday:

"Juli, you remember when you went to pick out your wedding invitations and you called me and said, 'This is too hard! I don't want to do this' and I told you, 'you have to do it just get it done and move on'. You reluctantly got off the phone and finished the task then called me with relief when it was finished. That doesn't seem so important or hard now compared to what you are going through now, does it?"

"No, it doesn't"

"See. When you are better...the 'little things' will really BE little. That is what you have learned."

"I hope you are right..."

Yeah Juli, me too.

March 23, 2010 - 10:30 pm

Juliana finally had her Botox booster today and as good as that is, and as much as we wanted it, and as much as she needed it…THAT is how bad it hurt her to have it. In order to find the small muscles in her hand that needed the injection they had to force her right hand completely open and flat, including her thumb. (I know those of you that have seen her are cringing now.) Chris had to be the bad guy and secure her left arm so she didn't react to the pain with force enough to harm the procedure. The exchange was a blood curdling scream followed by several good blows to Chris when the deed was done. I choose to believe that the worst is behind her. It will be a very long time before she can fully appreciate how far she has come. We can however appreciate it now.

March 25, 2010 - 4:15 pm

Juliana has made SO much progress in her mobility. The funny thing is, the last entry is 22 days ago and she can walk SO much better now. We don't even have to give her queues for what to do next and she just needs a slight amount of balance support. Getting to a standing and sitting position on her own is still not possible so it's not like she could walk completely on her own but, mechanically speaking, she is well on her way. So we are now in the middle of what we are calling 'Birthday Week' for Juli, which is really nothing more than pampering her a bit more than before. In her current state that translates to 'No Therapy' and that is all she asked for as a birthday present. That and going to Hamada. She is going to her dad's house for dinner tonight and tomorrow she will have a fun day shopping then back home to get ready for her big dinner. Then of course Saturday at Holsteins will be a whole new celebration. She didn't end up getting sick, though she certainly seemed like she would. It must be all the super vitamins she is being pumped with. Her body is reacting like a Sherman tank. (What exactly is that anyway?) Her right hand seems the tiniest bit more flexible and her ankle a little more pliable but I am looking for it so I could be imagining it. Her eye seems to be a tiny bit more open but I am probably just wishing for it again. I actually had a dream last night that it was open and I couldn't figure out what exactly looked different about her. Someday I am sure. We asked the doctor if Juli could travel by airplane at the end of May and the doctor advised against it. She said that someone that is not that mobile is at more of a risk for blood clots and the pressure from flying could break the blood clot free. We decided even if it sounded unlikely it wasn't worth the risk. The doctor recommended that she take a train. I recommended that she ride with Juli the whole way and hold the puke bucket! So as disappointing as it will be, it looks like Juli and Chris are going to miss Tessie and Matt's wedding in May in New York ☹

March 26, 2010 - 6 pm

HAPPY BIRTHDAY JULIANA!

24 years ago today an 8 pound 12 oz. beautiful little girl was given to me by God for safe keeping. He hired me to do the job of being Juliana's mom and I was instantly grateful. Prior to that moment, I didn't know what I would 'become' or what I would grow up to 'do'. The minute I held her I knew that I became her mom and raising her is what I was going to do. It sounds really cliché, I know but I felt God in the room when she was born and I have always said that my life was defined by becoming 'Juliana's mom'. I jokingly blame/credit her for my choice to go on to have 6 children. She set the bar very high for me and for the other kids. And although I can honestly say that I never took the job lightly, since I was only 20 years old when she was born, I didn't have a clue what I was doing. I let her teach me. I told her many times that she was my experimental child and to cut me some slack and that I would do better with the others. Sometimes, she didn't think that was funny. And here we are, 24 years later and in a way different place than I ever imagined and she still teaches me, defines me, and still doesn't think I am that funny. In fact, I made a comment about how all the comedians seem to die young and so, "I worry for me." She looked at me deadpan and said, "I wouldn't. You aren't that funny." Come on Jules.

Today she is celebrating the way she likes to: going out to eat, to the mall and just hanging out with Chris and Cheyenne. Tonight, a group of us are going to Hamada for her birthday dinner. Tomorrow we will see many of you at the benefit. I am hoping she will be able to stay most of the time but I suspect it will be too loud and full of commotion for her to be able to tolerate it for more than a couple of hours. My house has been a great warm up for a loud, commotion and music filled bar, but Holsteins will definitely have us beat. Lots to do so...on to the celebrations!

March 28, 2010 - 2 pm

Thank you to all of you who came out to Holsteins yesterday in support of Juliana. And a huge THANK YOU to Holsteins with Diana Ocampo at the helm for hosting and arranging it all. I had to do nothing but show up and enjoy. And that is exactly what I did. It was a great fun time, as it always is at Holsteins, and the outpouring of love was overwhelming. It was nice to meet so many of you that I had corresponded with, and others that have been following along with the updates. I still really believe that very support and the prayers that follow are the reason she is making such a wonderful recovery. We asked Juliana if she had a good time yesterday and she said she did. When asked what her favorite part was she said, "When I walked in and everyone clapped. I was surprised." That made me think that although Chris and I and our families feel the support from all of you through this medium, Juliana is not nearly as exposed to it. She is more isolated and removed and has been rather detached from the support...until she saw it yesterday. Don't get me wrong, we have been telling her daily about the impact she is making on her little world but I don't think she felt it, not the way we have. Not that is, until she heard the applause. She is still talking about it this morning, and is still surprised by it. This morning I read her the article written about her struggle published in the Southtown Star, and she listened quietly. She looked like she is starting to get the picture that she just might be newsworthy. I think if she could truly internalize how much of a following she has, she would be happier, more positive and more motivated. I know it has been a huge comfort to me for the last 6 months. It probably won't sink in for her, but more like seep in. We just have to patiently watch it happen. But her affect is still flat, her emotions and personality are still MIA with her voice, so her reactions to the world are somewhat hard to read. I know it will take more time. "Give it a full year" I was reminded yesterday and so we will. We might have to wait a bit longer for the Juliana we used to know to completely return but it sure was nice to have her loved by all of you...and really feel it.

Thank you all again... A round of applause back atcha.

March 29, 2010 - 7:30 pm

With the celebrations behind us, it's back to the hard work of physical, occupational and speech therapy for Juliana. She will have to return to the tasks, but this time, without the applause. Maybe we should record some canned applause as inspiration and validation to keep her motivated. She still hates it all and dreads it every day but the girl is nothing if not obedient. So, she completes the task, regardless of what is asked of her. We continue to be frustrated by her minuscule voice but try to focus on the fact that in addition to re-learning and practice and exercise, she needs the one thing that we can't control: Time. We are approaching the 6 month mark and the gains continue to drop in the bank a penny at a time. By my calculations we're just about at the 1/2 million mark. That's not too shabby when you look at how far she has come. The things we have 'purchased' with this half a million are worth even more than that: She breathes, she walks, she talks, she eats, she hugs, she kisses, she smiles...she lives. And that is just the direct deposit. How about the interest on that half a mill? My other children have matured a great deal in these six months in ways that only this experience can force you to mature. Juli was the matriarch of the siblings (I am sure there is a real word for that but I don't know it) so the others had to do their part to step up. They all did. My beautiful headstrong daughter Cheyenne did who never made things easy before (it's ok, she knows) now somehow chose to do all the right things. I wonder how much of Juli's shadow she was in. She probably doesn't see it that way but I am looking beyond the obvious and that is what appears to me. They each had to learn how to do a lot of little things without me and accept that absence without jealousy or anger. You would expect that to be a bit easier for the 22 year old than the 6 year yet they all seemed to just 'get it'. Friendships have been formed and bonds have been made, often in the most unlikely places. Tonight we got a food delivery from a very old friend, Ann Somers- Knight. She came all the way from Colorado and made us chicken marsala. Who gets friends like that?? I am the luckiest person alive, really. I can't say that my bond with my siblings is stronger because I am proud of the fact that it was rock solid to begin with so that just carried on. I do need to take a slight deduction for my house. It is paying the price because it is just a mess all the time. Sometime in 2011 maybe I will plan to care again about that. All in good time my pretty, all in good time.

Well Juli is sitting next to me telling me to stop typing because she wants to go lay down. I told her what I was typing and she said, "Oh, sorry… and tell them thanks from me too." There you go…straight from the princess' mouth.

March 31, 2010 - 6 pm

Breakfast food is SO overrated when you have chicken Marsala in your fridge…mmmm….and then yesterday Sandy Kudra brought us another two days' worth of food. I am NEVER going to fit in my bathing suit when I go to Hawaii in two weeks! So yesterday we asked the rehab doctor if we could possibly change Juli's anti-seizure medicine (now that everything else has calmed down) because she has had mild tremors since she started on it. The doctor said that the tremors are not due to the medication but instead just something that happens as a result of the brain injury. We had heard and read that but also knew that the tremors definitely started when she was changed to this particular medicine. I read all of the side effects and she really has many of them. Of course it could be a result of the injury but I think it would be worth trying another, right? Well the doctor and the nurse both said, "Juli is doing well, why change anything?" In fact the nurse actually said to me, "Since she is doing well, why would you want to change any medicine, just to change it?" Uh, yeah, *that's* why… We exchanged a few words and it once again was more of a battle of wills. Maybe I need to stop doing that. (When Juli is better of course…not now) You guys might not know this but I am sometimes not really a 'people person'. It's just one of the little 'features' that defines me. But back to Juli…so the nurse tells me that we would need to coordinate that with our neurologist anyway. Hmmm… this is the same nurse that was all bothered that we were using other doctors and NOT coordinating our care through the rehab doctor. Whatever, we will work through our neurologist. She did great at therapy, the Botox appears to be helping but, just like everything else, the results are difficult to see. She was able to write her name, with her RIGHT hand and do a pretty good job of it. That is definitely an improvement. She also walked pretty well on the treadmill but continues to stall on her speaking. That seems to be directly related to the amount of sleep she has and how much practice she gets. Today she got the day off from therapy and was SO glad. She can't seem to stop talking about how much she hates it. I try to tell her it is not forever but she is yet to be convinced. I hope she actually forgets a lot of this time. We are able to keep her braces on a bit longer but it takes some distraction to do it. Next week we go to see our new Neuro Ophthalmologist and I am excited to see if maybe something different will be offered to us. Considering this will be our fourth doctor of this kind, I have little hope. Let me put a prediction out there: He will say, "There is no way to know, we just have to wait and see." Here's hoping I am wrong.

April 1, 2010 - 5:30 pm

The nice weather has given us opportunity to take Juli outdoors for the last few days and she even got some sun. I know the sunshine makes me happy but it never really had the same effect on her although today she spent the afternoon at the park with her dad and she seemed to enjoy that. Either way, the vitamins are free so we took them. She got her new loaner wheelchair today and it is a much more slimmed down version from the monster she left RIC with 3 months ago...wow, has it really been that long that she has been home? This wheelchair will be ours to use until her custom one comes in 3 months. I was hoping by then she wouldn't need one then...but I am no longer sure if that is an attainable goal. Even though her walking mostly improves, sometimes her steps get wobbly and unsure and she complains of more pain than normal in her feet. To add to that, her left knee, presumably the strong one, snaps back when she stands as if she can't control her leg. I would guess we are weeks or days away from a brace of some sort on that knee too: She vows that she will not wear another brace. So with that back and forth in the 'progress' area, walking exclusively seems almost futuristic right now. I also wonder when the 24 hour care will no longer be necessary. Will that happen slowly as well? Will we gradually just start deciding when she can be alone for a few minutes here or there or will it not happen for years? I guess there are a lot of variables there. For example, if her 'dark thoughts' continue, leaving her alone would not be advisable. That is another thing that we really hope will go away as she improves. For now we just hang on tight and fight 'the battle of the braces'. So let's see… if it is true that recovery from a brain injury is like going from infancy back to where you were in adulthood, but all within a year to 18 months then Juli is approaching 'preteen' right now. That's about right so 'for your own good' doesn't really work. And even when you have all the hope in the world that things will once again be some shade of normal, there are many moments...hours... and even days where you can't even see it coming.

Well it's back to therapy tomorrow. It should be a great day because it seems when I sink low, Juli leaps forward. It's a fair trade.

April 2, 2010 - 10 pm

6 months ago today...

Half a year. Half of the holidays. ¼ of 2009, ¼ of 2010. Halloween, Thanksgiving, Christmas, New Years, Valentine's Day, birthdays, anniversaries, gatherings, outings, parties.

Those are the calendar milestones that we have been fortunate enough to be able to include our daughter, who is surviving and improving. The 6 months before that held just as many milestones, just not as much wisdom and respect for my wonderful life.

Juliana had a great day at therapy and once again did everything they asked. She talked well, walked well and spoke well. And then she came home to the hospital bed in the family room with her fist curled up and her ankles too weak to hold her up. I find it hard to convince her of her improvement when I can so easily overlook it. I was told, "It's not a straight road but instead a winding tree lined street that has a little bit less shade the further we go." I am so glad we have these 6 months behind us but I won't lie...I wouldn't mind fast forwarding through the next 6. How many times have we heard, "It's a marathon, not a sprint"? I have never been much of a runner no matter how you describe it so this just seems to go on. But, 6 months forward is nothing to complain about so, I won't. Thank you one last time to our Food Angel, Mary Dampf. It was a good and yummy Good Friday at hour house. Very Sleeeeeepy....Goodnight.

April 4, 2010 - 10 pm

I hope everyone had a very nice holiday. Ours started with Juli walking up the stairs and out the door to the car to go to Aunt Lori's for Easter breakfast. She then walked from the car into the house to a family round of applause.

She does like that applause. She ate, she got sleepy, and she went home and napped and then repeated the process to go to her dad's house. It sounds pretty normal unless you take into account that the simple act of leaving the house takes nearly 30 minutes. And although it is 30 minutes well spent, I get it now. I really do. I get why the doctors and nurses looked at us with pity and dread as we first decided to take on the recovery process at home. I get why they felt so determined to let us know that there was a 'long road ahead'. I get why people who had survived this feel the need to educate those that are going through it. I get all of that because that is where I am now. Chris learned of a family member of a co-worker who has just suffered a TBI and whose family is in the initial days of life and death struggle. When I hear those stories I get that same look on my face, the same pit in my stomach and the same empathy for the very long road ahead. I have become the very people I criticized for their pity in the beginning. This is a very long road. And every time we feel we have made headway, we feel as if we might have taken a wrong turn. Neither Chris nor I ever feel we are doing enough. We feel we are doing all we can but we continue to feel as if we have left stones unturned. How long does it actually take to learn to enunciate again? How long does it take to remember to swallow your saliva every time it collects in your mouth? How long does it take to learn you can't endanger yourself by unfastening your seatbelt in the wheelchair and leaning over? I just don't know, but I have been advised to be patient. That is another thing I fear I might not be good enough at. I got a new tattoo the other day. You see Juli, Cheye and I all planned to get matching ones before her wedding. Juli couldn't agree on any of our suggestions so it hadn't happened yet. So after her accident, Cheye decided to get a pink flower tattoo to match Juli's pink flower tattoo. So the other day I got a small one as well on my foot. So I asked the artist, "will this hurt and how long will it take." He said, "Yes, it hurts more on the foot than many other places and it will take about 20 minutes." I thought, 'as long as I know how long I have to tolerate it, I can endure it'. Well I feel that way now. I just want to know how much longer. I keep hanging on that year to 18 months marker we have heard about but if I don't see a little more trickling in, it is hard to be sure. So we just continue to wait. How long can you endure? You up to an 18 month novel? How long does it have to go before it is considered an epic? I don't know about you but I would like the cliff notes please. Happy Easter everyone.

April 5, 2010 - 10 pm

Another rockin day at therapy where Juliana continued to exceed their every expectation. If they decide she should walk 150 feet, she walks 160 without even knowing what they wanted. If they expected her to hold her balance for 1 minute, she will do it for 2 and not ask for a break. She uses her spare moments to try to pry her arm down or her hand open. She is also becoming less dependent on her cane...er..."magic wand". Yeah...so, she doesn't like to call it a cane. (We just go with it.) The girl wants out of this situation bad but she doesn't quite grasp that she does. Chris and I think they need to set their expectations higher but they are cautious to push harder. When we push it isn't always well received so we hang out in the middle letting her lead the way. She continues to feel defeated and depressed because she hasn't yet embraced the good fortune of living through a miracle. Could it be that she is TOO aware? Where many in her situation have memory or cognition loss, she seems to have that intact, which means she knows who she was, what she was doing and what was in the road just ahead of her. She also questions if Chris still loves her the same way. And truthfully, that is a tough one. We have all witnessed his love and commitment but is it really the same? Can anything really be the same after the life changes they have both gone through? I can't see how. I know that I am personally different, and so is every relationship that I have. Some better, some worse, some brand new and some are even missing. It's quite possible, (and what we all want to believe), that they will be far better off for having lived through this together. But if we were being honest and fair to them both, we would admit that where they will end up at the other side of this process is a mystery to us all. Relationships are tough in the most adjusted situations but the statistics for relationships in THIS situation are just not favorable.

Downer, isn't it? Yeah I know...I like to be informed but sometimes I read articles I wish I hadn't. And as Juli sneaks her way back to normal, Chris waits and supports and expects that the relationship will survive and thrive. I have grown rather fond of that young man and hope that this turns out as well for him as I do for my daughter. Speaking of sneaking back to normal, after walking to the bathroom, she walked to the sink to wash her hands, face and to brush her teeth. We joked that we could do a comedy routine as my hands come from around her back while I allow her to use me to keep her steady and, well, for an extra set of hands. It was nice to see her doing something so normal to her. Now if she could just sit in the sink…

April 7, 2010 -1 am

Juliana had her appointment today with her new Neuro Ophthomologist. He confirmed what we had been told before: The nerves in her eyes are severely damaged, particularly the right one; sight out of the right eye is unlikely but 'anything is possible'; the lower eyelid needs surgery; the upper eyelid is beginning to open; and there is no magic cure to fix her. What she really needs to heal is …time. He also referred us to an Ocular Plastic surgeon and recommended that we make an appointment with him and get the surgery scheduled soon. There is some damage to her eye, possibly from the eyelashes scratching against her eye, possibly from the pressure and swelling. It's hard to say. The scar on her eye may fade with time but it won't likely go away. Since the infection is mild and not ulcerated, there is still time to prevent further damage. And in the midst of all of that we got more confirmation that she is beginning to see light out of that eye. The improvement factor holds a lot of weight. Seeing Juli day to day I know I don't always recognize the gains she is making but I realized today as she sat in the doctor's chair that if I simply line up each appointment at the eye doctors, her improvement is clear and obvious. Oh, and this eye doctor…we like him. In fact, we started the visit with warning him that 'his type' of doctor has not been our favorite in the past. He quietly laughed and put us at ease. The appointment made Juli feel pretty good so she wanted to celebrate. And how does Juli like to celebrate? Yep, food. Yesterday Lina Pagan made another delicious meal and today Juli's dad made his famous tacos for her. The girl eats well, there is no doubt. (And ok, so do we) So glad I bulked up for Hawaii ☺…uh, 7 days from now officially.

April 9, 2010 - 9:15 pm

Well I have been trying to write this update for 3 days. Not because I have anything spectacular or devastating to report but just because…man…life is busy! Anyway, let me tell you what our lovely Juliana has been up to lately. A typical Juliana morning "before": Get out of bed, walk to the bathroom, wash your face and hands, and brush your teeth and hair. Walk upstairs for breakfast, walk to the sink to wash again. Clean a few dishes in the sink to help mom out. Walk to the computer to login to Facebook, check messages, chat a bit, chat with Delaney and Mackenzie too. Walk back downstairs to go to the bathroom, watch a little Oprah while chatting with the girls some more. Walk upstairs for lunch, then to the sink to clean up. Yawwwwwwwwn. Walk downstairs, walk to the bathroom then climb into bed for a short nap.

Well my friends, THAT is now also part of her "after" now. Normal never felt so good. Of course it all is slower and of every step still has to be taken with a shadow person assisting her with balance, but that is not a complaint. (Well not from us anyway. And to be fair, Juli isn't complaining about that either) (Juli even admit to being a little bit happy, usually when she doesn't have therapy. She also agreed with Chris today that she would basically work hard now and get this over with instead of dragging it out or not doing it and staying in this state. Attitude is everything. Today at therapy they started her on rolling over on her own to get her on her stomach. Those of you 'in the know' know where this is leading…that's right, they want to get her on 'all fours'. I can't explain why this is thought to be a good treatment but I know that many people have recommended it and her therapy has been building up to it. She isn't quite there yet but that is the goal. Tomorrow she is going to the dentist for full mouth x-rays. Her speech therapist want us to find out if there is a reason she doesn't open her mouth very wide when she talks. (She can sure open wide for ANY mouthful of food so I don't see how that could be the problem but there must be a reason they want us to find out.) Chris said she did very well in her three speech therapies today but it doesn't always translate to regular conversation at home. If you know what she is trying to say, you could surely think she is talking well. It's when you DON'T know what she is saying. You see, when babies begin to talk, it's one or two words at a time and you learn what they are saying as they learn to say it. With Juli, as her ability to speak is returning, she is using her entire repertoire of language and thought process so the words are very difficult to predict. Instead of saying "Eat" when she is hungry as a toddler might, she might instead say, "What do you plan to make for dinner?" or "If you have the ingredients I would sure like…" Yeah…when you don't know what's coming it can be frustrating to all. The other day she kept spelling something and I could not figure it out for the life of me. She spelled it over and over and I repeated the letters over and over and she was nodding in agreement that I had the letters right. But it still did not register. I was getting really annoyed and protested "T-A-C-O-S is not a word" until suddenly I HEARD what she said…and said, "OH, I am SO stupid!" As it dawned on me. Her eyes got wide with a combination of anger and relief as she shook her lemon fist. "I KNOW" she shouted, and I heard her very well. "If you only said everything that loud I would have known what you wanted to begin with!" I still get a good laugh about that one and of course, Juli got her tacos.

April 10, 2010 - 8:30 pm

I started reading the updates from the beginning yesterday and I only made it through about 2 weeks when I had to stop. Not only was it hard to see through the tears but it was also hard to remember how much fear I was hiding and how naïve I was back then. I remember very clearly learning that this was much bigger than I thought I could handle. I also remember reading in the book 'From Coma to College' how the patient's mother said something about how she is glad now that she didn't know what was ahead of her. As much as I count on 'knowing what to expect', it took probably 3 months for me to accept that this was going to be a multiyear process. And though I often feel tired and isolated, I am no longer afraid that this is bigger than I. Either the worst is behind us or I just might have grown. (And not just the 10 pounds I gained thanks to the comfort food I indulged in). I look back at what we thought back then and remember my sister Lori commenting on how I was in a 'coma of my own'. Chris and I have a very somber and humbled laugh at what we know now that we didn't know then. It was surely a different kind of coma. But, I think I have the cure for the 'uncommon' coma, or at least a respite from it. I think a little Aloha ought to take care of that, assuming I can leave the guilt and concern behind. I just started the Bob Woodruff story and plan to finish that on the flight there. Might not be the best 'escape' from the situation but I can be educated and liberated at the same time, right? We leave on Wednesday morning and my vacation starts when the car goes in reverse out of the driveway. Oh wait, we are taking a stretch limo so it will be pulling up out front, not the driveway! (Oh yes we are!) So the vacation begins when the champagne bottle opens. I know Adam is glad he jumped onto this vacation bandwagon. Think of me at 7 am Wednesday morning as I toast the start of a new era.

April 12, 2010 - 10:30 pm

I have really learned through all of this that everyone has a story, and they don't all have happy endings. In fact, if we were very frank we would have to admit that life is fatal. Not one of us is going to make it out alive. So along the way we will be sick, injured, sad, lonely, angry and even bitter. I look in the mirror each morning and am surprised that this hasn't taken me under. (I almost added 'yet' but that AIN'T happening) You see, I learn every day of a new situation of sadness and struggle and I alternate between feeling fortunate that we are healing and sad that someone else is going to go through what we went through. I can only hope that they are able to fight for their lives and don't overlook the joy because it absolutely still exists: Don Borling's wife, Amy Bullinger, Andrew Weishar, James Javier, Jerry Serrano, my brother Joe, are among those that have just recently been on my mind. I wish no one had to go through the agony but hope they are better off on the other end. Everyone deserves to feel as hopeful as we do on Team Juli, don't they? I wish that SO MUCH for Andrew, Amy, Jerry, James, Joe and Don and their families. Everyone deserves a chance to overcome something big. They deserve a team for support. They deserve to be surrounded by family and friends that care deeply and give of themselves. I hope those individuals have the good fortune that we have had and if I could tap into this wealth of caring for Juliana and share it with them I totally would. We are a powerful bunch. I have seen the magic come back to life in Juli and I really hope those people and their families can believe it and make it happen as well.

Speaking of our girl...Juli had a great day yesterday with her dad going out to breakfast, to a nature park then to a football game. She seems to enjoy getting out. Thank goodness the weather is improving so she can spend time outside on the deck at least. Now her friend gatherings can move outside. She is getting nearer to the end of her therapy sessions (end of May) and that will mean it might be time to make the next round of decisions. She will surely still need therapy so we may be shopping around at that time for a new facility. It's too soon to commit to that yet but we might have an opportunity for change. Although we have obviously seen great progress, maybe changing it up a bit wouldn't be so bad? The dentist didn't find anything concerning about her bite or her jaw so our next step is an oral surgeon to complete the diagnosis of TMJ or some other issue…some reason why she can't talk better. And although I have a hard time seeing improvements in her speech, those people that visit once a week or once a month even tend to say that she is 'much better than the last time'. As bad as it is to be 6 ½ months into this, that is also what is behind us.

April 14, 2010 - 6 am

Yesterday at therapy Juliana had a pretty incredible moment. While walking with her "magic wand" in her left hand and the therapist hanging on to the gate belt on the right, Juli set the wand down at her side and decided to keep walking. The therapist and Chris were impressed, not that she could do it because she has walked with only balance assistance before but because she recognized that she didn't need it and initiated that activity herself. Good work Jules. I also see that they are asking her to say one word at a time which does help to know what she is saying. I know we will get there; we will just have to watch that hair grow.

So ….The luggage is packed, the house is stocked, the guilt in tucked away and the limo is on its way. I am taking 8 days physical absence and hope the mental follows. Thank you all for your encouragement helping to alleviate the guilt of leaving at a time like this. I will be checking in with Chris of course to see how things are going but hearing the progress on the phone every day just won't be the same as being here (which is precisely the point, I know). I am hoping to come back and see something more than I see now and I don't know if I will be disappointed or excited. But what I do know is I will NOT be posting updates while in Hawaii.

So here's the deal folks: YOU are going to 'see' Juli the way I will see her…after a week away.

Hmmmm…now that I see it in writing it makes me look forward to coming back☺

~~Aloha ~~

April 23, 2010 - 6:15 pm

And now back to our regularly scheduled program....

First, you will have to indulge me while I tell you about my trip. (No, not about Hawaii which is as beautiful as you would expect, but about my departure) You see, since I needed a break visiting Dylan at school offered me the perfect location for that getaway. (Glad he wasn't in Nebraska!) I left with a lot of expectations around being away as well as for my return.

And much like everything else in this process, nothing matched my expectations.

I left to find peace and relaxation and what I found was that I was no longer distracted and hurried. The trip, (starting with the confines of the airplane for 9 hours) gave me the time and space to expose a much more broken person than I had admitted to being up to this point. My husband had to pick up the pieces several times during that trip while I once again appreciated his strength on my behalf. In my need to control what I was leaving behind, I probably insulted the most competent people in this equation: Juli and Chris. I worried, I warned, I prepared for help to come at a moment's notice...But what I found was what every parent truly hopes for their children: that they will someday grow up to find a partner who will be worthy of entrusting their child to. We have loved Chris as a son for many years but I have developed such an incredible trust and respect for him that I won't doubt his ability or his intentions again. And believe what you read folks, Chris Medina IS a wonderful man. He has taken this role of partner to my daughter to his heart from the very start and has done an incredible job of bringing her back to her former self. He told her one day that he wanted the 'old Juliana back' and she told him that she is still the old Juliana but she is the new Juliana too. I guess we will have to just enjoy getting to know them both all over again.

And of course my fondest reason for leaving... was to return. I hoped to step away only to return and be surprised by Juli's progress while I was away. But that is not what happened. There was no miraculous change any more than there was a 'moment' she awoke from her coma. Instead what I saw when I returned is was what had been there all along...subtle, graceful and preciously developing improvements. When I first came home she looked the same. She was in the same hospital bed with her leg braces on and her right arm held close and bent, her right eye still mostly closed, her voice too quiet to interpret. I held my breath, hugged my hellos and tried not to draw conclusions too quickly. I know Chris really wanted me to say that I saw something better, bigger, 'more' but I couldn't validate the work he put into the week right away. It took being with Juli alone all day yesterday before something happened. I dropped my wallet and the remained of my vacation money spilled all over the driveway.

Pennies. Well what do you know...?

I believe in signs so I took a moment to take stock:

Juli got in the car... no, NOT a car, my VAN, face forward, stepping up one foot at a time and then got into the seat. Although, of course, we assisted her, she did this four times yesterday as we went from appointment to appointment with only me to support her. That never seemed possible before. In fact, I never even attempted it before but somehow I just figured it would work and it did.

I watched her eat using her right hand, take medicine by mouth without being crushed and saw her smile with both sides of her face.

She opened her hand easily and pushed herself in her wheelchair right into the doctor's office.

She also acquired a habit while I was gone of holding up her hand to tell us the number of words she wanted to say and then saying them one at a time so that we could understand them. To think that all this time I wanted her to learn how to talk when maybe I just needed her to teach me how to listen.

I can't say that I am any more rested than Juli is healed but even though this is 'a marathon and not a sprint', I've seen enough mile markers to know that we are both headed in the right direction.

April 27, 2010 - 5 am

Since I came back the days have been passing quickly and I continue to see tiny glimmers of the old in Juli. I hate to be a broken record but it is still subtle and it is still happening. Gloria bought her the game of 'Blurt' and we play it every day to keep her engaged and to continue being impressed that she is still mentally completely intact because the girl is really good at the game. (It also gives Mackenzie another chance to work with Juli while practicing her reading skills). She is stronger walking and standing to the point where I am almost tempted to let her stand without assistance. I am sure that the therapists and Chris have tried this but I am not as strong or confident so I still hang on. I really long to see her show emotion (other than anger toward the therapists) and that 1000-watt smile is really the void. I also returned to a refrigerator full of leftovers from the many people who made sure Chris and Juli had plenty to eat so thank you Gloria, Maida and Pat Westergren! (Oh and Pat, I read your cards and letters to Juli all the time and feel as if we are following your story as well) Chris also took Juli out to dinner several times which I know she enjoyed. As she told me yesterday, "I will never say 'No' to going out to eat." I also got a pretty good scare on Sunday when I became really inexplicably sick. The scare wasn't me being sick, it was me wondering how the heck I was going to be able to take care of Juli when I couldn't even stand up. It turned out to be probably just a migraine but the sudden extreme dizziness, headache and vomiting made it impossible to even walk Juli to the bathroom. Thankfully Gloria arrived on the scene and took over mom duty while I puked my way through the day. When I finally emerged in the afternoon Juli was upset and a little mad. She asked me, "Were you hung over?" I promised her I had not had a drop to drink since I was in Hawaii and I had no idea what the problem had been. It made me realize how fortunate I am to have been healthy through this whole ordeal. Neither Chris nor I have had to really step back due to illness and I am so grateful now for that. I don't consider that good fortune random either so thank you all for the prayers and support that have kept us strong for the sake of my daughter. I mean, even though I had a pretty bad cold a few months back, it did not prevent me from taking care of Juli. But Sunday, man...THAT was a different story. Support groups are essential in the care of any sick or injured person and I urge all of you caregivers out there to heed the advice you will surely get: Take care of yourself or you will be in NO position to take care of someone else.

While on vacation we met a couple with whom we shared a conversation for a few hours. Near the end of our chat, the topic of Juliana's accident came up. The gentleman looked a little surprised and reflective as he started told a story of his own. "You know, until you brought up your daughter, I had forgotten about one of the most major occurrences in my life. When I was a freshman in high school my father fell three stories and also suffered a Traumatic Brain Injury. Just like your daughter he went through 18 months of rehab and all of the stages of recovery that you are talking about. It was a huge ordeal for my entire family and it defined our life...at the time. But I sit here today able to tell you that he recovered so well that I even forget about it as part of what happened to my dad and our entire family." His wife then chimed in..."And if I hadn't been told of the story, years after knowing him, I would never have even known." I was overwhelmed with happiness at that moment. And just like the song 'For Good' from Wicked that I like to sing to Juli states: "I've heard it said, that people come into our lives for a reason, bringing something you should learn and we are led to those who help us most to grow if we let them and we help them in return..." We didn't see this couple again but their story stuck with us. I believe we crossed paths so we could see a bit of the 'after' that may be our future. I would like to think that we added some value too...perhaps reminding them of the 'before' so they never forget how fortunate they are. I don't claim to really know why those chance meetings always seem to happen, I only know how I felt about it...just a little bit of relief.

There it is again.

April 30, 2010 - 6 am

A turning point...or...an awareness of what has been consistently turning? I think maybe that trip to Hawaii had some residual effects. It's like while I was spending my children's inheritance on the beaches of Waikiki I was banking something a lot more valuable. As much as I would love to be selfless and say this event is 'not about me' that would just be silly. This has become about all of us, right? So when I tell you about how I am interpreting the last 7 months as well as the months to come, yeah, it will also be how it affects me. You can tune out if you choose. I know that the readership is probably down to double digits even though the total number looks impressive. It's all good. I continue to document the little things for a variety of reasons. Mostly, to chronicle the progress for someone else to benefit. It started out with a different purpose: to keep family and friends abreast of Juliana's recovery. Now that we all know she WILL recover, I am watching and writing about the pieces of that recovery in the hopes that this chronology will help someone else know what to expect. If you know of someone who might benefit from our experience, let us know. I am ready to pay it forward in any way that I can even if it's just to listen and talk about what we have learned. When Juli balks at whatever stretches or exercises we make her do I sometimes remind her that this has happened to all of us and she is the only one who can get us out of it. So, yeah, it is about me and her dad, her fiancé, her stepparents, her siblings, her friends and her supporters...YOU. And she is working very hard at her recovery and it is paying off. Her therapists are consistently impressed at how much effort she puts into every task. You would think by talking to her that she is in complete rebellion because she absolutely hates therapy and as a result, the therapists too. But she does EVERYTHING they ask of her and achieves nearly every goal the first time they set it. Last week they had her playing UNO on her arms and knees. They began by saying they were going to help her to roll onto her stomach and prop up slowly onto her elbows (hoping to get her hands open and be fully on her hands and knees). I don't recall how long Chris said it took to get to that point but I do recall that he said she started doing it before they could assist her. She is gaining more control of her muscles and I see it in every move of her arms and legs. I was even able to stand her solidly several times yesterday without her braces. She wasn't putting weight on her right ankle but the left leg was strong. Her conversational skills are also improving. Her volume is a bit louder and her clarity is improving as I indicated before but it's more than that. Her voice is both a middle C and a D and she can hit other notes as well. The piano has been a good tool in helping her vocalize. She used to be able to plunk out a few basic melodies and she still can so it also gives her some home OT. She is also initiating conversations now, not just responses to us. She leans close for private conversations and uses her hand to cover her mouth when what she tells you is super-secret. Oh, by the way...Juli has forgotten how to keep a secret so beware all of you close friends, she has temporarily lost her filter for discretion! She spends more time thumbing through magazines than she was and she is now also watching TV, where before it couldn't hold her attention. She sat through Delaney and Mackenzie's talent show the other day and though she did get restless, it was 2 hours of staying put and she did it.

I asked her when she was going to start feeling as positive as the rest of us about her progress. I asked her when she was going to join us in putting the positive vibes out there and start visualizing her recovery completely. She said, "Maybe when it gets closer." That time has come. She needs to start seeing the end game so she can get there. I know that I have. I may have just been paying it all lip service prior to my trip but it was cathartic in many ways. I didn't see that right away, just as Juli can't yet see her own recovery. Funny how many times in our lives the situations have been parallel. It's time to develop and live that healthier attitude about this whole situation now and feel more in control, not just deal with the pain. The scars are healing nicely. Who am I talking about here? Could go either way.

May 1, 2010 - 10:30 pm

As many of you have witnessed, beginning in early December Juliana started shaking slightly with mild tremors. It isn't horrible; it's certainly manageable but prevents her from being steady with any hand movements. It seems worse when she is tired and all began at the same time she changed seizures meds. So with the guidance of our neurologist we have temporarily weaned her off the current seizure medicine to see if that is the cause of the tremors/shaking. Beginning today, she is fully off of the medication and as of this writing, although she is now asleep, she is still 'Shaky Juli'. We plan to give it a week. If after a week off of this medicine we don't see any improvement, in the shaking or in anything else, we will put her back on it. If we DO see an improvement we will conclude the medicine was the culprit and get a new seizure medicine. As much as we would like her totally off of meds, risking seizures is not worth it. So that is the plan for now. I will keep you posted on the outcome of that. In the week that we have been weaning her off though we have noticed a few other (coincidental?) changes. She is complaining daily of her legs and feet hurting and she is sleeping less soundly, but on the flip side there may be evidence of increased clarity of thinking. (It could just be time but I just don't know.) I would like to say her speech is getting louder and clearer (because I really think that it is) but since I have been saying that a lot lately I would hate to give the impression that she is a LOT louder and clearer: Just really 'one more day' clearer and louder. It is noticeable to me and definitely welcome….but you knew that because I complained most about that ☺

Another change for Juli is we are reducing the number of days she goes to therapy from 3 days down to 2 days a week. Since the insurance will only cover 60 day rehab visits until October 2nd we need to spread this opportunity a little thinner because as we have all learned, she simply needs time to pass. So while we wait for the state to come to their Medicaid decision, we need to delay the end of her current therapy days. Good thing we have the "Mad Therapist" on the case (Chris) to make sure the other days she doesn't truly get time off. Juli was happy with the reduction but what that will really mean is she will just hate it further into the year.

Today was a really busy (therapy like' in some ways) for her. She went to Chris's little sister Gianna's communion party from 1-3:30 and then Tessie's bridal shower from 3:30-7. From there we went to Starbucks to visit Chris at work. She spent the latter half of the shower with her leg braces walking through my brother's house, then out to the car, then into Starbucks then into the house, and down the stairs. That's a lot of 'I-am-getting-better-and-more-normal' walking. Juli cannot see it even though it's getting more obvious to all of us but her vision is skewed right now anyway. She said she really enjoyed the day and it appeared as if she did. But what was really cool is that getting her ready to go and taking her from place to place wasn't hard at all. I remember the ordeal of Christmas Eve...the drama of Joe's benefit and the prep and planning for Chris's show. It's all just slipping away. I am so grateful that my vision is crystal clear.

May 3, 2010 - 5:30 am

Yesterday was 7 months and it feels like a Wednesday morning in a very long work week. I keep giving these analogies of where we are in this process figuring it will offer some perspective, though admittedly I've never done this before so I am making it up as I go! Juli had a great weekend though if we are rating any day on the normalcy scale. We get constant reminders of how sharp her memory is from bands she remembers meeting in Nashville at Fan Fair in 1996 to punching/kicking combinations she learned 2 months ago from Gia. By all accounts, the girl is well over the worst part and just needs to physically catch up. However for Juli, 'perspective' is HER missing piece. (Maybe I should read her the updates...hmmm...) We continue to learn of people in very similar situations some progressing faster, some slower and some in the early stages of recovery whose pace is yet to be determined. I am clear on how this chapter of Juli's life will end and am starting to visualize a point in time when she might be able to live on her own. A few months ago I wasn't certain that would ever come to pass; but I can be totally grateful that she will be her old self one day. Convincing Juli every day (sometimes moment to moment) of that fact, is very challenging. As Chris and I talked about that very thing last night we concluded that we just have to keep plugging along; and as long as Juli continues to do what is needed to heal, we will have to just accept she won't like it. She definitely professes to be in more pain than she had been. She definitely is louder, and more vocal about her opinions. It's good to see but has a slight intimidation factor as well. Could that be the result of removing her anti-seizure medicine? We don't know but since the tremors continue still we will likely put her back on the trileptal at the end of the week and see if her heightened resolve and pain diminishes. I am actually not sure what to hope for since this is such a mixed bag. I want my daughter back along with her very strong personality but in some ways it is easier to move her along in her recovery if she doesn't have the wherewithal to object. You see when you are forcing someone to heal against their will and they aren't strong enough physically or mentally to protest, you can still accomplish the goal. But once she starts evoking her 'Free Will', we have to get more clever, convincing and firm. Chris takes the brunt of the abuse in this situation. Since he accompanies Juli to therapy each day she is associating him with the worst part of her day. If he takes pleasure in her hand and arm extension, she interprets that as joy for her pain in the stretching. When she walks over 200 feet successfully and he shares a proud moment with the PT, Juli interprets that as not caring that her legs and feet hurt. When Juli is able to use her right hand to perform normal tasks such as dressing herself, feeding herself and brushing her teeth, Chris watches even though she struggles through it. Juli interprets that as taking some pleasure in her struggling and spilling. So for all of you taking notes on your own journey...it's just one more day in the life of a recovery from a TBI. And all things considered, it's not such a bad day at all.

May 4, 2010 - 5:30 am

Juli and I watched the MTV True Life "I have a Traumatic Brain Injury" last night. I agree with her dad that my heart also goes out to all families who are dealing with this type of injury and subsequent extended recovery. I also agree that in seeing those young men, we are in a very good place. Juliana has none of the memory issues they speak of and she is cognitively intact. That seems to be the most debilitating potential to this injury and thank God, we have surpassed that. Her limitations at this point are left to physical and emotional and even her physical limitations are lessening each day. I think she needs to get out more and with the warmer weather upon us...it's time. She always took her greatest pleasure from socializing and often would come out of a bad mood simply by being in a situation where she had to just 'get over it'. Her job at Holsteins is a great example. She knew that even if she was having a bad day, she needed to be 'on' when she was at work because her tips depended upon it. Maybe I need to make her be 'on' more often....not sure. Now that Delaney started softball I told Juli that she is just going to have to become a softball cheerleader because I can't leave her home and I am not missing Delaney's games. Juli said "Fine" but we will see how long she can sit there before she runs out of patience. Her attention span is still pretty short and nothing really keeps her engaged for too long. We have been told "It's early in the recovery, just give her time." Early...really? I know that is supposed to make me feel hopeful but after seeing those folks in that show last night, it makes it crystal clear that recovery might be a lifelong journey. So if that is the case then my next focus is getting Juliana to come along for the ride...willingly. She indicated the other day that she doesn't like that Chris and I talk 'about' her all the time using 'her' and 'she' as if she isn't present. Fair enough. She...er...Juli... is not viewing herself as a patient but a participant and feels administered to instead of considered. So in order to really fully engage her we need to come up with some activities that will have her wanting more, doing more. The drudgery of her current schedule would not inspire action, I get that. The 'sheer joy of improving' to someone who has full recollection of what life was and what it is about to become is just not enough. I think we need to reinvent her life now and I don't feel like I am doing a very good job of offering that to her. I am going to have to go back to my creative roots from the days of teaching preschool to remember how to wrangle and please those individuals who have time, energy and limited attention spans and see what I can give her to do that might 'accidentally' provide therapy. Once we get the pool open that will be a great place to hang out. Creative and actionable ideas welcome.

May 6, 2010 - 3:45 pm

I have had a couple of very encouraging days with Juliana. First of all, the doctors are right, the medicine is not what is causing her shaking/tremors since she has been off of it for almost a week and still she shakes. It's ok, it was worth a try. Our decision now is whether or not to keep her off of the medicine altogether since we have seen indications which are perhaps coincidental, that she is making considerable improvement. For example, if the bed has the head raised a bit, she can get herself almost out of bed on her own. She has also started trying to get herself out of her chair. She is able to roll herself from her back to her stomach then to her back again. She can get up on her hands and knees (with considerable groaning, but that is ok too) She uses her right hand and arm a bit more, including to attempt typing and her talking is getting much better as well as 'other personal care' things that are much easier to manage. Now that she is willing to try typing we purchased a big keys keyboard so hopefully she can see the letters a bit easier and do her own Facebook messages. I have been her secretary for a while now but it's time for her to step in a bit. Some of you may have gotten messages from her, translated through me. She wanted me to let you know that we read your emails and she appreciates them. (Hey Juli, this is MY blog so shhhh... write your own)

Juli attended Delaney's softball game yesterday and for the first time I understood how offended someone who needs a handicap parking spot feels when it is smugly taken by someone who doesn't. We parked a block away and adjusted with drop offs, pick-ups and maneuvering to make it happen (pretty much the way we navigate our 4 level house.) The physical requirements of this task are not something we can afford to forget. For example, if I am going out with Juli, I can't wear heels. I can't trust my balance or grip when I need to stand or walk her. I need to think about what clothing works well for bending or getting dirty (much like having a very heavy baby.) Thankfully she is skinny enough!

Today while looking for new little things to do I handed her the bowling bag she called a purse. Now I had done this once before in the hospital but I couldn't know then how way too soon it was. Actually, looking back I am really glad I didn't know then what I know now. When, I gave her the purse, she went through it and attempted to put makeup on. It was so familiar to us that it was sweet. She looked through her wallet and shoved things all over the place. I had only just recently removed and discarded the clothes that were cut off of her at the hospital or they would have been in there as well. She even found a few pieces of window glass. It was eerie, like stepping back in time. And if that wasn't strange enough, she pulled out her camera and I loaded up her pictures. Now anyone who knows Juli knows that her camera is a walking photo album of the last three years. She used it to chronicle everything that happened to her and around her. It's interesting to see. So imagine my surprise when the most recent pictures were taken an hour before her accident. I see that smiling beautiful girl who had no idea that she was moments away from losing a year of her life. It's sobering still... just not as sad.

Mother's Day 2010 - 8 am

When I woke up I went to Juliana's bed just a few feet away and noticed she was awake. She immediately started saying something that I couldn't understand. I asked her to say it louder and clearer and it wasn't getting either. She started to spell it and I tried to figure it out. She started "...A-P-"

"Oh," I interrupt, "you want Apple Juice?"

"No" She tells me and begins again, "A-P-P-L-Y-"

"Apply?" I say confused. "What are you talking about? Man I wish you could just talk clearly!" I said this getting more annoyed than I should. Then after a few more attempts at guessing 'applesauce' and other nonsense I finally got the whiteboard and asked her to write it. The first letter she wrote made me instantly figure it out and feel ironically good and guilty all at the same time. That pretty much sums up the last 24 years for me anyway. She was saying, 'Happy Mother's Day'

Yeah, the first thing on her mind this morning was to wish me a Happy Mother's Day and I was annoyed at her attempt. So my 'Mother's Day resolution' is to be a better mom, live up to the expectations of my kids because regardless of anything they have yet to learn better, they deserve the best from me. Happy Mother's Day all you moms out there on Team Juli.

May 11, 2010 - 6 am

There are other things coming to our attention and we aren't sure what to think of them. On Mother's day Juliana was a bit more clingy to me than normal. At first it didn't really concern me and I didn't really notice it. But then as the evening wore on she wasn't content with me being in the same room, she wanted me NEXT to her. Separately, but also becoming a 'thing' that day was her renewed energy, or agitation, which grew stronger the later it got. She even sat herself straight up from flat on her back in an attempt to get herself out of bed! (Yes, that is a positive, if it can be valued on its own) Apart from the times of agitation and fixation, mostly she is only interested in either eating or lying in bed isolated. She doesn't really just lie there quietly though, she is still wanting...something... but even she doesn't know what it is. When we have to tell her 'no' about something she becomes fixated on having that very thing. At therapy, they are noticing a decline in her attitude and participation. They are concluding that she is more aware and more mentally 'intact' than we first thought and also more than she is letting on. Her increased awareness is also uncovering the other things we are seeing. Their diagnosis: severe and increasing depression. We knew this was a possibility on the horizon and have seen the signs ourselves. In fact, since nothing really seems to make her happy, we really already knew. Trying to find a way to "fix" or "help" her is proving to be tricky. She is on an antidepressant and we will likely increase it after we hear back from the doctor. She is aware enough to understand what has changed yet not capable enough to take back her old life. We go on and on about our certainty that she will return to her normal self but honestly, not everyone does. In fact, most never do. As you know she was very social before the accident. Now her limited ability to connect with people, as well as life going on for the rest of the world has limited her environment to mainly just family. It's the way this thing works. If it wasn't for anger and agitation, we would see very little emotion at all. This is definitely not the Juli we all knew and we wonder, she wonders, what and who she will be on the other end of this. We go back and forth between being discouraged and sad and positive and hopeful. She never really gets to the latter even though we could line up many reasons to be hopeful....if you look at what she has as better than dying in the accident that is. She doesn't see it that way. I am researching vacation ideas, creative therapy and activity options and anything that might get her to want to improve or at least BELIEVE she can improve. We are reaching out to others who have been through a TBI but that is proving to be less optimistic than we care to admit. We want to hear stories of complete success with no traces of the tragedy that is behind them. Instead what we learn about is a lifetime struggle to get back to the basics, a constant fight to do the normal things normally. Being thrilled that she is alive and improving is the most grateful stance to take but day in and day out we are forced to reconcile the reality of the life she may be LEFT to live. I can see why she would she would think being grateful to be alive is sometimes hard to swallow.

Tomorrow's another day.

May 13, 2010 - 11:50 pm

So we made Juli a deal: If she makes an attempt to see the bright side, tries to think about the good things and not focus on therapy and how much she hates it, we will allow her to take off this Friday (tomorrow). She was so excited she hugged and thanked us and was on her very best behavior...for a while. It didn't take long before she was trying to wear us down to 'call her off' for Monday too. She is relentless! I tried every trick in the book too: "Juli, if I don't make you go to therapy it is considered child abuse" or "The doctors are requiring that you finish your therapy" or my favorite total lie that I will surely need to go to confession for, "Since the police had to arrive on the scene to take you to the hospital, we are required by LAW to send you to therapy". Ok so before I get 'reprimand mail' for being so obviously dishonest, she believes none of it so it's all good. We felt justified cancelling therapy because, like I have said many times, she simply needs time to pass, so the days we skip just move to the end and on we go. It's not like she isn't getting therapy all the time at home anyway. I asked Juli, "What do you do at therapy?" She said, "Walk, talk, and use my right hand." I definitely led her to that simplified answer to make my point which I am sure YOU can see is that therapy is just relearning to live life. "Juli, WE make you walk, talk and use your right hand and you don't hate US?!" But the irony is lost on her if for no other reason than, when she gets an idea...ANY idea...she cannot let it go. Ever. It is a drive like I have never seen before. It's actually what is dragging her out of her hell and she doesn't even see it. Someday, looking back she will because our words are not completely penetrating. We did increase her anti-depressant and although I know it takes time to work, she has definitely had better days these last few. We are getting her out more, like it or not, and I think that might be helping...her. Traveling with her is still a lot of work but it's worth it. She doesn't like to spend too long in any one place so we have to choose places that don't have a large time commitment still. But she really is making incredible strides. Her balance and walking are so good now that our assistance is getting less and less. She is working on getting out of bed but I am a little afraid of her actually mastering that one. Unless that success is accompanied by additional maturity and attitude improvement, we will be in a whole new world of fear. Her shaking still continues, the anti-seizure med is still off and we will wait it out just a bit longer. We are also still waiting to hear back from the ocular plastic surgeon. Apparently the tradeoff for finding a 'nice' eye doctor is that he is less responsive. The good news on her eye though is this: her right eye is almost half open and she is able to see light and some shadows. That means we have high hopes again for that eye. I even caught her trying to use her right hand without being prompted. We got some books on CD and we are trying to have her listen to that for a while. I asked her if it was interesting and she said 'No' but she knew some of the facts of the story so at least she is listening. Since her emotions are the slowest to progress, we can expect that 'interested' might just take some time. Speaking of emotions, we caught her smirking twice today. She denies that she was smiling but we all saw it the first time and Chris saw it the second time. 2 more days until Dylan comes home. Yeah! Another team member at ground zero.

May 17, 2010 - 8 pm

The 'new' Juli can't keep secrets OR promises.

I really hope all THAT changes back! You see we kept our end of the deal, cancelled her therapy on Friday and instead of her trying to be happy about it she couldn't stop begging us to call her off of therapy for today. And that started about 2 hours after she promised to not speak of it for the whole week. I wish I could say that it's cute or funny or even a little tolerable but she gets angry, really angry. She punches herself, throws her braces and kicks her wheelchair. Don't get me wrong, I am grateful she has an opinion and is expressing emotion but it is such a fixation that I have been weighing the cost to benefit. I talked to Chris today about ending this therapy arrangement in case it was doing more harm than good. His first reaction was of course, reluctance and I totally understand. After all, it was only a suggestion not a firm conviction. I am still just a mom who is figuring this all out as I go. There is a safety in continuing to do what we are doing. It feels like as long as she stays in therapy, we are actively admitting she will still get better.

Then, totally without my suggestion the therapists recommended the same thing to Chris and Juli today. They confirmed that some people progress better at home and frankly, they have hit a wall with her, emotionally if nothing else. They are afraid that her depression will prevent progress. So, it seems that Juli might just get her wish after all. That puts us once again, into new territory which may be in home therapy. Her discharge date from RIC in Homewood is currently May 28th so we expect to have our next steps defined for us soon. But even while we are novices, Chris does amazingly interesting and dedicated 'therapy' all on his own. In fact on Friday, for her 'day off' he walked her out of the house, down the deck stairs to the pool, up the pool deck, back down, around the pool and back to the house. We have a pretty deep backyard so that was impressive. Chris planned to tell the therapists how she spent her 'day off' so they would know that even though we let her stay home, he kept up the good fight. I am sure they were impressed because that is further than they were EVER able to get her to walk. Maybe they felt they couldn't compete! So we will see what is around our next corner but I am confident that summer has lots of chances for real life therapy. And as soon as we open the pool Juli will have a whole new opportunity for therapy that I think will be fabulous. You got it…POOL CLEANING!!

May 19, 2010 - 11:45 pm

Very interesting.

Today we had the good fortune of meeting a beautiful young lady who took time out of her busy schedule to come all the way out to the suburbs to meet Juliana. She stayed for a few hours and talked with me and Juli and learned a little about our current situation. She had been reading some of the updates and like many other people, wanted to help, wanted to offer support, wanted to talk with us about our future. But this particular beautiful 24 year old visitor had something even more precious to offer: Experience. She suffered a TBI when she was 15 and she was at our home to tell us…no… SHOW us that there is a possibility of life after Traumatic Brain Injury. If she wouldn't have told me she suffered a terrible injury and went through much of what Juliana is going through, I wouldn't have been able to tell.

In fact, she must surprise many people with that admission as she handles school and work and a downtown apartment on her own. She didn't try to paint a picture of ease and simplicity though. She tried to offer encouragement with caution, optimism with realism and gratitude with empathy. She reiterated the fact that we have heard more often than we care to admit: This is a very long process. I listened to her story of recovery and heard many similarities and many differences. I saw a girl that got her life back and was able to do it in just 2 ½ years….yeah…so….2 ½ years? Really? That was a little sobering. I mean, I'd heard that before but I was still stuck on other estimates that we had heard which were closer to the 1 year mark. I again remembered the look of pity on the nurses' faces and avoided a mirror to see my own. I looked around my family room littered with 'Juli supplies' and equipment and then to my young daughter shaking gently with her half closed eye and clenched fist and wondered how we are all going to get her to that other side. As her current therapy draws to a close and we explore our other options I see a calendar of blank spaces where appointments used to be. I am no longer sure how we will measure our progress or our completion. Sometimes I am still surprised this is our life. I know that is Juli's thought every day…every time she can think those thoughts. I am sure we will have an opportunity like that beautiful and engaging young lady we met today. In fact I have never doubted it. What is deeply unknown is how and when we will get there. But I do know this: after today, though I sigh a little deeper to prepare for the potential of a longer road than I expected, I also smile a little more securely at the prospect of seeing my daughter return to me, just as Nicole Mayzner returned to her mom: Eventually.

Fair enough, she is worth the wait.

Thank you Nicole. You will never really know how much your visit affected me.

May 21, 2010 - 6 am

Tomorrow starts the last week of day rehab therapy. Our next step will be to schedule in home therapy. I think that the key to success will be for Juli to connect with the therapist. Maybe they can even be someone that she can view as a friend and not a therapist at all. I will see what my options are there. We are opening the pool next Sunday so that will begin our new home therapy as well. It will take some coordination to get her in the pool since her braces will have to be off yet she will have to go down the stairs into the water. I will let Chris figure it out the first couple of times then follow his lead. He is working hard to learn all that he has to do to help Juli once she comes home. I know he feels the pressure of her improvement because he has the most to gain by her full recovery. I predict this summer will see a flood of improvement, you watch.

Juli has an appointment on Wednesday to get another CAT scan in preparation for whatever the Ocular Plastic surgeon will be able to do. Her right eye continues to appear to be opening and the lower lid no longer sits on her eye but it is starting to look like she has a bit of a cloud over part of her eye. I hope we didn't wait too long to take care of this problem. Then again, with the improvements in her eye the doctor may determine he should do nothing at all. The next appointments we need to schedule are with an ENT specialist, a vocal cord specialist and a dentist who specializes in TMJ. Hopefully I can get all of her appointments in before her next schedule of therapy starts. I just never knew there were so many specialists necessary for one human body.

Friday night Juli's good friend Donnie Slattery brought over a delicious dinner and hung out with her for a few hours while she obediently (covertly) exercised in a variety of ways. All the while she begged Chris to take her upstairs. Of course since he said 'No' then she just couldn't let it go, she continued to ask. As soon as day rehab therapy officially ends I wonder what will replace it in Juli's obsession....hmmm...

Today we will enjoy the beautiful weather outdoors at Delaney's softball picnic. I can't imagine Juli will want to stay the whole day but I am going to try to make her as comfortable as possible so she can change from sun to shade, sitting to lying down. It's got to be better than just hanging out in our living room, right? Donnie, my husband, is going out of town this afternoon for a few days so that means that I am on my own for...everything non-Juli, which is what he is managing through all of this. I will really have to rely on Dylan, Cheyenne and Adam to be around and that is not as easy as it sounds. Speaking of Adam...guess what phone call I got the other night that I NEVER wanted to get again? Donnie called me and said, "Janet, Adam was in a car accident. It sounds like it must have been pretty bad."

My heart stopped.

"How do you know?" (At the time I couldn't tell you why I asked THAT question first but later I reasoned that knowing who told him made me gauge the severity.)

"Adam just called me."

PHEEEEWWWWWW-AA !

"Is he ok?" I asked this with caution but I immediately (no logic, just intuition?) knew he probably was.

"I think so."

My next call was of course to Adam who confirmed that he was fine, he was rear-ended and no one was hurt, but his car and the car who hit him were not drivable. So readers take note: If your child must have a car accident THAT is the kind of situation you want to be in. The only problem now is that Adam is without a car for a while. I'll take that problem, thankyouverymuch.

May 26, 2010 - 6 am

It's funny how this whole ride continues to point out to me how good people are. Maybe this shouldn't surprise me or choke me up still but it does. Take the Sunday softball day at the park for an example: It was by all technical and specific definitions, ' a failed operation'. First of all, Juli and I made it to the parade but not without cuts and bruises as I was again reminded that I am not as strong and coordinated as I really need to be. And even though it took more than an hour to prepare and to actually get there, we ended up leaving the park less than an hour later. But during the course of my attempt to stay the whole day, Juli and I were constantly offered help, company, assistance, concern, and support. In that regard, every few minutes I kept thinking silently "thank goodness 'so-n-so' is here otherwise this would be much harder or much more uncomfortable." We are so blessed. I think that really we all are and we just don't always see it. Unfortunately, in addition to being reminded how good people are, I was also reminded yet again that this world is so NOT accessible! Even the simplest of tasks like going to the bathroom, can prove too difficult to attempt twice. That is at least, when you are pushing a wheelchair through soggy grass, then needing help carrying it up then back down a couple of stairs. I had to look at the park for places and routes that would make staying even possible. The world itself is inconvenient for anyone less nimble and that was really why we ended up leaving the park.

I felt bad in a way since so many people offered to help anytime I needed it, assuring me that all I had to do was ask. Old friends were there to make me feel less 'separate'. New friends were there to help pick up my slack with the other kids. Neighborhood acquaintances and park officials were doing everything they could to help us navigate an uncomfortable and undesirable situation. Juli and I were both uncomfortable with the attention when we really (naively) just wanted to blend in. Is that how others with a disability feel? It doesn't feel very good. My heart broke for those that deal with this every day. I told Juli, "remember all of this help and support when this is no longer your life. Take none of it for granted." And since the single bathroom trip was a 20 minute adventure in character building, I decided it was not going to be worth it to stay for the day. Those of you who know this 'current Juli' know that we could be taking 'the bathroom tour' every 15 minutes. I just couldn't see inconveniencing everyone all day long and monopolizing the one good bathroom for the majority of the day. I ended up feeling like our staying would detract from other people's ability to fully enjoy their day. So we wheeled back the two blocks to the car and just went home. Doesn't that sound pathetic? After everyone was SO willing to help? I probably should have fought the good fight a bit longer for Juli's sake except for the fact that I was basically forcing her to stay to begin with so... who was I actually doing it all for? Delaney and Mackenzie got to stay and enjoyed themselves regardless if I was there. We arrived back home scratched, bruised, exhausted...and it was barely noon. I hope I have the physical stamina to keep this up. I hope Juli gets stronger faster than I get older and weaker! So apart from feeling completely inept at being able to take care of my daughter on my own, I was humbled to realize that I don't HAVE to do it alone.

Now if I could just feel comfortable accepting help....

Well...'comfort' might just be a luxury I cannot afford this year.

May 28, 2010 - 1 am

So you might have seen that Juli typed a message to all of you with her new keyboard. She is getting better at it but her shaky hands and her skewed vision make her typing imperfect. After she typed what she wanted to say (and she decided on her own what to write) I just went back over it and took out the double letters she accidentally placed as she shook and typed simultaneously.

Tomorrow is the end of Juliana's day rehab at RIC Homewood. And although they did a fabulous job of progressing her walking and use of her right hand I can speak for the entire family when I say that we are glad it is OVER! Don't get me wrong, Juliana still definitely needs therapy. She is not able to independently do much of anything yet so obviously, we have a long way to go. But she has been SO obsessed with her hatred for therapy and the therapists that it's almost impossible to communicate with her about anything else. It is a very immature fixation that is a result of how her injury is manifesting itself. In our little bit of research we did learn that the location of her injury could cause this type of behavior along with a lack of impulse control...oh yes, we are seeing THAT too. I probably can't describe it accurately enough but let's just say, if she feels it or thinks it, she can't filter from there. So if you really don't want to know if those 'pants make you look fat' I wouldn't bring it up around Juli. Even when you ask her or beg her not to say something or do something....(or maybe BECAUSE she is asked not to say or do something) it becomes the single thing she must say or do. If you ask her not to put 3 toasted cheese raviolis in her mouth all at the same time, well, she just doesn't care that it will make her choke and make Cheyenne scream and me dig in her mouth to retrieve the wad of cheese. And now, with her increasing strength and mobility we have the added concern of how she might be able to do harm by not listening to us. She reaches and bends and often times, falls. I feel like I have been here before.

She went for her CT scan of her orbits yesterday to see if the swelling near her eye has decreased. Then the ocular plastic surgeon will determine what he can do to help Juli's eye heal. Her eye is starting to open more and more though, all on its own.

I have to get back to packing and hopefully get some sleep soon. Don and I are leaving in the morning to go to New York for my niece Tess' wedding to Matt. I am so looking forward to the short 2 day get away to let me regain my strength to deal with the rest of her 'adolescent phase'.

June 1, 2010 - 6 am

So here we are, at the next juncture: "Do it yourself therapy". As it turns out, in the eleventh hour the rehab facility was "uncomfortable" leaving Juliana for so long with unskilled therapy. Knowing that skilled at home therapy would not be taking place and that the day rehab was being seriously rejected by Juli, we came to a compromise. We would continue with moving her along as we have been and go back there every other week for a day of "evaluation" (sssshhhhhh, don't tell Juli they will be doing therapy). The plan (as communicated to Juliana) is that they will continue to monitor her progress to ensure that she really is 'doing better at home'. Then if it appears she is not, she will resume day rehab. At least that is the way we explained it to Juli. In reality we may have to wait until October for approval of the next60 sessions of therapy, but other things are in the works as well. She seemed to be ok with that solution and has shifted her depression from 'because of therapy' to 'just because'...*sigh* This is all a bit of a moving target and we all just put in our time and hope to see the results in the long run. It's just that this run takes longer all the time. There is continued progress though as Chris tries his very best to stretch Juli back to her former self. I really have to hand it to the boy: He is giving it his all. And when Juli reaches whatever potential she will reach, if they are no longer the people that they intended to be and find themselves parting ways, he will surely be able to do so with a clear conscience. NOT that I expect that mind you but we are all trying to be realistic. I care enough about him as well that I don't want him plagued with guilt over something he could not control. But all that doom and gloom aside, he was able to do something pretty awesome while I was in New York enjoying an awesome wedding with the BEST wedding food ever (Matt and Tess: bravo, kudos and congrats...LOVE to you both!) Chris was able to get Juli to do some walking WITHOUT her leg braces! This is a huge step and potentially more premature than the therapists would recommend but, have no fear, Chris is incredibly careful and attentive so he was surely doing it with the greatest of support. Not to mention the guy is as strong as an ox and could lift her up at a moment's notice. (Wouldn't necessarily know that to look at him, right? Yeah, he has many surprisingly wonderful qualities). So Juli took several gentle and precise steps without her braces in an attempt to strengthen her weak ankles. He will continue to work on that in the coming weeks. He is also spending time helping Juli with her balance, when she doesn't fight him that is. You see we have learned that the nature of a traumatic brain injury is how it manifests itself so individually for everyone. Juli has no memory gaps or obvious learning deficits. But what she does have are emotional limitations (she still shows very little emotion) and immature reactions. She might be mad at me for this someday reading back but she is similar to a preadolescent in her responses to things. She has always been quirky and particular and Chris has even acknowledged that a lot of what he sees in her today is similar to how she was before. However, what he is looking to regain is what he fell in love with: the parts that made all the quirky particular things worth navigating through. That is the missing link at the moment. We keep hearing, "well, its early in the recovery process yet". That should help us hang on to hope but even as she walks and talks just the tiniest bit better, a smile now and then would be a nice little bonus to fortify us all. Come on, you have seen the pictures, many of you knew the girl, her smile, her personality, her...WAYS all filled a huge space in our lives and our home and our hearts.

The space is still reserved though, we just have to believe she can move back in.

June 2, 2010 - 8:30 pm

We had another special visitor. Well of course ALL of our visitors are special but this one was particularly...well...informative. You remember Nicole, our new TBI acquaintance? Well she came back and brought her MOM who traveled all the way from Texas and chose to spend an evening with us! She was really a mom after my own heart. Sure there are many differences in the recovery path each girl traveled but it was nice to meet someone who survived what we, the support team, have survived. I asked her when she walked in, "Tell me everything I need to know." She laughed and said, "Everything? Well, 'everything' is that your daughter will be fine. That's 'everything' enough." (Doh!) It was a joyous and pleasant meeting full of something I rarely find: complete understanding. They are a family of faith and love and I can see that is what took them bravely through the tough times. We shared, compared and had a very nice visit. Dayle Mayzner was just as lovely and engaging as her daughter and I am so honored that they chose to spend their time with US. As I said though, as with all brain injuries, you can find similarities, but our course of recovery is unique to Juli. And although Juli continues to show improvement (and I do my best to be grateful and happy about that), it is still a physical, vigilant, hands-on effort for all of us. Juli is inching back to herself and we are traveling with her toe to toe. That also means as she gets stronger, yet not yet independent, the risk increases with her abilities. She is stronger than I am anyway so if she goes down, we both go down and it has happened multiple times. That is where our stamina is consistently tested. I remember the saying so clearly: "It is a marathon, not a sprint." Dammit, they were right again. Sometimes I feel like I am on 'pause' because so many days resemble so many others. (Groundhog Day, but darker and WAY weirder). Maybe if the only challenge in my life was Juli's recovery it wouldn't seem so overwhelming but, to be truthful, my life had its share of color and texture before the accident, as most lives do. I thought I was good at managing it all too. I don't think that anymore. Now, I just let the tide take me, I really don't have the energy for much more than that, much to the dismay of my other demanding children. Ok, perhaps too honest today so I will stop and just say, Juli told me, unsolicited, that she loved me 3 times today. Yep, I was pretty happy about that. Of course I had to ask 'why' (Note to moms: don't ASK, it will ruin the illusion). In fact, I won't ruin yours by telling you her answer. After all, if you really think about it… does it even matter 'why'?

Right, that's what I thought too.

June 7, 2010 - 5 pm

We made three attempts at using the pool for Juliana's therapy and discovered that we need to learn more about how to utilize that resource. Just getting Juli into the pool is a workout for both her and whoever gets her there between the trek down the stairs, through the yard, up the stairs then into the pool...phew! Once we finally catch our breath we are too tired to help her do anything more than get in. I had very different expectations for it though. I guess I expected that with her ability to feel weightless she would be free to walk and maneuver on her own. But it seems that in addition to everything else, she will also need to learn to swim again. For whatever reason I completely overlooked the fact that she can't walk because of her brain's inability to 'get it all together', not just because she isn't strong or coordinated enough. So 'walking' in the water won't be any more successful than walking on the floor...yet. She is not able to keep herself upright or even tread water yet so it's just one more thing that is back to basics. Tomorrow she goes back to rehab for her "evaluation" day. She is not completely fooled by the term but the reduction in her obsession over therapy tells me that she is not as worried or aware of it as she was before. Both Chris and I are concerned that we will not be able to move her any further along without continuing professional help so we may have to make some unpopular choices for her own good. Juli continues to be completely aware of her surroundings and we try to be grateful for that. Stringing together our own sanity and happiness gets thinner all the time because the act of caregiving continues to be just as physical as it is mental and Juliana is finding it very hard to see 'the bright side' in any of this. She sees herself as 'completely there' mentally but stuck in a broken body. I am not sure I agree with the 'complete' part but she needs some mark of independence to the rainbow on the horizon. If she could either walk or talk effectively, I think it would make a huge difference in her outlook, which would in turn make our jobs easier. I keep waiting and working for those days in the hopes that the benefits will start multiplying exponentially. Might just be another misguided expectation though.

June 13, 2010 - 11:30 am

You still out there? We are still here. I was beginning to feel like updating so frequently was a misrepresentation of the pace of Juli's recovery. The more time that passes (8 months and 9 days to be precise) the more we know that time more will have to pass. Progress has slowed, probably in large part to not going to outside therapy, which we will be rectifying soon. Chris has done all he can but Juli is much more comfortable objecting to Chris and me than she was the therapists. Some people do better at home. That does not appear to be the case with Juli, at least not right now. And so unless you are counting the pennies, the increments are undetectable to the outside eye.

We have had a bit of a change that deserves mentioning since it has been the topic of conversation in our house the last week. It's kind of an 'unknown' that took us by surprise and Chris and I don't quite know what to think of it. I will be interested in your perspective. You see, when you aren't expecting something, it's easy to miss all the signs. 'Signs' of something changing or being altered and so you are taken off guard and your reactions to it are slow. As you may know, it is an interesting balancing act of monitoring Juli's progress against what we might be doing, or not doing, to help her progress. We spend most of our time and energy trying to learn the best combination of therapy, stimulation, medicine and motivation to get her back to herself.

In fact, sometimes it seems like the only thing I do. Devoting this much time and energy will pay off some day and all I can hope is that I have done the best I could to keep her safe and happy and on the fastest track possible. Yet, in spite of our attention to detail...every so often there is something happening just under your nose and you just don't see it. I actually should have expected it, it is typical and normal and predictable. I have known the players in this game long enough to know what they are capable of yet; when 'it' happened it opened old wounds and confirmed new directions.

Ok, so maybe I am over dramatizing it and some might think it is not a big deal. In fact they might think that there is no reason to even mention it to this readership. Some might even think that it is indulgent to tell you the details of what happens in this process. I figure it this way, you have had to endure all of the good bad and ugly up until now, so, why not...full disclosure, right?

Here it is:

Chris made Juliana laugh. It was pretty monumental when you think that up until the last week or so she has been void of any emotion other than anger. No crying, no smiling, no laughing no real sign of what made Juli...well... JULI. But they were watching Night at the Museum 2 and when they got to the part where Abe Lincoln came to life Chris asked Juli what she would do if she saw Abe come back to life. Juli said, "I'd shoot him." After Chris laughed and teased and collected himself he asked her why and she said, "Because he is supposed to get shot." Chris said, "yeah, but not by YOU!" And he broke into animated laughter and much to his surprise, and Juli's, she laughed too. It was small, it was maybe even a little scary for her but it was real and recognizable and so darn cute. I just underestimated how funny Chris could be even though he has me in stitches once in a while as well. I underestimated Juli's recovery and while we are looking at her feet for changes, it was happening in her face. I kick myself for not seeing the emotion emerging so that it could be brought out sooner but, here we are making all of us...even Juli now, happy.

Have a happy week.

June 15, 2010 - 6 am

Today is actually the day Juli goes for her "evaluation". I thought it was last Tuesday but I was off by a week. In the two weeks she has been out of therapy (really? only 2??) we have accumulated several questions for the doctor and the therapists. She seems to be complaining more about pain in the last week so we need to talk to the doctor about this new occurrence and devise a plan to help her with that. We surely don't want her in pain but we also need to know the best way to handle it from those that understand the complexity of her condition. I expect we won't get many answers since this is the game of "Time" but we will be starting her back on the therapy schedule. She will probably fight, object, and obsess during all her waking moments at home but she will shine at therapy so we will all just tough it out. We have to keep forging ahead because getting stuck is a very bad thing at this point. One bit of update that is not so encouraging: The ocular plastic surgeon reviewed previous CT scans and compared them to the one taken last month and concluded that the damage to her optic nerve and muscle will likely be permanent. And although he would like to proceed with the surgery to turn out her lower eyelid, he does not recommend surgery on her upper eyelid to attach her eyelid muscle to her eyebrow muscle because 1. There is no guarantee that muscle is any more effective than her eyelid muscle, 2. She could have difficulty closing her eye (eewwwwwa) and 3. Her brain matter is still protruding into the orbits and according to him, her CT scan has not changed (improved?) at all. I was pretty down after that conversation. All along I have been telling Juliana with great confidence that she will eventually return to her old self and now, with the slowed progress and the bad news about her eye and her scan, I am wondering if I have lied to her. I am also wondering how I might have to teach her to live with her limitations once they are fully known. We have been living with the idea that all of this is temporary from the hospital bed in the family room to the lack of vision in her right eye but it is getting harder to look back at 'the old Juli' because I fear I need to adjust to a whole new world…and help her to do the same. I keep hearing that it's too early in the recovery process to think about that but my 'look at the bright side' is clashing with my 'you need to prepare in advance' so I am not sure what to do next. I am not giving up hope that she can recover fully and in fact, if I stay connected to the positive signs, in spite of the doctor's prognosis on her eye, it is defying all logic and opening up a little more all the time. So that is just one more indication that we…all of us…medical professionals, therapists, and plain old mom, just don't know anything for sure. I heard a good quote the other day: "Time heals almost everything. Give time, time." Considering we don't have any other choice, we will be doing just that.

June 18, 2010 - 6 am

Juliana went back to RIC Homewood on Tuesday for her "evaluation" and did extremely well. In spite of the fact that she had almost three weeks off of skilled therapy she continued to progress. Upon arrival she was tense and upset and Chris was once again reminded how much Juliana did not want to be there. And once again, in spite of her very obvious dislike of the whole activity, she was focused on being a perfect student. Her arm is able to extend another 10 degrees and her hand is able to extend another 5 degrees. She was able to walk a longer distance without stopping than they ever attempted before but her gait was less steady and balanced. That is something they will want to work on getting back in line. They also noticed that her right eye was open more than they remembered. The speech therapist was impressed by how much clearer and louder she was and Chris said he could even here her outside of the room. All things considered, it was an extremely successful evaluation. She will go back today and then again four more times over the next two weeks. Then we may be doing home therapy for a month or so after that. How and when and where she gets her therapy is a moving target but insurance is a tricky business and we are learning all that as we go along. We have been able to get Juli in the pool again and as usual, after five minutes in she is ready to get out. Since it is a 30 minute process to get her into the pool, I wasn't budging until I got a return on my investment. So, for 2 hours we laughed and played and had a good time...even though she hated every minute of it. (Yes children that IS called teasing but moms are allowed when it is for the greater good). Though she moved around the pool with me begrudgingly, I was finding it easier to get an occasional odd laugh out of her and that is wonderful to know. To see the tiniest glimmer of her personality coming back...well...A personality coming back, (it still doesn't seem familiar)...it does feel a little like a reward. Even though it is only half a smile with what looks like a painful laugh, we know it to be the same kind of progress we have seen all along: small, awkward and differently executed. The fact that we can call it 'progress' at all is that we hang onto as the days go by looking just like the ones before it. As I tell Juliana, she is not going through this alone because this accident happened to the whole family and we are all forever changed by it. I find myself dealing with everyday situations much like my daughter does as I navigate the new logistics and priorities: a bit more awkward and unsure. And just as it does for my Juli, the world looks different to me now as we both adjust our focus. Sometimes it actually even works.

Good luck at the show tomorrow night at the Beat Kitchen to Chris and the Able Body!

June 23, 2010 - 6 am

You ever stop and think that life is a series of resetting of expectations? I have been thinking that a lot lately. I think about what I originally expected in Juli's recovery to what I think now and it has been a very long and winding road. (Of course you know that, you have seen the changes). Well I am kind of thinking that I shouldn't expect, and instead should just 'see'. Expectations are really about the future, what will or might happen and maybe that puts the focus just out of sight of the right now. I alternately believe in a future that resembles the past and one that resembles nothing I know. I no longer have a preference and am really trying to stabilize today. For Juliana, back in therapy with no foreseeable end, she has a long slow road. We are looking at managing the long term effects of this injury which include pain and sleep. Where once we had 'expected' the pain to get better and disappear, we are learning it might be a lifelong condition, even if she regains normal functionality. Where once we had expected her need to rest would be reduced, we are learning that when she wants to sleep to let her sleep even if it seems an inordinate amount of time. As the recovery takes its slow and steady pace we accept it just a little more and try to modify our home, our time, our schedules and yes, our expectations, to include this situation in a much longer haul than we would like. It's not good or bad but it is...

In the meantime, we are working to get her leg braces adjusted for better comfort, learning to walk her more accurately and use additional skills like typing to improve her speech. (I am not sure how typing and speech are connected but they have studies to prove the correlation). Juli continues to hate it all and obsesses as she did but with our increased acceptance of her need to sleep, the result is, we hear it less. (Heeheee) Next week Juli and I will be managing without Chris as he drives across country to take some much needed time off. I suspect it will be similar to my trip to Hawaii: different than he expects. (Ah....there it is again, that devil 'Expectations'.) He will take some time for himself and take a slow drive to Vegas and we will keep on keeping on back here. I will also be taking Juliana over to William Tell where her wedding is scheduled. We had asked if we could move the date (not get any money back mind you, just move the date again) and they want to see Juliana for themselves. I understand that they have no reason to believe us, it's business and not personal, but I had to warn the coordinator that she will feel very uncomfortable when we show up so they can "ask Juli some questions" and they won't be able to understand her. Guess they will have to get their expectations reset as well.

June 28, 2010 - 11 pm

I feel that although I don't update as often, I think of doing so every day. You know when you wake up from a dream and you feel all day like you were in the middle of something you meant to get back to only to recall, wait, that was my dream, it just seemed really real? Well I keep thinking, "Wait, who was I just talking to? Oh, yeah, it was the Facebook page." So since I have been holding back I might have missed a step or two but I will try to get as much in as I can.

Chris is gone, left for his road trip to the west coast...or nearly the coast. He left me an opportunity to embark on an adventure all my own as I took the week off to spend with the kids, especially Juliana. We do have what I find to be a pretty cool accomplishment: Juliana's laughter. Well...since it is still a jumble of laughter and crying or whining it is not truly what anyone would recognize as laughter. In fact, anyone stopping by might think there was a delicate siren going off. But all the same, WE know what she is doing. And now the subject matter (thankfully) has moved beyond assassination. Now we can get her to laugh or 'craugh' as we have coined on any number of topics. It has become our favorite pastime. I am going with Juliana to therapy tomorrow and plan to ask a few questions of the doctors and therapists in hopes of confirming that what I am seeing is really as good as it feels. Her balance and walking are still taking a very slow road to recovery and that means she still requires a lot of physical attention. Her talking hasn't improved much either and that frustrates us as much as Juli. We have an appointment with a voice specialist in July so we may take a new path at that time. She is now finally scheduled for her eye surgery to fold out her lower eyelid. That will be August 3rd. In the meantime her upper eyelid continues to open eversoslightly. I will post a picture. You will notice her right eye has what appears to be a slight film over it, almost appearing to have changed colors. That is because of her lower eyelashes periodically resting on her eye. It may get better after that problem is corrected but there is no guarantee. Her vision is still limited and her tremors continue. Sometimes they even seem to have increased but she can stop them if she concentrates on staying calm and nothing else. And in spite of what she can't yet do, it still feels like there is quite a bit she can. For instance, Chris taught her how to fold socks the other day. Hey hey! Maybe he can show the other 5?? Seriously the good thing about that is she had to use BOTH hands. The more reasons she is forced to use her right hand, the more it becomes useful. She is also going to be spending a bit more time on the computer so for those of you that have Juli as a friend on Facebook, I encourage you to send her a short email with a question or two that she can read and respond to. It will be great practice for her vision and her typing skills. Please do keep them short though because it will be a tough read with her vision so off.

And please, even though we don't 'chat' every day, please know that I am still grateful for the followers that are praying for my daughter. It is a daily effort for us to keep her progressing and without your support; we wouldn't be able to do it. While you are at it, say a little prayer that Chris gets the well-deserved physical and mental rest that he has earned.

July 1, 2010

We went to the William Tell Banquets at the Holiday Inn in Countryside yesterday for our appointment to discuss the particulars of Juliana and Chris's wedding date. They did feel uncomfortable for just a moment or two but we got in and out of there in 15 minutes. It seems they want us to NOT select a new date at this time and just get back to them when we have a definite date. At that time, we will draw up a new contract (undoubtedly new prices) and go from there. Fair enough. I oozed how kind they have been and how accommodating they are and I am sure when the time comes they will treat us fairly...they of course said they would see what they could 'throw in' when the time comes because they want Juli to have the beautiful wedding she deserves. (So I capitalized on their discomfort just a bit....it's all good) Damn straight. So, it was uneventful and no harm done. My husband asked me to start walking out while he stayed to ask them a few questions…

Don: "So, why did we have to COME here for this to be taken care of? I didn't hear anything that couldn't be handled over the phone."

Food and Beverage Manager: "Oh we just wanted to discuss this in person to make sure we were all on the same page."

Don: "This could have been handled over the phone so it seems to me like you wanted us to come in person because you needed proof."

F/B manager: "Oh no Mr., Barnes that isn't it at all. We believed you, we just thought this would be more… personal."

Don: "Well if you wanted 'personal' we could have invited you to the house instead of making us drag Juli 40 minutes each way."

F/B Manager: "I assure you, we believed you we just wanted to make sure that we all agreed on the new situation."

(Don skeptical and not convinced)

Don: "So, what IF this wedding is never able to take place."

F/B Manager: "We will discuss it with the owners at that time but we have seen tragic situations before and they have always handled it fairly regardless of the fact that they COULD by rights keep funds already presented to us."

Don: "Thank you for your time, we will be in touch…and we look forward to whatever you will be 'throwing in'."

That's the way Don rolls.

I have heard from Chris a few times and he seems to be thoroughly enjoying his road trip. As you have learned, he is not your typical male. He is creative and introspective and sensitive so what some guys would see as an opportunity to bar hop across the country, Chris sees as an opportunity to see nature. He is marveling in the canyons, the sand, the mountains and the sunset. I expect his creative juices are getting replenished. I also hear the yearning for Juli in his voice. I would love for him to return to grand advancements but just like my escape to Hawaii, he will not see a big difference. We have been working on lots of little things and trying to get her outside as much as possible. Since I took this week off and the weather has been incredible, it makes that effort easier. I am shocked how much easier it is to handle all aspects of my life with my job not in the middle. Not that they haven't been incredibly accommodating at work, because they have but being off gives me one huge thing to NOT worry about. I am trying to bottle this temporary calm so that when I am back to full time next week I can sustain until the next respite.

Today Chris's journey takes him to Vegas. Let's all wish him a little luck since he has certainly earned it. He is not much of a gambler but even if a few dollars in a slot machine yields him a few more...that is one in the Win column and we just don't turn ANY of those away these days.

July 7, 2010

Chris is back and both Juli and I are glad. I mean, I managed, and in some ways it was easier...you know how moms are, it's just easier to do it yourself sometimes. Not that I was without help but I was definitely without THAT kind of help. But while he was gone I was off work so that made taking care of Juli much easier. The beautiful weather didn't hurt at all either! Chris was thrilled to see her and spent the first couple hours intermittently quietly crying. What can I say...he is the sensitive type. Anyway he had a great time on his road trip and claims to be 'totally recharged for another 9 months'. Yes team; it has been 9 months...sigh...much different than other '9 months' I lived through. That particular length of time was not lost on Juli who even said that she could have had a baby by now.

So you may recall we took her out of therapy temporarily for a few weeks, then put her back in to complete the sessions allotted by insurance. Well next week those full day outpatient sessions come to an end until October. We will be pursuing in-home therapy for two months and then we will see where we are. Who knows, there may be some significant progress to be made. The more time that passes though, the more that we wonder how much of what she can and cannot do, is here to stay. I am still encouraged by her progress and have great hope in the possibilities but since she still remains completely dependent it all just feels...how should I put this...'longer than temporary'. As a family we are trying not to give up all of our former life and entertain at our home frequently as we always have. Boating and camping weekends will probably not happen this year and many other outings aren't quite the same of course but I am happy my home is a place I love to be. But as much as I enjoy what we can do, I can't help but always feel guilty that Juliana can't do the same. She still doesn't enjoy much of anything and that just makes me feel even more guilty. Progress for her is still slow and in some cases we fear we may be backsliding. I know that we are still fortunate in that we have not faced many medical crises that face people with brain injuries have such as seizures and additional injuries or memory loss so really, I am very grateful still and am seriously NOT complaining about where she is. As I have said many times, she is my daughter for life, regardless of what she can do for herself. I am merely trying to lay it all out for a reality check. I can say for certain that "1 year" will NOT mark her recovery. That was probably just in our heads anyway.

In an effort to fight her increased muscle tone (which may be contributing to her decline in her ability to walk) we put her back on the muscle relaxers. It was not our favorite option but it is a path we did not explore for very long the first time and her minimal amount of medicine now seems to point to the timing being right to try something new. She seems to be talking less clear now as well though I wouldn't be surprised at all if that is a result of the muscle relaxers. It is such a tough balance. Tomorrow we go to the voice institute for a long awaited appointment to have her vocal chords assessed. I am not sure what they do exactly but her dad has experience with this doctor and it seems this doctor will be able to tell us if her limited talking is due to something physical. We will see.

July 10, 2010

"9 months is really such a short time..."

Hmmm....tell that to a pregnant woman and see if she agrees; or the mortgage company waiting for the payment; or a wife waiting for her husband to return from Iraq; or a cancer patient enduring chemo; or a young lady recovering from a traumatic brain injury (and her family).

But that was part of the really good news we got from the Bastian Voice Institute. It started with, "9 months is really such a short time in the overall recovery process of a brain injury." Which then led to: "Juliana does not need to return because her vocal chords, larynx, voice box, and swallow are perfect." He was very impressed with her quick response time to vocal commands, her clear understanding of all that he asked her and even her ability to enunciate the sounds he requested. He said more than a few times that for a brain injury such as Juliana's, she is making remarkable progress and we all just need to be patient. Then I asked my unanswerable question (not because I expected HIS answer to be any different, it's kind of just to add to my catalog of the many ways to say, "I don't know.").

"So if she is in 'perfect working order' can we expect her to eventually speak normally again?"

(Do I even need to tell you his answer? Probably not, you should be able to guess that one by now)

In any case, his advice, other than to wait for time to pass, is to force her to vocalize ALL THE TIME. Any sound we can think to have her make, make it. Any noise that we hear from her, enforce it. Any words that she says make her say it again. Ok doc, I got this one. So the relentless teasing will continue because that gets her really going with both volume and quality. It appears painful but she admits... (You ready for this)...she enjoys it...AH. At last. It gives us something to work on.

Full day therapy at RIC in Homewood is done for now and next week we will start with in home therapy. Who knows, maybe we will get a therapist that really connects with her and that is where great strides will be made. Throughout this whole 'short' 9 months I have vacillated between complete confidence and sullen reserve but the raw hope itself never fades. So on this day, where I am feeling hopeful and confident I think about the 9 months I was pregnant (x6) and realize that those months were nothing at all compared to the many years I have enjoyed my kids (ok, and sometimes I just tolerated them) . And when I think about the hard times in my past, they are gone and over and barely a memory. That is our future here: seeing this as the distant past.

July 18, 2010

Juliana was a lovely young child. I can't remember her being mischievous or bratty or acting inappropriate. I always thought of her as kind and respectful, patient and sweet. As I plan to 'look back' on THIS time, I hope I can see it through the same rose colored glasses. Because...if I think REALLY hard, I do recall that we used to call Juliana 'Veruca' after the character Veruca Salt in Willy Wonka. (Yep, those of you that know that character are seeing where this is going) I also recall her intense NEED for things being a complete distraction to others. I also recall her brother Adam coming along as the 'supporting player' right from the beginning. Yes, if I remove the glasses, perhaps like every other child, she had her moments of being juuuuuuust a little bratty. And in the course of her recovery we have been told that it is like going from infancy through to current day in the space of a year. Well I can point out at least two few flaws to that: 1. My earlier estimate of where she was in her maturity was overestimated and 2. (As previously admitted), it will take much longer than a year. I know this because right now, she is being a total brat. And as I publicly admit that to 3790 potential readers I must also say that I loved the little brat back then and I love the big one now. In fact, as much as I can say she is being immature, I am truly beaming that this is my new problem. You see I re-watched the videos of her early days of recovery where we were thrilled when she moved her head from side to side. I was forced to remember the swelling and the bruising and the tubes that seemed so permanent we were garnering a medical degree. I recalled the desperation for some indication of recovery but reliving all of that didn't make me as much sad as it did nostalgic. So then when I respond to Juli's current yell for "MOM!" and I arrive just to realize she just wants attention, it is a type of 'bratty' that I am really pretty happy to handle. Granted, (as Chris will Amen) handling the girl on very little sleep has a whole new challenge to it, but that is the fallout we accept from trying to tend to her AND reclaim our social life. But it's ultimately all good because our new problems with her revolve around her increased strength and abilities. She attempts to get out of bed (badly and harmfully) and won't stop even when we are begging her to. She demands to go to bed or out of bed or in a chair or out of chair and if she doesn't get what she wants (re-enter Veruca) there is an adult sized/toddler like tantrum. We all have bruises to wear as our battle scars. I have taken to calling her Veruca again these days and instead of being insulted she simply says, "That's right".

Sigh…what's a mother to do? We have our little mantra that I keep telling Veruca…er…Juli as she complains her way through the day: "How are we going to get past this?" And she responds with her half of the drill she almost hates to say anymore. Words that I will boldly accept as MY current plan as well: "Go through it".

So…through it we go

Home therapy begins tomorrow and will last for about 8 weeks. Then we will see what the best course is beyond that. Who knows where she will be then but I am certain she will be 8 weeks further along than she is today. If that takes her beyond the tantrum stage, I will welcome it. If it doesn't, well guess what? I will welcome that too… but maybe with a just a little more armor.

July 24, 2010

Well we had another reminder that this is not necessarily a straight line to recovery. We can't expect only forward movement and we are still in a medically tenuous position. I guess if you really think about it, we are all walking ticking time bombs of one sort or another. You may recall we had reduced her medications in the past few months so that we could get her to a more natural state. That meant removing her muscle relaxers, anti-seizure meds and adding in vitamin supplements to pick up some of the nutritional benefits. Well on Wednesday morning we faced the dreaded setback in this TBI journey when Juli had her first seizure. It was scary and sad and definitely sobering but it was also the safest and best of situations possible. She was in her bed, surrounded by pillows and it was very mild in comparison to the possibilities. We have been told that the seizure itself holds very little to worry about. It is the danger in what happens during the thrashing that is the real unknown. So I will continue to feel fortunate that our wake up call to this risk was given to us in a safe environment. After talking with her neurologist we of course put her back on the anti-seizure meds. She had also been slowly put back on the muscle relaxers as a result of increasing muscle tone. These re-introduced drugs, in combination with the seizure have produced a 'backtracking' type of effect. It might be our imagination or it might be just the lingering exhaustion that is a necessary byproduct of a seizure but she is certainly more difficult to understand again as her talking is largely reduced to sounds again. This is frustrating and sad for me as it interferes with each moment of the day. She continues to attempt to communicate frequently and that is good, right? Well it would be except the result is a constant attempt, with a high failure rate, of understanding her. I don't know why her speech has not improved more when it is the only discipline of therapy that has constant and repeated attempts. Patience runs most thin in this area on both sides of the equation.

Speaking of therapy, her in home therapy is continuing though it is not quite to the level we received at RIC. Maybe it is because we are just ramping it up or maybe it is because they just offer less but so far, what they have done for her Chris does on a regular basis much better. The boy could become an OT or PT if he wanted to but he wants none of it. He said, "I do this because I love HER, I don't expect I could be as successful with someone I didn't."

In addition to the (temporarily?) reduced functionality, her blood pressure is starting to be a concern. It flares as well as her heart rate and has actually prevented the visiting PT from working with her. I wasn't convinced he was accurate and thought maybe juuuuuuust maybe he was looking for an excuse to not stay but then I checked it myself (I know, I know) and sure enough it was really really high. She has been practicing relaxation techniques and when it works her blood pressure goes down a bit and her tremors temporarily subside. It's really quite cool to see her control herself and acknowledge that she has control but deciding to do it on her own has not been possible yet. We keep trying and eventually it will become a habit, right? Here's hoping...

July 27, 2010

"If we all threw our problems in a pile and saw everyone else's, we'd grab ours back" Today I couldn't agree more. It seems so horribly unfair when you hear news about a 19 year old boy who fights so bravely and positively against cancer only to be dealt a surprising and significant obstacle. Andrew Weishar, all of us at Team Juli are praying for you.

Juli is recovering nicely from the seizure, her voice seems to be coming back and so is her strength. No independence yet but I feel we are at least back on track. We are continuing to practice getting in and out of bed, in and out of her wheelchair and maneuvering around the house. In another naïve thought I had hoped the wheelchair would be so temporary she wouldn't need to learn how to use it. I know better now. Her home therapy is starting to ramp up a bit but we haven't hit our comfort level with the new therapists yet. Chris is still the best resource she has by far. I do her stretches and exercises with her too but it is pretty hard to bend a foot back in shape that is contorted and tight. That takes the strength that Chris relentlessly puts into it.

We have some interesting things coming upon us with a new and improved hospital bed (thanks Jim!) and her new wheelchair (only waited 4 months for that) and then of course the eye surgery next Tuesday. I am not sure what will be the outcome there but she will at least have her eyelashes off of her eyeball (ewwwww and owww!) We spent this evening at Piyo where Juli participated as much as she could, even though it was pretty clear, she was only interested in the Reeses promised at the end.

Nothing more I need to share on Juli tonight, I am pretty distracted at Andrew's situation even though I am more than a few steps removed from his inner circle. He is my son's age and longtime friend and I would not wish what he is going through on anyone or any parent for that matter. As much as what we are going through is at moments horrible, in this case, I will keep my own troubles thankyouverymuch. I would like to please ask each of you to say a prayer for Andrew as he heads to Mayo clinic in search of his miracle.

Please.

August 2, 2010

We decided to make Juli take the 2 hour drive with us to Michigan to spend the day at the beach. SHE decided she would spend 5 minutes...twice. The rest of the time she was content to stay at the cottage and have snacks and take naps. It really defines her 'dog days of summer'. I really hope that interest in life is on her horizon but no one will tell us if that is something that 'comes back' or not. We keep trying though and once in a while she appears to like something but not really very much. Tomorrow is a big day though: Juliana will finally have her surgery to repair her lower eyelid. I am going to trust that this doctor, who is very nice, came highly recommended and is a plastic surgeon, will do a safe and beautiful job. Juli gives a thumbs up when I ask if she is excited about the surgery but I have yet to see 'excited' on her these past 10 months. That's right folks. For those keeping track, it was 10 months ago today. On that day 10 months ago we had no idea what this day would look like but I thought we would be planning a wedding (again). Her speech therapist works her pretty hard on drills of articulation and we may be seeing a slight improvement. Her physical and occupational therapists are nice enough but the treatment is very passive. In fact, they are 'discharging' her next week. Her PT said that insurance wants to see big gains in order to keep paying for in home therapy. (Well that makes all of us buddy). It's a shame that throwing money at this won't speed it up. And while we wait we are seeing deterioration in the flexibility in her right hand. I bet we are in for another round of Botox in her fingers. And as the story goes (I could just rewrite old posts it seems) it looks like we are headed back to day rehab which will mean tantrums and fits and protests, etc. As she gets stronger and more annoyed with the whole thing, the pressure will increase on Chris to be the bad guy. He takes the heat like a champ though. Chris still sees the girl her loves and ponders the 'when she gets better', never 'if'. He laughs at her expressions when they glimmer through and proudly (and loudly) says, "There's my old Juliana!" He treats her like she is a princess to be adored, even when she is threatening bodily harm. The end result is worth it, at least that is our best option, and so like it or not, back to therapy we will go. Her blood pressure continues to be elevated and she sweats like…never mind, I was going to quote my dad but remembered the audience here. Those who knew him, fill in the blanks. But seriously, it has got to be a result of the meds she is on because I seriously have never seen anyone soak their shirts with sweat while lying still in 70 degrees and a fan! We are going to look into that a bit further. Comfort is a priority so we are happy that she got a new comfortable bed and a new wheelchair… her 'permanent chair' (which turns my stomach to admit we are actually THERE) but it is high quality device and brand new so I appreciate that. Wish us luck tomorrow!

August 5, 2010

Surgery went well. No problems, complications or setbacks. Isn't that what you always hope to hear? Her eye is healing nicely although the swelling and redness and repeated medicine application is oh so familiar. It is nice to know that even though it appears that her eye is back to square one it is actually on the path for healing. They said she would be groggy most of the day but that wasn't the case at all. In fact, less than an hour after surgery she was eating an egg McMuffin followed by complaining to Chris that he was holding out on the hash browns. We were also warned that she might have difficulty talking for a few days (can you just hear me groan?) and that as soon as the soreness goes away she will be fine. That wasn't the case either. In fact, she is louder and clearer than ever. She still has no breath control so she can't sustain her talking for more than 3 seconds without being winded. It's really the strangest thing, especially considering, the girl can sing...er... could sing. She has been practicing singing happy birthday so she could impress her brother Dylan who turns 20 today. It's so hard to believe that he is out of those teenage years. He will be going back to college in Hawaii in 15 days and I am SO not ready. He has been a great brother to Juli, especially these last few months and has been a huge help to me. Not to mention, the boy is just 'gooooood people'. Come on, if you know him I KNOW you agree. Juli begged him not to go to Hawaii last year because she was convinced he would die. Yes, that was the 'irrational-even-before-the-accident' Juli. She no longer worries about that but she said she is going to miss him. Happy Birthday Dylan, I will miss you too ☹.

As Juli is becoming more and more aware of her situation, her anger and frustration are taking on new qualities. She often says that she hates 'this' or, 'being dependent', and that no one understands her when she talks. I asked her why she never cries. I am pretty sure she just can't show that much emotion yet but my thoughts were confirmed when she answered my question: "I cry constantly...inside." I also asked her how long she thinks the rest of her recovery will take, given that we have been through 10 months already. She said, "Another year". I was surprised that she was able to understand it all enough to guess so well. Her personality is definitely still in the process of returning but we will wait it out with her. Dylan will just wait it out in Hawaii.

August 9, 2010

There is a recurring theme in our house in August: "Happy Birthday". Today it is true for my lovely 10 year old lady, Delaney. She has been a charming wonderful, beautiful girl with the warmest personality from the moment she was born. With Delaney's arrival in our lives a corner was turned where our family was officially blended. She was loved immediately of course but it forced a lot of changes in a family which had previously only been built on 'My' children. The older kids all embraced their new little sister but her arrival is what got a 14 year old Juliana thinking that maybe she DID in fact want children after all someday. It would take the arrival of Mackenzie three years later though for Juli to truly realize the most passionate goal she ever had: to be a mom. And today when Juli and I talked about Delaney becoming 10 and what we might do for her birthday, she interrupted me and said: "I hope I get to have a 10 year old daughter someday." Of course accident or no accident THAT couldn't be guaranteed so I just told her that I hoped she did too but if she didn't I believed it would not be because of THIS situation. I asked both Delaney and Mackenzie if they think Juli will be back to her old self one day. (I like the honesty that young kids can't help but convey) and they both, without hesitation, said "Yes". Taking reassurance anywhere and looking for signs everywhere, I choose to believe my young soothsayers. And speaking of looking for reassurance and signs, it seems we are destined to have people cross our paths who have walked it as well. Again, Traumatic Brain Injury is as individual as a healthy brain but the similarities in the story always resonate. I was talking with someone who is relatively close to home, (literally in fact: she is the sister of my neighbor) and learned the circumstances of her TBI many years ago and it had an eerie ring to it. As she walked in our house to see Juliana, I watched her have the same reaction as Nicole and her mom had a few months ago: She has been 'here' before. From the hospital bed in the family room to the wheelchair, walker, cane, bucket of medicines and other assorted medical supplies, it brought back memories of a pivotal yet forgotten time. Isn't that strange? Isn't that wonderful? It wasn't sad, for either of us I think. It was nostalgic and reflective (for me encouraging) and the way she has come to terms with it all was truly inspirational. She is now a mother of two happily living a very normal healthy life who admits that her accident, as tragic as it was at the time, made her who she is today and a person she is happy to be. How can you really knock that? I mean, I by no means recommend this path for a way to 'find yourself' (as if!) But it is very clear to me that we are all here to live our lives with purpose and sometimes that means that we have to find our purpose deep within the very hardest of times. Who knows if Juli will have a 10 year old daughter some day? Who knows if being a mom is in her future at all? Let's not try to predict that far. Let's just take the day and make the most of it, both the good and the bad because sometimes they may be necessarily coupled. There is a line in a song by Darryl Worley that I am hearing right now… "I love this crazy, tragic…sometimes almost magic…awful beautiful life".

Oh, and once again, Happy Birthday Delaney Irene Barnes.

August 12, 2010

Last time this month, I promise…Happy Birthday Donnie. I couldn't let my husband's birthday go by when he has stood by me these last 10 months taking care of everything else around me so I could be available for Juliana. He chose to stay in the background letting Chris and I make the decisions, learn the therapy, administer the nursing and have the day to day control while I let go of everything else around me. It turned out to be a choice that I relied on when things were hard and still now when they are just tiring. He was taught well, learned by example exactly how much of you it requires being a caregiver and for that, I am grateful also to his family. So even though I tease him mercilessly about getting old, he is still the strongest man I know and I am lucky to have him in my corner.

But heck, you don't want to hear about another family birthday. You are tuned in for an update on Juliana, so here it is: She had an appointment with the neurologist the other day who confirmed what was obvious to us: Juliana is still making improvements. He reviewed her recently increased list of meds and confirmed that she still needed all but two of them, which we have now begun to reduce. We asked if he had any idea when we might expect the tremors to go away and he answered predictably then prescribed another medicine to 'try'. Once I started doing my own reading on the internet, I learned this drug is a bit of a 'Swiss army knife' of medicine which includes possible side effects that sound worse than the tremors! Considering the serious medications she is on already, we decided to wait a few months longer and see if the tremors subside on their own. She does seem to have a certain amount of control over them but when she is stressed, upset or trying hard, they are pretty noticeable. Later that day she went to the Ophthalmologist where he also confirmed that her right eye is opening much more than when he last saw her. He doesn't think her vision improved (though our testing of her vision seemed to yield better results). I asked him whether glasses would improve her vision and he told us with nerve damage glasses won't help, but come back in 4 months and 'we will see'. Again? Ok. So that is her medical round up.

Her behavior at home is a bit more positive. She engages in conversation more, even if she prefers to spend most of her time in bed, and she is definitely getting easier to understand. She even shows a bit of a sense of humor. It's odd humor but we are laughing just the same. And just like old times, she questions Chris when he leaves the house and pays attention to every detail around her. She is also getting closer and closer to being able to transfer from her bed to her chair on her own; she just has a few more skills to master. I will take some pictures of her in the next couple of weeks and maybe even post a video to give you an idea of where she is in her progress. Thanks for hanging in here with us, it means a great deal to have you still caring about my daughter. I still believe that the continuous positive wishes and prayers, emails and cards in the mail (Pat Westergren, Hallmark must LOVE you!) All of that are what have taken her so far on her journey. So thank you for that. And because you have helped Juli so much, again I ask that you use that energy to add Andrew Weishar to your prayers because he will be undergoing a dramatic and radical surgery Thursday at Mayo clinic to fight his aggressive cancer.

August 13, 2010

So obviously by now you realize that Juliana is not my only child ☺ She is the one who started me down this parenting path which changed my life for good (and usually for THE good as well). But having Juli encouraged me to have...well...more. And while being the mother of 6 kids does not make me an 'expert' by any means, it does make me experienced. The two are often confused and I personally don't want the responsibility that comes with being an expert. An expert knows the answers. Someone who is experienced has lived the questions. Parents...we are the latter. I am here to tell you that my experience has taught me many things through the unfolding of events since October 2, 2009 that I probably should have been learning all along. You know when your children are small and start to exhibit those signs of brilliance or amazing talent? Come on, you know what I am talking about... when Junior hits a home run and you are having visions of a Cubs center fielder or little Sally sings so beautifully that you are certain she is destined to win American Idol? We see the best in our children then construct this vision of their life and then go about trying to help them get there. I did it...well, that it what I tried to do. I put my kids in every activity that they showed an interest in and then felt the pains of defeat when they decided they were no longer interested. I will be honest, I was disappointed sometimes. But now I am learning, while I reflect where I thought Juliana would be at this time in her life, that the vision and the dream was not where I should have put my expectations. We don't know what life holds for us. We don't know if we will be dealt a devastating blow of an accident or an illness or a death to take that dream from us. I know that experience has taught me that I don't want to have expectations for anything beyond today. I want to love my kids right now, for the people they are and not worry about the people they will become. I am sure some of you think this is foolish and short sighted and maybe it is. But MY experience has taught me that I don't get to decide anyway so why set myself up for failure? I love them today, why not just revel in that? Dylan is getting ready to leave for Hawaii in 7 days and I am going to miss having him around so much that I physically feel pain. That is the other side of love and I am so grateful that I love him that much. He didn't become the center fielder for the Cubs in spite of the promise he showed in his youth but you know what? I love him just as much for the wonderful person he is right now. And Juliana is not Mackenzie's nanny, Chris's wife, or the next American Idol and I have some serious adjustments to make in what I expected but she is still a person who has an opportunity at a life of her own and I love her just the same. It's kind of freeing actually, to let go of my expectations. I know parents out there going through some major issues with their kids and if you are reading and taking anything from what I have experienced, please let it be this: Once you let go of what YOU expected your child to become, your grief subsides and you make way for whatever they were destined to become anyway.

Juli laughs differently but she laughs. She can't sing anymore (yet?) but she still chooses to try. She can't walk but she can move around. She can't talk clearly but she made sure she said Happy Birthday to all of us. She can't baby-sit Mackenzie but she can still influence her. She can't walk down the aisle but she can still tell Chris that she loves him. And even though she isn't the girl I pictured, I love her just as much. Throughout numerous school projects or home activities I have always told my kids this: "There are no mistakes in Art, only changes". Our children are our Art and although I myself am still learning to take my own advice, I am learning to love the changes.

August 19, 2010

After months of practice and months of time passing (which as we know is the REAL ingredient to accomplishments in a brain injury of course) Juliana was finally able to get out of her bed and into her wheelchair 'without assistance'. I would have ended that sentence with an exclamation point because it IS pretty darn awesome but let me replay the effort and you will see that it deserves the more reticent punctuation. For Juli to get out of bed it requires coaching or queues on each of the movements:

" put your feet flat, now spread them apart more. Good, now reach for your chair, reach further…that's right lean forward, more, lean even more. Remember, 'nose over your toes', that's it, keep leaning. Now pull! Pull Juli, pull yourself forward, keep going, don't stop, hang onto that handle, come on…wait, your feet are slipping. Here, let me stand in front of your feet so they stay in position, ok now try again. Pull yourself now. You can do it. Let me wipe the sweat so it stops falling in your eyes. Ok, keep going. You are almost there. Don't let go, no, don't give up you WILL be able to do this easier one day, I promise. Really, there is so much you can do easily now that you couldn't do before. We will practice this so many times each day that you will be able to do it with ease some day (groan from Juli, sigh from me). I know, just keep pulling, you are SO close. Yes, you are doing it. Yes! A little further, up and…over…you are THERE! Yes! Hey you did it, you really did! You got into your chair all by yourself! I am SO proud of you, SO PROUD! Aren't you proud of yourself? (Thumbs down from Juli) Well that is ok because I am proud enough for both of us."

So as you can see, that laborious effort is an extraordinary accomplishment that I am so grateful she can achieve. And it is true; it will become easier one day I won't complain. 'Normal' life will be upon her someday and THIS day will be a distant memory, maybe even forgotten. I will do my best to remind her of how far she has come, how much Chris has been supporting her and how many people (you) care about her recovery. She has always been a gift to me and she is still a gift that keeps on giving. And in her altered state we still find ways to laugh and tease to make this all just a little more ok and we are…ok that is. My hopes for her continued recovery are that we see more improvement in her spirit. She has little interest in anything and that is a bit restrictive for all of us as we can't really take her anywhere and expect cooperation. But I have seen so many horrible things come and go, 'this too shall pass'. I can't and won't be sad about this. Sure there are moments when I feel like I am trapped in my family room or annoyed that she only wants to lay in bed but both Chris and I see the light at the end of the (still VERY LONG) tunnel getting brighter. I remember when THIS day was the only thing we prayed for…

Prayers do get answered.

August 23, 2010

3800 strong…so many voices in prayer. But there is one voice that has recently gotten stronger and is joining our fight: Juliana's. What you might not have known, (because I chose not to make it an issue) is that before the accident, Juliana doubted the existence of God. She was at that point in her life where she was believing that religion was a construct of man and based on the need for individuals to have something to hold onto. On those two points we agreed. Where we parted ways was in her belief that the Higher Power was not at work. I felt like a failure in this department because I was unable to do my 'job' of convincing her that my beliefs were right. I was unable to persuade her to consider that God makes things happen and believing will change your life. The best I could do was convince her that believing made ME feel better. So I lowered my expectations and tried the "wouldn't you rather consider what I believe and be right, then consider what you believe and be wrong?" But still, she was undeterred. The funny thing is, regardless of her religious practice she had the spirit of a believer. I am not going to try to convince you she was without flaws. Who would actually be that naive to believe it anyway? But she was passionate and dedicated and committed to her family and friends. And regardless if her career ideas were scattered, her love for the people in her life never was. I always felt she was a believer waiting to happen (again). Well this whole experience has been sobering for our family and many of you following along. Just the sheer length of time we are required to endure this has given us pause. And during this time, Juliana is gratefully emerging from a fog, from the trenches and in the process she is evolving into someone changed. And with that, a precious gift…

Juliana is starting to pray.

I have been praying all along on her behalf. You have been praying all along on her behalf. Chris, although previously dabbled in the sentiments of

Juli in her denial of a Higher Power, has been praying all along on her behalf. And now, Juli is praying for herself. She told me a few weeks ago that she "Apologized to God for not believing in Him." I was moved, but still a bit skeptical. After all this is also the same girl who judges good days and bad days by the fast food place she frequents. I didn't want to push her (which has probably always been my maternal fatal flaw) but I wanted to explore that further. I was curious what she was expecting from 'making up' with God. Was she bargaining for her release from what she calls 'a private hell'? Was she looking for a miracle instant cure? Was she thinking she needed forgiveness? As it turns out, she was hoping for all of the above. I just have to hug her and try to tell her that we have to trust this all happened for a reason and someday (soon she said) she will believe it too. It felt a little like taking advantage of her in a weakened state but I still believed the baseline "It can't hurt"...so now, we pray together. We made a list of very specific things to pray for (thank you Ann for reminding me to do that) and it includes all of the incremental improvements she wants and needs. It is both a personal list including things she really wants for Chris and a generic list but it is what she is thinking about, and what I am thinking about too. As I struggle to maintain patience especially when I am really tired (or hungry...but that is a whole other flaw of mine...I digress) I try to focus on how far she has come and how grateful I am that she will have a future. I try to ignore the fact that as we approach the end of 11 months of this recovery that she is still years away from full functionality and I will need to continue to live in this altered state with her. Not just passively watching her go through it either, but actively adjusting my every day activities to accommodate the limitations she has to face and the attention she requires. So I pray hard for her release from this, as well as mine. It feels selfish sometimes and sometimes I too want to have a tantrum as I sleep on the couch and wake every few hours to her need for something erroneous (White Castle at 3 am...really??). So I pray that she gets to the point of taking the reins of her recovery and joining me in prayer is a step in that direction. I am starting to document (go figure) the goals that we have for Juli and hope to design a personalized little program for her: 'Healthy, Happy and Independent' I am calling. And in doing that, define the tasks that need to be accomplished to reach each of those goals. I am starting to take people up on the offers to spend time with Juli sharing their particular expertise so that Chris and I don't plateau in our ability to assist.

We are also going to start her back into therapy which she will surely hate with a passion. That will mean the prayer list will grow to include MORE tolerance, strength, and patience. She will only be able to 'go along' with me on that one until her brain heals enough to compensate for her odd fixations, irrationality, and immaturity. (For those of you that have been around her you recognize what I am talking about.) Those of you reading along, I am not sure what state you picture in your mind from what I tell you but she is like a 'half-Juli' on her good days.

So if you so choose, (and far be it from me to expect you to share in my beliefs, I am just glad you are here), take a peek at my shopping cart for God and see if there are any items here you would like to request on our behalf: To smile often, to laugh often, to feel happiness, to talk louder, to talk clearer, to enunciate, to articulate, to open her right eye regularly, to open her right hand effortlessly, to stop shaking, to regain balance, to walk without braces, to walk without assistance, to regain full eyesight and last on this list (but near the top of hers) is to have Chris succeed in his musical career goals.

Amen.

August 27, 2010

Shhhh….can you keep a secret? Well it won't be necessary for long because she will know in just a few days. Juliana is going back to therapy. You may hear a loud roar or a terrible clap of thunder about 9 am on Monday, this is your heads up. We are actually taking her to a new place with new hopes and expectations. We all know it's the best thing for her even though she doesn't believe it. Chris and I can't do it alone and we need to see her continue to improve. I have been feeling particularly frustrated and restless lately as I see this go on and on with very little progression. I start to panic thinking, 'Will this ever change? How will we get past this routine of 24/7 care to a degree of freedom?' I figured out that this whole process is cyclical. I don't mean her progress really, but how I think about it. I have a day or so of self-pity for being in this situation, then anger that my daughter was taken from me and a stranger given to me to take care of. Then self-loathing for worrying about myself at a time like this… (Yes, I have just admitted to all that dirty laundry. I am not in the mood to pretend this is easy even though she is alive) Then that wave passes and I feel tremendous sympathy for my daughter who answers, "What do you miss most?" with, "Everything because nothing is the same." And cry for what she can't do, and how she spends her day going from the bed to the chair to the bathroom to the bed and wants nothing more. I get angry that she should have to lose so much even if 'it happens for a reason' and 'she will be far greater on the other side of this'. Yeah yeah, I know all that because I have said all that. You could probably even quote me. But listen, this is white and black and every shade in between. And I just have to be glad that none of it stays for long. The sadness and despair make way for the next wave which is encouragement and hope and beauty and a future. Truth? I hate this. More truth? I will survive it. Even more truth? We will all be stronger, wiser, better people on the 'other side' of this. Most truth of all? I am SO ready to get there.

September 2, 2010

So…she figured it out even before she left the house. In fact, she must have overheard us talking or something because Sunday night she started the campaign to "call her off of therapy". I ask her why she hates it so much and she said, "People think they are helping but they aren't." I asked her if I was included in the 'people' she referred to. She said "yes" Hmm. "So Juli, why do you think I do what I do for you?" You know what she said? You know what I got? I got air quotes! That's right. She said, "Because you 'care' about me." Oh, yes she did. (Did you expect her answer to be logical? She DOES have a TBI you know.) Well it's ok. Lucky for her I am a mother of 6 who has seen and heard it all and have become quite resilient to childish attempts to wear me down. For better or worse, I was not given children who were perfect angels, children who never made my heart stop or my blood boil. Instead God blessed me with normal kids just like yours and when all is said and done, I wouldn't have it any other way. The years of experience have toughened me enough to easily withstand a few sticks and stones from a child with a brain injury. So tonight when she begged me to call her off of therapy Friday with"…pretty please with sugar on top and whip cream and a cherry", I just laughed and said, "Uh, that would be a 'no'."

The new place seems to have a handle on where Juli is in her recovery and they have a realistic and optimistic view of how they might help her. The therapists are probably just as qualified as those at our last rehab but no matter how hard the last ones tried to break through her wall of resistance, Juli was not ready to cave. The change in venue will buy us a bit more time to allow her to come to her senses too. Chris is learning some new stretches to help Juli and soaking up everything they are teaching him, as he always does. The boy could surely be a Physical Therapist on the other end of this but he assures me that unless he was madly in love with every patient, he just couldn't do it.

I continue to have the greatest frustration with her speech and have enlisted reinforcements in that area. I know it bothers Juliana too because when I asked her to explain why she always wants either Chris or me with her she said, "Because you two are the only ones who understand me." (Not as much as she thinks….shhhh). We don't have a magic decoder ring; we have just put the time in service. So I want to turn that all around. Talking to her and making her talk to us is going to be my push as we enter into the fall. I believe if Juli could be more understandable, she would have the ability to reciprocate in conversation opening the door to her (previous) specialty…socialization. So, that is the plan as we check off one more month on the calendar, (wow 11 months ago) and think about our goals for the next 11 months.

My goal…is to stop needing these kinds of goals.

September 8, 2010

Juliana's new therapy location comes with new therapists, goals and methods. Considering we were at a plateau prior to this, change is a good thing. The Physical Therapist there is trying to walk Juliana without her braces. She feels that she can do it and is willing to give it a try. If you recall, that was one of Juliana's specific prayers so I pointed that out to her as an indication that God hears her and is responding. She acknowledged what I said but still holds the position of 'hating therapy'. I guess that is the real kicker here. She knows this is good for her, acknowledges that she needs to improve, recognizes that she can't do it on her own yet she resists the help. She doesn't resist the actual tasks because she still very obediently complies with any request. But the obsession with hating it is consuming. I just don't get this whole brain injury recovery, even after all these months. My daughter who previously loved her friends, family, music, TV, magazines, children…doesn't seem interested in any of it at all. Visits with people still only hold momentary interest and any of the other items from above hold none at all. This girl who was defined by her magnanimous personality, pretty much from birth, is void of expression, emotion, and motivation. The young lady of animated speech and joy of singing is monotone and monosyllabic. The girl who smiled from ear to ear in even the silliest of occasions must be forced to attempt the smallest of grins. What kind of therapy brings THAT back? She is getting stronger, I can see that, so we continue to capitalize on what works and try not to focus on what doesn't but it still confounds me when I just want to see the girl I spent so much time chatting idling with for hours about reality shows that no one else really cared about. Now she is one of 'them'. We are trying to get creative. Focus on singing, art, cooking, visits with babies but her involvement is very short and her attention span even shorter. You know what is also odd that I have been distracted by? She won't make eye contact for very long. I know when babies are small they have a limit to the stimulation they can handle through eye contact and will look away from your intent stares. I knew this, experienced it plenty in my years in day care but I am seeing it now with Juli. We all know that this recovery is like going from infancy to adulthood all over again but the path of progress is NOT linear. So what she originally learned at 6 months may not occur until the end whereas something that was nearer to maturity may have already been achieved. I guess it all depends on what part of the brain was injured and how it is finding its way to recovery. And this complete unknown is why we can get no answers. Every brain injury recovery is a new journey and very individualized …and very unpredictable.

September 13, 2010

Juliana completed a week of therapy at her new location without anyone going with her. Sounds like progress, right? Well I am not sure they would see it that way. In fact, on her second day unaccompanied by us, she was unattended by them long enough for her to unbuckle her wheelchair seatbelt (I warned them) and fall out of her chair. (She was fine) This led to a phone call to us stating that they would "prefer if someone came to therapy with her". (Of course they would…makes their job easier, right?) Apparently they were unaware that she needed constant supervision. (Perhaps I should ask them to read along with you guys). They also said that Juliana 'refused' occupational therapy. ?Really? How does that exactly work? I was a bit surprised that they accepted her refusal as an answer. WE are certainly able to work around her objections to gain her cooperation, albeit unwittingly. And finally they said....get this...they can't understand her when she talks. Ummmm... tap tap tap....hello...she is there for SPEECH therapy, can you please provide that?? Yes I am being a bit critical but I do not have the patience of a saint; that would be my beloved mother-in-law, Irene. While she was on this earth I learned a lot from her but not quite enough to endure this all as gracefully as she could. So I just have to say that all of that therapy hoo-hah was more than a little disappointing to me. After all, if Juliana were not broken, she wouldn't be going there to be fixed, right? So the end goal of helping Juliana remains and once again, we will adjust to meet that goal. And once again, Chris has rearranged his work schedule to go to therapy with Juli and 'show them how to help her'. No one is as successful in her therapy as Chris is anyway. I know you already know this but that man is a godsend to me and my daughter. Chris and I have also had a few heart to hearts about how we can escalate her recovery, and how we can't and some of those talks are both hopeful and painful. We recognized that we might have slacked off a little bit in our home therapy so we have committed to a 'full court press' on her stretches, exercises and routines. Juliana is still not on board with her own therapy so we are taking significant abuse to accomplish our goals but we just can't let up. We are approaching the one year mark and that looms heavy as a failed expectation of mine. We see her potential and both Chris and I are eager to push her to whatever she can achieve. I am still very confused as to why her speech has not improved more because that has been constantly practiced since she began talking 9 months ago. But then again, this whole recovery confuses me. She is by all accounts, 'mentally aware and cognitive' yet she still has behaviors that confound and astound us. We don't know how to encourage her desire for anything and no amount of interjection of previous interests seems to spark her former joy....yet. How do you find a missing personality? How do you repair an emotional deficit? How do you create a lost desire? I think that her friends might hold the key since they were so important to her before the accident but so far, even that hasn't made much of a dent. She is depressed and discouraged and I have to admit, many days it is a physical effort to not go down that dark path with her. Juli and I were so close before this all began that I almost can't see where she ends and I begin. In my grief over missing her so badly, I have to remember not to lose sight of all that is most precious so me: my handsome loving sons, my beautiful vivacious daughters and my strong and loving husband. She does have some very cute moments and endearing qualities peeking through on occasion but it remains difficult to recognize Juli for who she was on October 1st. I don't want that girl to fade from my memory. I don't want to forget her voice. I don't want to allow this stranger to own my daughter's memories and body but I get no say so in that at all. My son Adam uses Juliana's old phone number and has kept her recording on the phone. Sometimes I call hoping he won't answer just so I can hear her say her name again. Weird, huh? She isn't gone, she didn't die, she is right here. I am looking at her as I type but. God forgive my selfishness...it is sometimes hard to find comfort in that. So, Chris and I will keep working hard to get her physically and vocally to a point of independence and understanding and hope that the rest follows. We don't seem to get a choice but to wait anyway. I will continue to pray, and pray with Juliana too, that someday I can look back as others have and say "Oh, yeah, I almost forgot about that...."

September 22, 2010

Attitude is everything.

Yesterday we connected with another former patient from RIC who suffered a brain injury two weeks before Juli. Chris and I wanted to see how she was doing, talk to her family about what they have been experiencing and compare notes on doctors, medicines, therapies....really everything. And it was a good day for that because Chris had just returned from a grueling therapy session with Juliana that left him discouraged. As you know she doesn't like therapy. (Yes, I did just make a gross understatement but, point made, let's keep going). Well it must be said that most of the time, in spite of her intense dislike, she does what is asked of her. The difficulty comes with her reluctance to want what is helping her. She will admit that she needs therapy to improve, will acknowledge that she wants to ("I demand it", she chants) get better and she even acknowledges the logical connection. But then that TBI logic steps in and she fights the whole process anyway. Her tremors go from severe shaking when she is upset or over stimulated, to nonexistent when she is resting or very calm. So, in a therapy setting she is upset and over stimulated and then the tremors prevent an effective therapy. Chris reviewed video footage from her rehab at RIC and found that she has not improved since then in her ability to walk, and she may have in fact regressed. This was concerning to me, and his sullen appearance when he got home was equally concerning. He wasn't sure if it was Juliana's bad attitude that got in the way of her bad day at therapy or maybe it was his. It is clear that this has all taken a toll on him although he has continued to plug away. So with his (temporarily) defeated perspective, we packed up Juliana to attend this dinner meeting with our 'kindred' family. It seems that once again the timing was right. Have you ever experienced that where you hear something and you pay it little attention until circumstances align when suddenly, the information resonates with you? I have seen that many times through this last year. Well in meeting with this family we concluded that there is SO much more in the rehabilitation field that can be done for Juliana that we have yet to explore. Juli had Botox 1 ½ times so far, this other girl has had it 4 times and it on her way to her 5th and the results have been remarkable. They switched her sleeping medicine and found that their daughter not only slept all night (which is still rare in this house) but it had an additional impact on her speech. They have also had their daughter fitted several times for modified equipment to use as her progress increased where we have not received anything new, and the current equipment had only minor alterations in all these many months.

So needless to say, I will be making some phone calls to see if Juliana can go to the place they take their daughter. They like the doctor there who they said "is aggressive and not afraid to try something new". Sounds like our kind of doctor.

In addition to what we learned, Juliana seemed to have learned something too. I had asked her in preparation for the meeting if she was looking forward to it. She gave me thumbs up, which of course is always a good place to start. But then she asked me something I found a little strange. She said, "Is SHE depressed?" It is clear to us that Juliana is very depressed in spite of the medication to help that problem. It is also clear to us that for better or worse, a lot of her depression comes from the fact that her memory and mind are intact. So as her former self stays trapped inside this limited body with limited ability to communicate, she wallows in her depression daily. And although I wasn't sure if this girl was depressed, from the conversations with her mother, it certainly didn't sound like it. That fact was confirmed as soon as we arrived and she waved and said "hello" and admitted that she was "very happy". She has also temporarily lost her short term memory and her long term memory is a bit cloudy. There probably is some correlation there. Juliana can't forget what she is missing, what she is lacking and what is no longer happening for her. She lives with the realization that the one thing she wanted most (a baby) is now moving further away from her, where this other girl might not yet remember all that she was. Ignorance surely can be bliss, right? So by the end of the dinner, Chris was encouraged by the possibilities, but we were both beating ourselves up about not doing more. Juliana was also affected though it was not apparent until later in the evening after she had said, "I Love you" several times, unprovoked. SO, as Chris takes a few days off from the day to day grind here I am determined to stay staring straight ahead at all that can be done; no time to concern myself with what we didn't do and with Chris on the back side of encouraged, it's my turn to be the cheerleader. Lord knows it has been reversed often enough; you guys have had to read through those dark times, right? Well not right now. The encounter was helpful for us all and today is a new day with new possibilities. Things are looking up.

Time to make some phone calls… (Maybe not right now, it IS only 5 am).

September 29, 2010

Well…

We went to the doctor and started Juli on some new sleep medicine. The hope is that, of course she will sleep all night, (though as I type she has already woken twice ☹) but also that we could achieve a miraculous improvement to her speech. It's a long shot…documented results are inconclusive… but we have talked to people who claim that this particular medicine, designed for a good night's sleep, might work for improving speech impaired due to brain injury. I gave Juli the first dose tonight so I will be anxiously waiting to see what tomorrow brings. It's funny after almost a year I am still looking for a miracle to turn this thing around. Some of you might be thinking " but I thought she was getting so much better?" Well you are right, she certainly is but it still takes a really long time to get to a million dollars by saving pennies. The distance between where she started last October 2nd at 3:30 am and where she is now is miraculous. And to go the rest of the distance, we will need to summon more of the same. Juliana's depression is pretty much debilitating her. We heard from the beginning that those individuals who happily and eagerly approach their recovery will improve faster and go further. As I recall that statement, it makes me nervous and sad. Anyone who has been around Juli in these last months knows that she is anything but happy or eager. Her resistance to everything from therapy to phrases that have to be repeated, even things she once loved…is palpable. But even with that, I still see glimmers of hope in her response to what she most wants to improve: her attitude. I hear her carry on normal conversations, even though they are confined to the limits of her articulation, they are not limited by her words. I hear her make jokes about herself even though she doesn't know she is being funny. I see her really SEEING us when we talk and knowing that her sad self is inside trying to be normal. She said "I want to be happy, I just can't". So although she is trapped in there, she is so IN there that I can't help but feel encouraged (when I am not exhausted at least.)

We are also beginning the adjustment process for her anti-depressant medicine. First, we will wean her off slowly. ("Isn't that counterproductive for what you are trying to achieve?" you ask) Well actually, there IS a method to our madness. You see, since Juliana is still physically dependent she doesn't really have the ability or opportunity to harm herself at this time. So if we suspect that there is even a chance that the depression might be caused by the medicine, or medicine combinations she is on (it happens more than I knew) the best time to try to see how she is without it, is now. With therapy, time and 'magic' Juliana will be strong and capable enough in the next year to act upon her serious depression. Before that time comes I want to be certain we have ruled out the medicine as the culprit. After we have weaned her off, if she is either worse or the same, we will look for a different anti-depressant since the one she is on is clearly not working and we will work on getting her on course. This diversion from our disappointments at therapy will stop us from being too impatient as we wait for the next evaluation of her physical, occupational and speech progress which will take place on October 12. Our plan is to get her into the RIC in Willow brook for some aggressive progress.

Good things are going to happen. I just know it…stay tuned.

ONE YEAR: OCTOBER 2, 2010

I want to go on record for saying I NEVER expected to be doing THIS still 1 year later.

Yes, ONE YEAR....

Please watch for the second volume, the continuation on Juliana's progress as she fights to come back and the exciting developments that happen in the second year of her recovery. You will be truly amazed to witness what a support system can wish into being when they all join for a common cause: For Juliana